Karen Blixen's
SEARCH FOR SELF

Karen Blixen's SEARCH FOR SELF

THE MAKING OF *Out of Africa*

Patti M. Marxsen

LOUISIANA STATE UNIVERSITY PRESS
BATON ROUGE

PUBLISHED WITH THE ASSISTANCE OF THE NOLAND FUND

Published by Louisiana State University Press
lsupress.org

Manufactured in the United States of America
First printing

Designer: Barbara Neely Bourgoyne
Typeface: Adobe Minion Pro
Printer and binder: Sheridan Books, Inc.

Jacket photograph: Karen Blixen on safari.
Courtesy of the Karen Blixen Museum, Rungstedlund Collection.

Cataloging-in-Publication Data are available from the Library of Congress.

ISBN 978-0-8071-8607-7 (cloth: alk. paper) —
ISBN 978-0-8071-8648-0 (pdf) — ISBN 978-0-8071-8647-3 (epub)

for Kate

beautiful daughter, trusted reader,
enduring light in all seasons

Life can only be understood backwards,
but it must be lived forward.

—Søren Kierkegaard

Out of Africa is one of the most dangerous books ever written about Africa, precisely because this Danish writer was obviously gifted with words and dreams.

—Gikuyu novelist Ngũgĩ wa Thiong'o, 1980

CONTENTS

Acknowledgments xi

Abbreviations and a Note on Names xiii

Prologue 1

PART I. *Memory and Vision*

1. Thinking Backwards, Moving Forward 13
2. Origins of Imagination 27
3. Truth and Revenge 39

PART II. *The Mythmaker's Art*

4. Metaphors of Truth 49
5. A Trace of Erasure 60
6. In Search of Vanished Time 72

PART III. *Contested Legacies*

7. Otherness as Revelation 91
8. Karen Blixen's Closet 112

Photo Gallery 131

9. On the Question of Feminism 137
10. I Had a Farm in Hollywood 153

Appendix: A Brief Chronology of *Out of Africa* 169

Notes . . . . 173 | Bibliography 187

Index 195

ACKNOWLEDGMENTS

It is my pleasure to thank early readers and Blixen enthusiasts who were kind enough to take an interest in this project first imagined in the midst of the pandemic. I was planning my reluctant departure from Switzerland after fifteen years at the time and felt drawn to rereading *Out of Africa* as I gradually dismantled my home. The analogy with Karen Blixen was not lost on me, although she had long been a fascination in my literary life. As I thought more about a book, I gradually realized that many friends, including talented writers whose work I'd come to know through the Geneva Writers Group, shared my fascination with this "mysterious woman." Yet I soon learned that the name "Karen Blixen" had the power to pique the interest of many more who recalled the larger-than-life 1985 movie of *Out of Africa* as well as avid readers "all over the map." To Christy Begien, Alan Harmer, Peggy McIntosh, Susan Tiberghien, Barrett Travis, and Deborah Wetmore, among others, thank you for nurturing my confidence in a book that took a while to find a form. In time, my daughter Kate—to whom this book is dedicated—supplied invaluable editorial suggestions, especially as we puzzled through the meaning of "safari style" in the life of Karen Blixen. And in the world of social media, Elvis Bego kindly made time to solve a few important mysteries from his home turf of Copenhagen and his annual visits to Rungstedlund. Meanwhile, my community in Maine has been helpful in other ways, not least by getting my mind off the project with early morning chats at Zoot café or, later in the day, a creative cocktail at 40-Paper.

Much of what served me well in imagining a book on the meaning of memoir in Blixen's life was a trip to Rungstedlund in the summer of 2019. I'm a firm believer in "shoe leather research" as well as every other kind of research. Karen Blixen's house with a view of the sea, her dark bedroom under the rafters, the green room overlooking the garden, and the garden that blends into the now protected woodland known as a bird sanctuary brought the "frame" of her inner life into view. Needless to say, the cooperation of the keepers of memory at the Karen Blixen Museum and the archivists at Denmark's Royal Library in Copenhagen deserve more gratitude than one might realize. Their work, and generations of scholarship, have made the life and work of Karen Blixen a deeply engrossing study.

Finally, I realized from the beginning that this book was in very good hands with LSU Press, thanks to the eternally responsive senior acquisitions editor James W. Long. If he is a gatekeeper par excellence, those whose work makes well-made books possible under the leadership of Alisa Plant and Catherine Kadair constitute an author's dream team. As I look at this book on the table and slide it onto my shelf of other works devoted to Karen Blixen, it is a great pleasure to realize that my modest contribution has found a place on the LSU list of other thought-provoking books about this remarkable woman. Among those, two translations from the Danish hold "pride of place" as treasured books on Blixen's inner life: *The Pact: My Friendship with Isak Dinesen* by Thorkild Bjørnvig (trans. Ingvar Schousboe, 1983) and *The Power of Aries: Myth and Reality in Karen Blixen's Life* by Anders Westenholz (trans. Lise Kure-Jensen, 1987). The existence of such books has motivated my own attempt to understand a formidable subject, as have the generations of scholarly works I engage with here. Apropos, it should be noted that the talents of thoughtful and accomplished peer reviewers, copy editors, indexer, and designer have made this book better than it might have been.

A book is a journey and yes, "it takes a village" for which the author can only be grateful.

ABBREVIATIONS AND A NOTE ON NAMES

LFA	*Letters from Africa*
OA	*Out of Africa*
SG	*Shadows on the Grass*
SGT	*Seven Gothic Tales*
WT	*Winter's Tales*

In Denmark, Karen Blixen's true identity behind the pseudonym "Isak Dinesen" was tracked down in 1934, shortly after *Seven Gothic Tales* was published. From that point on, she used "Karen Blixen" for works published in Danish and "Isak Dinesen" for those published in English. In the interest of readability, I use "Blixen" throughout the body of the text. Please note that the author name used in citations, which may be "Karen Blixen" or "Isak Dinesen," corresponds to the edition of the reference. Also, in my notes, where first names are spelled out only at first mention, I break this rule for Ingeborg Dinesen and Isak Dinesen to avoid the potential confusion of two people named "I. Dinesen" and also spell out the full name in notes that reference Aage Westenholz in proximity to sources I cite by Anders Westenholz.

Karen Blixen's
SEARCH FOR SELF

Prologue

Out of Africa found its form in the village of Skagen, Denmark, in the late autumn of 1936. The remote spit of land at the northernmost point of the province of Jutland was as far as Karen Blixen could get from her coastal family home north of Copenhagen. At fifty-one, she felt a desperate need for space and solitude in order to return to her adventurous, younger self and the "book about Africa" she had finally begun to write about her seventeen years in colonial Kenya (1914–31).[1] She had good reason to feel hopeful about her writing. After all, her *Seven Gothic Tales* (1934) had met with positive reviews in America in the wake of publication by Random House. Furthermore, she had more or less overcome that awful feeling of exposure that seemed to surround her like a conspicuous cloak once the true identity of her pseudonym "Isak Dinesen" was revealed, a troublesome feeling that only added to the negative criticism ignited by the Danish version of *SGT.* As she ferried through the Samsø Belt to the Jutland Peninsula in late September 1936, she surely took pleasure in the way her mind was fully focused, *at last,* on the new book well underway.

It is not difficult to imagine Blixen behind the wheel of her blue Ford Roadster as I drive through another coastal landscape nearly a century later with my own book—this book—floating toward completion. In this way, my rereading of *Out of Africa* begins with two minds in motion as my own attempts to understand hers at that critical moment when the book she wanted to write reached its "point of no return." For Karen Blixen, this occurred only when she was far enough beyond the shock of her final departure from Africa in 1931 to write the memoir that remains in print nearly ninety years later.

What is it about *Out of Africa* that speaks across generations? Is there a universal secret concealed in its multiple genres and manipulation of memory? What accounts for its meaning as an enduring cultural artifact? Should we read her "words and dreams" as artful illusion or as dangerous deception, the latter suggested by the late Gikuyu novelist and public intellectual Ngũgĩ wa Thiong'o in 1980? The essence of his famous critique is that Blixen dared to aestheticize what was, for his countrymen and women, a painful period of humiliation in the guise of Great Britain's "civilizing mission" in colonial Kenya. First and foremost, reading *Out of Africa* today means reading it in light of what we now know about that era in which Blixen's role has been accurately described as "the oppressor as well as the oppressed."[2] Yet we must also read it as a feminist text because it captures a moment long ago when women were trying to figure out how to claim a space in their lives as independent thinkers with aspirations beyond the domestic sphere. *Out of Africa* also exists as an early piece of travel literature from an era when the opportunity to travel for pleasure was the province of elites with leisure, money, and aristocratic lineage. And like all good memoirs, *OA* tilts a retrospective mirror toward the reader. All we have to do is catch those reflections and read between the lines.[3]

Many people feel as if they "know" Karen Blixen because she became an icon of American culture in 1985 when Meryl Streep's voice introduced the author to a new generation with a memorable voiceover of the book's nostalgic first line: "I had a farm in Africa, at the foot of the Ngong Hills." Like the opening line of a fairy tale, those words announced the crossing of a threshold into a distant past. From there, it was easy to accept Sydney Pollack's golden, cinematic vision of Blixen's years in colonial Kenya as "true." After all, the film was based on a memoir, a genre assumed to be true in a sense that goes beyond factual accuracy of time and place. Yet as memoirist and literature critic Sven Birkerts points out in his deep reflection on Vladimir Nabokov's *Speak, Memory,* "The intersection in memoir of 'real life' and representation raises a big question," a question that he settles with a jarring response: "Every remembered moment, every characterization of a person, every suggestion of causality—*everything* is staged."[4]

Maureen Murdock expresses a similar skepticism in *Unreliable Truth: Memoir and Memory* when she writes that "we can never separate the remembered event from our imagination: They stick together."[5] This notion of reimagined events as sticky pieces finds an echo in Susan Tiberghien's concept of memoir as both an artistic and a spiritual "way of the mosaic." With that metaphor, taught for decades in her international writing workshops, Tiberghien urges writers to bring the "pieces" of memory—with or without imagination—into a whole. "You look for the various colors and shapes. You move them around to find different patterns. You form pictures of your life with them."[6] For Tiberghien, the goal is always wholeness and yet it is no secret that the wholeness of any mosaic depends on well-organized fragments. Yet another way of understanding such wholeness is expressed in Judith Lee's approach to Blixen's narration of self as a carefully constructed mask. "The form Dinesen has given to the information about her experience constitutes a mask," she writes, before proceeding to deconstruct that mask through a philosophical lens.[7] It is, as Lee reminds us, the form as well as the content of *Out of Africa* that readers must recognize since both are shaped by the narrator's struggle as she confronts the loss of the indebted coffee farm that serves as a kind of scaffolding for her identity. In this process, the themes, imagery, and emotion of Blixen's *Letters from Africa* are integral to understanding her memoir, where they often appear revised and reimagined as literature.[8]

The result is far from a factual account, although some, including Judith Lee, would argue that the right way to read *Out of Africa* is as "autobiography," a form of life writing that implies adherence to facts. In the twenty-first century, "memoir" has largely replaced the once-popular form of autobiography, in part for the freedom memoir offers to a particular time and place or a particular experience within a long life. As I read it, *OA* is an intimate tale of Blixen's seventeen years in Ngong presented as a vast mosaic of jagged shards surrounding the core of her inner life. The truth that matters here is internal, while the external world, apart from the world of Nature, is only described as needed to locate people and places. This approach accounts for Blixen's ability to spark postcolonial critique, which tends to foreground the sociopolitical injustice of minority populations caught in the hungry jaws of imperial power. Yet in keeping with Tiberghien's idea of consciously arranged pieces and Birkerts's certainty that "everything is staged," Blixen's memoir exposes a kind of privileged self-absorption in which her "search for self" becomes the primary subject to the exclusion of history.

Out of Africa demonstrates a critical premise of memoir—that the recollected self can actually be reinvented *through writing*, not unlike the narrator of Marcel Proust's voluminous novel *In Search of Lost Time*. Like Proust, Blixen foregrounds the power of sensory *mémoire involuntaire* (involuntary memory) to elevate and activate the presumed truth of inner life as a marker of modernity. "We should approach a memoir not as a verifiable account but as a projection of the memoirist's *I*," Birkerts writes.[9] The "I" we encounter in *Out of Africa*—and in virtually all memoirs—is naturally sympathetic with itself because it is the self that is at stake. For over a half-century now, Blixen's readers have known that British colonialism and the land grab that went with it formed the foundation of her presence in Ngong, a region of modern-day Kenya about fifteen miles southwest of Nairobi, to say nothing of her family's generational wealth that made it all possible. Yet it is only since 1980 that scholars have "called out" Bror and Karen Blixen's exploitation of land and labor. Even as she writes sympathetically of "squatters" (i.e., displaced African people) on her land, she never explains their existence or their political status with the moral clarity that David Ward did in 1989: "The right of settlers to 'have a farm' was secured by murder and sustained by extortion. People who had never lived in cash economy were forced into it by hut taxes and poll taxes, devices to make the 'native' work for total strangers, on land which had been his, to produce a crop he could not consume."[10]

In this context, Simon Lewis points out that Karen Blixen's role as *fermière générale* actually required her political awareness since she was, by 1922, personally responsible for the collection and delivery of the squatters' taxes to government offices in Nairobi, even though she had been complaining about the "Hut Taxes" in her letters since 1914. In the face of this history, it is difficult to "square" Blixen's self-congratulatory relief toward the end of *Out of Africa,* regarding her negotiated agreement with the British Colonial Administration to have all of the squatters on the land she could not keep resettled in the nearby Dagoretti Forest Reserve. "As for me myself, the settlement of the squatters' fate was a great appeasement to me. I have not often felt so contented."[11] Her concern for those more than two thousand people is supported by the words of the developer who bought the farm in 1931 and attributed its failure to Blixen's "stubborn devotion to the Africans." His point was that she might have had room to plant maize (corn) and breed cattle, had she been willing to evict squatters from her land.[12] Understandably, postcolonial scholars are not moved by such acts of "generosity." Lewis's summation of the terms of engagement speaks with eloquence when he writes that "in the same way that colonization might be fundamental to culture, so taxation is essential to colonization."[13]

In the chapters that follow, I grapple with these and other problems of ambiguity, contradiction, misreading, and erasure woven into the fabric of *Out of Africa,* even as I focus on the essential subject: the author's search for self. Understandably, that search draws the writer into a deeply personal sense of ahistorical time and a process of staging that excludes a great deal of relevant information. As a foreigner living alone in a British colony, a modern woman living alone (throughout the 1920s) in a male-dominated society, and an artist eager to reclaim her sense of self shattered by her departure from East Africa in 1931, Karen Blixen expresses the same ambivalence toward political reality as she does toward chronological dates. One expression of this is her persistent vision of a generalized place called "Africa" that was, in fact, a conglomeration of distinctive territories, tribes, cultures, and ethnicities that eventually became the fifty-four independent nations that exist today. This "flattening" begins with the title of her book and extends to every experience she has, whether it is in Nairobi or the Ngong Hills or at the port in Mombasa or on the border of German-controlled Tanganyika (current-day Tanzania). It is understandable that postcolonial scholars find this irritating, to say nothing of inaccurate, as Simon Lewis does when he suggests that "her having the farm is no more a political act than Old MacDonald's having of his farm in the nursery song."[14] It *was* a political act, of course, that took Karen Blixen herself, and millions of others, time to understand.

Tanne Dinesen (Blixen's maiden name) was shocked when her fiancé, Baron Bror von Blixen-Finecke, made a unilateral decision to switch from their plans for a dairy farm on 700 acres of Great Britain's East Africa Protectorate to the purchase of the Swedo Coffee Farm and the 4,500 acres they later expanded to encompass 6,000. Not only was the scale of this impulsive purchase enormous, the soil and altitude of the highlands southwest of Nairobi would never be conducive to a profitable crop. To make matters worse, Bror quickly realized that he preferred Masai women and safari life to coffee farming, and so the struggle of farming fell to his inexperienced wife, whose family was financially invested in the adventure. In 1922, Karen Blixen reluctantly signed a pledge drafted by her mother's brother, Uncle Aage Westenholz (aka Chairman of the Board of the Karen Coffee Company), that named his niece as salaried farm manager. The infamous pledge also separated Bror from farm operations and all property rights as the couple's divorce proceedings crawled through the British bureaucracy until the break was finalized in 1925. From 1922 to 1931 Karen Blixen lived an oddly individualistic life as a Danish woman working in Britain's new Crown Colony of Kenya with a small circle of relationships that included trusted servants, a succession of field managers, her Swedish friend and fellow farmer Ingrid Lindstrøm, and Denys Finch Hatton, her aristocratic British lover.

Blixen's brother Thomas Dinesen was also part of her African world during his long visits in the 1920s to support his sister's dream. As her dearest, lifelong confidant he was, in many ways, a significant part of her

African experience as well as of her writing career. Not only did he engage with her life in Ngong, he purchased property nearby, climbed Mt. Kenya, and enjoyed safari life before returning to Europe in March 1923. Thomas also traveled back and forth—from Denmark to Ngong—with their mother, Ingeborg Dinesen, twice (in 1924 and 1927) on visits that lasted months at a time. His absence from both the memoir and the 1985 film is a significant act of omission, especially since he was in Ngong with Karen when their sister Inger (Ea) de Neergaard died two months after childbirth on June 17, 1922. Yet even with his support, Karen's bursts of optimism fluctuated with increasingly intense periods of despair throughout the 1920s. It was then, as we know from her letters, that she turned to writing at night to escape her feeling of being "buried alive."[15]

Tania, as she was called in Ngong, worked diligently at complex tales set in the nineteenth century, anecdotes of life in "Africa," and edits to an early play for publication in Denmark. She also penned a rigorously philosophical essay on "Modern Marriage and Other Observations," sent to Thomas in April 1924 and first published posthumously in the 1970s.[16] Yet she was reluctant to think of herself as a serious writer until *Seven Gothic Tales* was published in the United States in 1934 as a Random House Book-of-the-Month Club selection with two stories written in Ngong.[17] The same marketing boost accounted for strong sales of *Out of Africa* in the United States in 1938 as Random House became her lifelong American publisher.[18] Three more volumes of tales were published in her lifetime—*Winter's Tales* (1942), *Last Tales* (1957), and *Anecdotes of Destiny* (1958)—of which *WT* was especially successful because, in addition to the hardcover edition, an "Armed Services Edition" designed to fit in a soldier's rucksack was financed and distributed by the nonprofit Council on Books in Wartime. In her last years, Karen Blixen worked on *Shadows on the Grass* (1961), her second memoir and final book that serves as a kind of epilogue to *Out of Africa,* in which she poses a critical question that hints at her long-standing awareness of the irreversible damage done by colonialism in Kenya: "What business had I had ever to set my heart on Africa? The old continent had done well before my giving it a thought; might it not have gone on doing so?"[19]

A year later, on September 7, 1962, Blixen's spinal syphilis, long settled in her digestive system, led to her death from "emaciation."[20] Since then, a long list of books about her life and work have appeared in English, beginning with Robert Langbaum's insightful *Isak Dinesen's Art: The Gayety of Vision* (1965) and a chatty biography by Blixen's friend Parmenia Migel, who indulged her subject in *Titania: The Biography of Isak Dinesen* (1967). In the 1970s Danish opera singer Frans Lasson became the widely respected editor of Karen Blixen's letters and archives. Thanks to him, and Blixen's long-time assistant Clara Svendsen, we have *The Life and Destiny of Isak Dinesen,* an annotated "album" of photographs dating to the nineteenth century, as well as the essential volume *Letters from Africa* and another volume of letters from Denmark, as yet untranslated into English. There is also a shelf of memoir literature that includes Thomas Dinesen's memoir *My Sister, Isak Dinesen,* Svendsen's own memoir, a deep reflection by Blixen's friend and Danish poet Ole Wivel, and Thorkild Bjørnvig's riveting, confessional memoir of his relationship with the aging Karen Blixen translated as *The Pact: My Friendship with Isak Dinesen.* In 1983, Judith Thurman's *Isak Dinesen: The Life of a Storyteller* won the National Book Award in Biography and the centennial year of Blixen's birth was marked with Sydney Pollack's blockbuster film in 1985. On the other side of that "mass hysteria," as Frans Lasson described it, a new audience was eager for more.[21]

I've thought a lot about how to approach this singular writer, this eccentric woman, this prolific artist of reinvention who overcame a crushing sense of failure in 1931 and reversed the plot of her life within a few years. Her reinvention was, however, more than a tale of overcoming hardship. Blixen's radical break with her life in colonial Kenya threatened to become a radical break within herself forever entwined with the memory of her father's suicide by hanging in 1895. Ever since, Karen Blixen had struggled to keep Wilhelm Dinesen's spirit alive by keeping *his* vision of *her* alive as his clever, creative, adventurous daughter. Blixen scholars generally agree that her 1931 departure—with its overlay of grief at the sudden death of Denys Finch Hatton months earlier—echoed the original loss of her beloved father that had long been Blixen's "ground zero" for all losses of all kinds. In that sense, Wilhelm Dinesen was always her original audience and, as Jane Kramer wrote in 1986, "the first of her fictions, the prototype for all the elusive aristocrats in her life."[22]

That first, destabilizing loss explains her psychic need to write her way back to an idealized version of herself within the idealized world of "a farm in Africa" in which she enjoyed the adventurous, aristocratic life of a baroness living at the center of a very small universe. Yet *Out of Africa* is not only nostalgic within Blixen's own biography. The deep, historical layers of nostalgia found in *Out of Africa* were cleverly deconstructed as a "triple nostalgia" by African literature scholar Thomas R. Knipp in his 1990 study of three European women writing about their experience in Kenya in the first half of the twentieth century: Karen Blixen, Elspeth Huxley, and Beryl Markham. In Knipp's view, these "literary ladies," as he calls them, drew on the (then) presumed emptiness of the Africa they inhabited, the "recent past in imperial Europe in which the creation of a fictive Africa was possible," and "a much younger European world—both feudal and Edenic—evoked by this fictive Africa."[23] As persuasive as this analysis is in light of Blixen's first readers, who were, as Knipp notes, people of her race and class, it does not fully explain the memoir's unending popularity ever since and/or its popularity with non-European readers. One of the remarkable achievements of Karen Blixen's prose is, clearly, its ability to appeal to generations of readers, each of which finds relevance, meaning, and their own mysterious link to the nostalgia embedded in her sense of a lost world.

In a long, reflective letter to Thomas in April 1926, Karen Blixen responded to her brother's advice that she should "cross out all your past idiocy and do immediately what you ought to have done long ago—." Her reply is poignant in its hopelessness when she writes that "I cannot see the way," not even to hell because "the devil is expensive to talk to" and "I, personally, have squandered those assets of my youth, of time, of work, of personality with which I could once have paid for it—and am now insolvent."[24] Five years would pass before Thomas met "Tanne" in Marseille as she made her way down the gangplank of the SS *Mantola* in a state of mental and physical exhaustion. It was August, a perfect time to pause for a few days in Montreux, Switzerland, from which they took the funicular up to the village of Glion and climbed the steep streets for a consultation about anemia and depression at the Clinique de Valmont. Back home in Denmark, Karen Blixen spent months in recovery, much of it sitting alone in the garden behind the house she grew up in that has since become the delightful oasis of the Karen Blixen Museum and Bird Sanctuary at Rungstedlund.

Returning to intricate tales set in the nineteenth century helped Blixen to organize her days, hone her craft, and rediscover a sense of purpose, as the trunks shipped from Ngong remained unopened in the attic. Only in the wake of the Danish publication of *Seven Gothic Tales* did she find her way back to the other book she had long envisioned. Committing herself to it in 1935, at age fifty, and working steadily throughout 1936, allowed memories to return, pages to accumulate, and a uniquely nonlinear structure of episodes, observations, parables, and stories to emerge as a narrator named Isak Dinesen took over. Then, as the autumnal equinox approached in September, the time was finally right for a period of isolation in the remote village of Skagen. There, she would find the solitude she needed to reinvent the young woman she desperately wanted to have been. She believed her story was worth telling, if only she could clear her mind of the present. She felt a sense of truth just beyond her grasp as one memory led to another. Then suddenly, it seemed, it was done by early spring—or almost done—like a promise finally kept after so many years. To her great relief, and in her heartfelt assessment, "No one came into literature more bloody than I."[25]

PART I
Memory and Vision

CHAPTER ONE

Thinking Backwards, Moving Forward

My little African travel accounts . . . become mbuni (coffee berries) before they get to my pen.

—Karen Blixen to Thomas Dinesen, 1926

Karen Blixen's life, like many twentieth-century lives, is documented in black-and-white photographs. Other scenes and scenery described in her *Letters from Africa* recall weather conditions, tribal customs, and the "surround" of untamed Nature. With Judith Thurman's award-winning biography *Isak Dinesen: The Life of a Storyteller,* Blixen's life expands backward in historical detail and since 1985, Sydney Pollack's interpretation depicts her as a romantic heroine. Yet beyond such angles of vision there is another view and another context that involves her search for inner truth through writing. This level of comprehension constantly reaches back into the emotional sediment of lived experience as it gathers meaning forward into the ever-changing present. I am conscious of these many layers of representation as I trace Blixen's journey to Skagen, Denmark, that began on September 21, 1936, "for several months with the goal of completing my book."[1] By then, she was finally ready to isolate herself with the manuscript described to her brother over a year earlier as "a book on the Masai."[2]

The ghostly gesture of Ingeborg Dinesen's hand waving from the window probably reminded her daughter of all the other early morning departures from Rungstedlund. Karen was, no doubt, wearing a coat in late September, although the color, texture, and style vanish in a vague silhouette of a slim woman with streaks of gray hair as she slips in behind the wheel of her Ford Convertible Deluxe Roadster. I know the car is blue and I know she purchased it used with earnings from *Seven Gothic Tales,* but the only photo I can find of her with it was taken earlier in the year on her mother's eightieth birthday—May 5, 1936. In that moment Ingeborg Dinesen is dressed for an outing and seated on the running board in a black coat, as if waiting to be taken out to lunch. This commemorative photo includes a *papier mâché* "dummy" propped up behind the wheel in front of a homemade sign that reads: "Chauffeur Isak at your service for one hour daily." Karen/Isak is smiling, almost laughing, as she leans on an open door in a stylish suit, cloche hat, and checkered scarf.[3] I pause for a moment at her comic use of the pseudonym she took so seriously as part of her literary identity.

It is easy to lose sight of her for a moment as she rolls onto the Strandvej (Beach Road), away from the L-shaped house with its long lace curtains pooling softly on polished floors. Such a long journey within Denmark was unusual for her, although she had traveled quite a bit in the two years since the publication of *SGT,* which gave her a newfound sense of freedom and the funds to go with it. For that, she would always be grateful to Thomas Dinesen's connection with American editor Dorothy Canfield Fisher, who had passed the manuscript along to a friend at Random House in New York. As for the Danish edition, it was delayed by translation issues, the author's poor health, and what appears to have been both arrogance and ambivalence on the part of Reitzel, the Danish publishing house owned and operated by Blixen's brother-in-law Knud Dahl.[4] The ordeal of finally bringing *Syv fantastiske fortællinger* (Seven Fantastic Tales) out for Danish readers left her feeling unappreciated by everyone including the translator, the publisher, and her younger sister Ellen Dahl. Never again would she concede so much authority, especially when it came to Danish translations from her writing language of British English. Those, she would do herself.

Blixen could not be sure what she might accomplish from a small room at Brøndums Hotel in a village huddled on a remote spit of land at 57.72° N, 10.59° E. She knew something of Skagen, however, since it was located on the edge of Jutland not far from her father's ancestral estate of Katholm on the Djursland Peninsula. Long before memories of life in Ngong took hold, Karen (called "Tanne" as a child) was transported to Katholm for a month-long stay every summer with her mother, four siblings, and their nursemaid called "Malla."[5] That geographical connection to Wilhelm Dinesen's life and her paternal ancestors surely made her 1936 "writer's retreat" feel less remote. Perhaps the familiarity would allow her to relax and reclaim her memories of Ngong in the bright, uninterrupted solitude of sea and sky, even if the farm was at the other end of the earth. If nothing else, she hoped to align herself with that distant world on this autumnal equinox and find her way to completion in the months ahead as her book evolved beyond a feeble collection of anecdotes, autobiographical notes, and travel vignettes.

Blixen had learned to drive in Africa where rutted roads determined the speed and no one ever knew what might happen along the way. In September 1936 she was, in a sense, driving toward her vision of those "African years" as she turned her back on the shimmering Øresund (Sound) that would soften through the hours into silver, then violet late in the day. By the time she reached Skagen that afternoon, the oil lamps would be lit in the parlor at Rungstedlund and by seven o'clock the night sky would unfold like a blue velvet curtain. In the intervening hours, the car would be her silent companion, as good as a reliable horse taking cues from her hands and feet. The excitement of departure might even have triggered childhood memories of traveling on the Strandvej to the rhythm of carriage horses with Mother and Father, two sisters Inger (Ea) and Ellen (Elle), and baby Thomas bundled on Ingeborg's lap before Anders arrived to take his place in 1894—all pressed against each other with a rough, woolen blanket tucked across their laps.

Blixen turned onto the same road in 1936 with her tiny black Corona typewriter in the boot of the car, eyes staring straight ahead, gloved hands gripping the steering wheel as Bror had insisted when almost every drive in Africa involved some sort of urgent business or unwelcome surprise. But what could be more urgent now than a voyage backwards in order to move forward according to Søren Kierkegaard's familiar maxim: "*Life can only be understood backwards, but it must be lived forward*"? Until 1936, the challenge of those words had only been something she deployed in the context of inventive tales. As she set off for Skagen, she must have realized anew that the words of the great Danish philosopher meant something deeper and closer to the truth of a living, breathing *self*—a self with a past propelled by memory and its own visions of time. If nothing else, she had come through a year of emotional turmoil and months of diligent work with enough wisdom to confront the project that had been waiting ever since her departure from Ngong in 1931—and years before that, if she were honest.

The necessary courage emerged—though she could not explain how or from where. Whenever Blixen pondered such questions, she fell into an internal debate in which fate opposed self-determination and notions of God's Will fell short of human logic. Her sense of being innately rebellious, "Lucifer's child" as she liked to say, had led to fictitious journeys in which her characters often concealed their inexplicable lives behind a mask. The new book would require a different journey because it involved self-exposure and a painful journey backwards to "Ngong," a word that represented a distant place and fleeting time on the vast continent of Africa. How to describe that place through her senses had become a central question—with the sound of chattering Gikuyu children or the lion's roar? She would think carefully about that. She would also have to remember the presence of Denys dozing on the veranda and the metallic sound of the gramophone, his gift to her, now stored in the attic and utterly silent since his death in 1931. Her only certainty as she drove toward Skagen was that in order to "unpack" her memories she would have to turn her back on the snug clutter of Rungstedlund with its Danish voices, Sunday visits, and the fragrance of baked apples. It was too easy there, like a nest folded upon itself in which a lifetime of pain had been deliberately dulled by routine. Tea by the fire. Stories read aloud. Old Pedersen driving the carriage. *Mother's hand at the window.*

Seven Gothic Tales was written in English in the green room overlooking the garden at the back of the house, although the first of those tales emerged at night in Mbogani House in the mid-1920s as Blixen, by then divorced and living alone, wrestled with issues of destiny and identity, especially in the lives of women. One of the early tales, "The Dreamers," begins in moonlight as travelers in a dhow sailing along the east coast of Africa exchange stories enroute to Zanzibar. Gradually, they realize that they have loved the same woman in different expressions of her identity. Within this long tale—eventually "built out" as a series of tales—Blixen's first, symbolic self-portrait emerges in the form of a renowned opera singer who has lost her voice in a disastrous theater fire. For Pellegrina Leoni, the only solution to life's tragic losses becomes an audacious claim to a level of freedom that allows her to avoid a fixed identity. In "The Dreamers," wisdom is allied with a self-protective mask that irritates her lovers, inspires a true friend's loyalty, and sets the world tumbling out of control.

Sometime late in 1931 or early 1932, the act of writing became a kind of mask for Blixen that helped her recover from her fragile state of mind and body in the wake of her return to Denmark. This painful process encompassed the invention of a literary persona called "Isak Dinesen," a name that first appeared on the cover of *Seven Gothic Tales* in 1934. Shielded by the mysterious name and layers of imagination, those complex tales set in the nineteenth century became a way for Blixen to shutter her mind against the losses of her farm, her friends, her beloved Denys, and ultimately the loss of a version of self left behind. In that sense, *SGT* kept death at bay, not unlike the legendary storyteller Scheherazade who kept herself alive by entertaining the Sultan with tales told throughout 1001 nights. It is no accident that Scheherazade is evoked at the end of the first "gothic tale," "Deluge at Norderney," when death-defying dawn appears on the horizon and a clever old woman, Miss Malin, ceases to tell her tales after surviving a night of rising flood waters.[6]

By the end of 1936, Blixen had read *The Story of an African Farm* by Olive Schreiner (aka Ralph Iron), a novel based on a woman's nineteenth-century experience in South Africa.[7] She also reread her letters from Africa so lovingly kept by Ingeborg Dinesen. Although she often concealed her deepest thoughts from her mother, Blixen's *Letters from Africa* constitutes her first writings about her life in Africa like a hall of mirrors filled with reflections of Farah, Kamante, Bror, Denys, the ever-present *totos* (African children), Chief Kinanjui, and the old, chattering women who called her "Jerie," which means many things in the Gikuyu language including "one who pays attention."[8] Within her deeper corridors of reflection she would have found memories of that time when Grandmother Mary Westenholz (called "Mama") and an all-powerful network of aunts, uncles, and cousins were alive. Those people—and especially the women—shaped the limits of young Tanne Dinesen's self-awareness even as they opened the wider world to her through the personal experience of books read, deaths observed, rooms inhabited, and houses visited, each with its own fragrance and light.

The sensory presence of animals—especially horses and dogs—moved through Blixen's memory of childhood like shadows she could "feel" as well as "see," including Father's dog Osceola trotting ahead on woodland walks. She might recall her dreams of becoming an artist and then, suddenly, those days of shopping in Naples with Mother and Elle before she boarded the SS *Admiral* for Mombasa on December 16, 1913, and the strangely final feeling of waving goodbye from the ship that would take three weeks to reach the Port of Aden, which appeared as an explosion of colorful chaos. Suddenly—how could she forget?—everything around her calmed when a tall man wearing a Somali turban stepped out of the crowd to greet her with steady eyes, just as Bror had assured her would happen. His face was the color of caramel and his eyes did not move at all when he addressed her as his "white lady boss": "I am Farah, *Msabu.*"

In *Shadows on the Grass* (1961), Blixen refers to Farah as her "major-domo," her "essential person" who quickly became her trusted guide, servant, translator, house manager, and loyal friend. By the time she wrote that chapter devoted to him and the age of seventy-six, she understood how *thinking backwards* allowed her mind to sink *into* depths of memory, like a deep sleep where everything became real again. She bid him farewell for a second and last time in *SG*, reliving that moment when their lives merged and parted once and for all: "As I watched his dark immovable figure on the quay growing smaller and at last disappear, I felt it as if I were losing a part of myself, as if I were having my right hand cut off, and from now on would never again ride a horse or shoot with a rifle, nor be able to write otherwise than with my left hand."[9]

There is no documented recollection of Blixen's 1936 automobile journey from Rungstedlund to Skagen, although Karen Blixen's first biographer, Parmenia Migel, includes a lively account of it in her 1967 book titled *Titania: The Biography of Isak Dinesen.* Blixen certainly circled the fjord at the center of Denmark's Zealand ("Sea-land") Province, which took her to Roskilde, then drove north to the ferry terminal at Zealand Point (Sjælland's Odde in Danish). From there, she boarded one of the Great Belt ferries that had been in operation since her childhood to cross the Kattegat Strait, eventually disembarking at Aarhus. From this point, Migel dramatizes the drive north, through Aalborg into northern Jutland as "two hundred kilometers of icy roads," which seems unlikely considering Blixen's September departure. In any case, she probably reached Skagen late in the day, assuming an early morning departure from Rungstedlund, as the route taken in September 1936, as described here, is approximately 325 miles. Like Pellegrina, Blixen allowed herself to reject the past at will, as she had done earlier in the day when she turned away from the tidy comportment of Ingeborg's house in search of an "escape" described by Migel as a place where she "could feel quite certain of working undisturbed by intruders." Migel's powers of mind-reading continue in her telling of how Blixen made her way north feeling "ill at ease" and wondering "if it had been a mistake to choose this lonely refuge."[10]

Ultimately, having become a disciplined writer through the work of *SGT,* Blixen quickly adopted a routine in the small, seasonally quiet community of Skagen, where she was known to entertain villagers with stories of her life in Africa, possibly testing them out for further development. As daylight dwindled, she often took a break by going out for a drive past what Migel describes as a "lifeless lunar landscape" of dunes and sometimes got out of the car to walk on the beach as far as land's end, called Grenen.[11] Such details could only have come from Blixen herself, even if Migel's undocumented embellishments seem designed to please her subject. What remains indisputably factual, however, is Blixen's immersion in contrasting worlds as she wrote of Ngong in Skagen, Denmark, where cold, blustery walks were followed by hours of work into the night as she recaptured memories of animal migration, aerial visions from Denys's airplane, conversations with Somali women, and the accidental shooting of a child by another child. Somehow, it all appeared on the page in a serene voice.

In preparation for Skagen, Blixen must have reread "Ex Africa," her poem written in 1915 from a hospital bed in Denmark. This poem expressed her early sense of the timelessness found in the world she was just beginning to discover. It was first published in *Tilskueren* in 1925 under the pseudonym "Osceola," the name of a heroic, mixed-race Seminole Native American much admired by Wilhelm Dinesen. "Ex Africa" clearly meant a great deal to her as it also gave birth to her working title for the book she was writing, even if Robert Haas at Random House would talk her out of high-minded Latin that might be off-putting to American readers.[12] Yet in its echo of a classical ode, "Ex Africa," like the memoir she would eventually write, took her back to those nights near the Equator where darkness fell so suddenly: "I need a long time to gaze upon you, / Great Lady moon, to see you again / as I saw you before every night /—ah, in the vanished nights gone by." She was ill and disillusioned about Bror on that first trip home, during which she endured her first arsenic treatment for syphilis. Yet she seems to have realized, even then, that Africa would become an important part of her life, with or without Bror: "Long sparks flared in the cool, sharp night. / Each of us reads a thousand signs rising in the flames and glow of the fire." Clearly, her sensory memory was at her fingertips long before she was ready to write the book that made her famous with the English title *Out of Africa.*[13]

In Skagen, Blixen's thoughts necessarily turned from poetic imagery to structure, voice, pacing, and the essential challenge of connecting a prolonged narrative across varied experiences and a vast range of emotions. How to go *backwards* and bring it all *forward* as a tale of many moods that would stand as true to life? How to find the essence of experience? How to become a memoirist? That was the new question she struggled to answer after years of indulging her imagination with intricate tales. Was the book she still thought of as *Ex Africa* going to bend inexorably toward another exercise in imagination over truth? She must have understood, by the end of 1936, that making it work as a continuous narrative would require a tale of *personal experience* that she embodied but also wanted—somehow—to protect. Not unlike the narrator of Marcel Proust's *In Search of Lost Time,* a work with which she was familiar, Karen Blixen's voice would have to be controlled but passionate, honest but without an overflow of emotion, specific in its observations but cognizant of the complexity of life flickering around her.[14] Above all, it would call for a modern voice—a woman's voice—that spoke plainly and yet conveyed the grandeur of a timeless world and the loss of it in real time. As Susan Brantly notes, "Dinesen had such a strong emotional link to her material that it seems to have taken her a while to find the right tone."[15]

The long process of thinking her way back into a book about Africa had started and stopped so many times and only began to move forward after *Seven Gothic Tales* was published in 1934. That spring, she explained to a journalist from Denmark's *Politken* how liberating it felt to set those tales in a previous century: "With the past, I find myself before a finished world, complete in all its elements, and I can thus more easily recompose it in my imagination."[16] This was an important distinction from the book she only began to speak of publicly that year when, in another interview, she confronted a blunt question: "Why not write about Africa as a first book?" Her answer came naturally and clarified her thoughts: "One must have things at a distance. In my tales I have put a whole century between me and the events [of life in Africa]," she replied, knowing that the underlying question was "Why bother to write those crazy tales?"[17] As she waited impatiently for the Danish edition of *Seven Gothic Tales* to finally appear in September 1935, yet another interview was published in *Møns Folkeblad* (People's Magazine). There, she explained that her next book would be about Africa, but unlike her tales it would be a story of her own lived experience "in which all things are true, where everything that is told truly happened." As a woman then-unaccustomed to the spotlight, she understood that her claims might sound ambitious. She nevertheless dared to add that "It shall be the truth about Blacks."[18]

During the long months between American and Danish editions of *Seven Gothic Tales,* Karen Blixen was filled with an obsessive sense of uncertainty that Judith Thurman describes as "a crisis that had certain familiar hallmarks," including melancholy, numbness, and fatigue.[19] It was a sign of progress, internally and on her desk, when she realized that the great effort of her first book had been a kind of brush clearing or, as she would say years later, "like a scream, a lion's roar [because] I could not write *Out of Africa* before the pain abated."[20] If anyone understood this, it was Thomas, who had believed in his sister's project from her first mention of it in 1926 when she wrote to him in a self-deprecating mood: "[My] little African travel descriptions that the *Flesborg Newspaper* is now kindly waiting for are meant to mimic the angels' hymns of praise, and I can't do that anymore; they turn to *mbuni* (coffee berries) before my pen can touch them."[21]

Of all people, Thomas Dinesen understood the adventurous allure of his sister's life in Ngong, having lived, worked, and traveled in the region himself on three long visits in the 1920s and even climbed Mt.

Kenya in 1923.[22] He surely smiled at the polite understatement of the letter Blixen sent to her Random House editor in New York on March 24, 1934, shortly after *SGT* was published in the United States with the pseudonym "Isak Dinesen" on the cover: "I have got a few short, quite truthful accounts of my life on the African farm, particularly about my relations with the Natives. I have to have these published under my real name, as they deal with real facts and people. I should like to get them out in a *good* magazine, if possible, and I suppose that this cannot interfere with our contract, *since the stories cannot in any way be classed as a book.* Will you give me your kind assistance to find such a magazine, if you think it could be found?"[23]

Unfortunately, the mood of that hopeful note could not be sustained, and so she decided to spend time with a wealthy friend in London early in 1935. There, she met erudite literary lights—Aldous Huxley, Stephen Zweig, George Bernard Shaw—who might have laughed at her, had they seen her a year later heading for Skagen. A kind man from Putnam, her U.K. publisher of *SGT,* might have scratched his head as well, after escorting her around so diligently to bookshops and parties.[24] Even Albert Schweitzer might have found her amusing when she met him in London after an organ concert. As one of the most famous Europeans to establish a hospital on the African continent (in French Equatorial) in the twentieth century, he listened patiently to her idea of a children's hospital for the Masai, before discouraging her, with a kind smile.[25] Did he sense her lack of confidence? Or her emotional frailty?

The one person who always took her seriously, regardless of her mood, was her brother Thomas. When she asked if he would come to visit her in Skagen he was more than ready to oblige. He would come to talk with her and walk on the beach and sit by the fire at Christmastime, despite his own family obligations. But primarily, he would come to listen to his sister read from her newborn pages and steady her uncertainties with his presence, as he had always done. As 1937 began, Blixen's edits and elaborations of memories filled hours and days in the shelter of her small hotel room with a writing desk at the window in hopes of returning to Rungstedlund with something good enough to send to New York where Robert Haas was, by then, eagerly awaiting his chance to read her second book.

The nearness of ocean is something you can sense in a coastal village as the wind off the water picks up and the day fills with the soft sounds of waves and gulls. I imagine that Blixen's thoughts moved toward the sea as she approached the village so carefully chosen for her writer's retreat. Was she truly "ill at ease," as Migel writes, or simply tired after a long day of driving and thinking and feeling her way forward? Perhaps she was thinking about Pellegrina, that voiceless opera singer she created, when the small, brick structures of the village came into view—Pellegrina, a wounded artist, as all artists must be, whose source of power was "magical because she is invulnerable."[26] In *The Pact: My Friendship with Isak Dinesen,* Thorkild Bjørnvig recalls a conversation with Blixen in which he said "You are Pellegrina," and she agreed wholeheartedly, because "the loss of her voice corresponds to my loss of the farm and Africa."[27]

The walls at Brøndum's Hotel were lined, then as now, with cheerful, summertime canvases of sand and sea, boats under sail, and women in long dresses walking together on the beach at twilight.[28] After settling in, soup and a plate of rye bread were offered with a small carafe of red wine. She must have savored that hour, feeling restored after a long day of driving, thinking, and summoning her courage. As 1936 came to an end and a new year began, dreams merged with memories and a way to write her story gradually took shape as a book by March 1937.[29] By then she had a readable draft that only needed a good edit easily done at Rungstedlund. Her final manuscript arrived in New York in August, and *Out of Africa* was published in the U.K. in November 1937, concurrent with the Danish and Swedish editions, all slightly ahead of the first American edition a few months later in 1938.

Within Susan Brantly's discussion of how the book was received in different cultures, it is interesting to note that Danish critics initially indulged in attacks against Blixen while Swedish reviewers appreciated her avoidance of racist tropes, one of whom wrote that "it is foreign to her to see them [Blacks] as people of a worse quality than the white race."[30] British reviews were mixed on that point, and some did not understand her feelings about colonialism at all. Meanwhile, Sir John Squire wrote that "what is new in this book . . . is the sympathy with the local population, who were there before we came and the oldest of whom cannot help feeling, when they are called 'squatters' on our farms, that we are squatters on theirs."[31] As for the American edition successfully marketed as a Book-of-the-Month Club selection, it sold 99,000 copies in 1938, a figure Brantly compares with the paltry U.S. sales in the same year of *Facing Mt. Kenya* by anticolonial activist Jomo Kenyatta, who would eventually become Kenya's first president. "Dinesen reached such a large public not only because of her extraordinary literary talent, but also because she was a white European who sought to influence, but not offend," writes Susan Brantly.[32] For all her reported snobbery and blindness of privilege, Blixen clearly knew how to communicate with Anglophone readers on both sides of the Atlantic, even as her posthumous reputation has included a persistent postcolonial critique dating to the era of the Mau-Mau Rebellion (1952–58) and Kenyan independence (1963) as well as waves of scholarship that seemed to coalesce around a negative consensus in the 1980s.

Meanwhile, literary scholars have never ceased to admire Karen Blixen's storytelling talent while feminist scholars have often focused on the writing of her memoir as a self-portrait of modern womanhood in all its complexity. As a measure of that complexity, the feminist perspective exists in opposition to Sydney Pollack's midcentury male vision of *Out of Africa* onscreen that dominated the Academy Awards in 1985. More recently, Blixen's writing resonates in the context of our problematic human relationship with the natural world that she appreciated so deeply during her years in Ngong and which Danish literary scholar Peter Mortensen has explored so thoughtfully. For all of these reasons, Karen Blixen's memoir completed in a hotel room on a remote, wintry point of Denmark has become one of the Random House Modern Library's 100 Best Nonfiction Books of all time. As one title on a list established in 1971, *Out of Africa* manages to speak in new ways to each generation as it lives up to the Modern Library's vision: "We hope to continue to remind readers that today's classics are often the works of yesterday's avant-garde; and that what we call the literary canon is an ever-fluid collection of great books—books that gain their significance from readers engaging with their themes across the centuries."[33]

CHAPTER TWO

Origins of Imagination

We were not observers, as children today seem to be from birth of their own accord; and not utilizers, as they are brought up to be; we were creators.

—Isak Dinesen, "On Mottoes of My Life," 1959

Long before the literary persona of Isak Dinesen existed, a child was born in Denmark to the improbable marriage of Ingeborg Westenholz, a quiet Unitarian, and the adventurous Wilhelm Dinesen. Both were raised in the Danish province of Jutland and together they brought five children into the world who enjoyed the privileges of a prosperous, loving family that included a trio of sisters born in the 1880s followed by two brothers in the early 1890s. In time, Karen Christentze Dinesen—called "Tanne" by her family—would outlive them all, with the exception of her brother Thomas, a decorated war veteran whose memoir *My Sister, Isak Dinesen* (1975) remains the best portrait available of Karen Blixen's childhood and youth.

The garden was just beginning to bloom with wild tulips when Ingeborg, then twenty-nine, gave birth to her second daughter on April 17, 1885. This birth, like all the others, occurred at Rungstedlund, the site of a former inn with its forty acres of woodland and meadow situated on the Beach Road between Copenhagen and Helsingør (Elsinore). By the time Wilhelm and his widowed sister Alvide purchased the property in 1879, it had long been an ideal spot for rest and refreshment, as well as home to dairy cows, herds of swine, and the families that tended the animals and worked the farm. Thanks to the right to distill brandy acquired in the eighteenth century, generations of travelers stopped at Rungstedlund over the years to gaze at the blue haze of Sweden across the Øresund from a small veranda.[1] One guest in particular, the Danish poet Johannes Ewald (1743–1781), slept beneath the rafters in the room that Karen would eventually inhabit as her own. Perhaps his ghost still hovers over Rungstedlund today, casting a glance toward the sea and drifting along the sloping path to Ewald's Hill, where Blixen was buried in the dappled light of an oak tree beneath a simple stone slab that reads: "Karen Blixen." No dates, no lines of verse; no more, no less.

It's not difficult to imagine what Wilhelm envisioned when he first walked the property in 1879, as I did in the summer of 2019. My route was a well-worn path through flowering fields and trees full of birdsong behind the L-shaped house museum. The benches in the bird sanctuary today are named for birds—Nightingale Bench, Woodpecker Bench—and a field of wildflowers seemingly gathered and held in place by woven willow fencing follows a curving path to the ancient oak and humble gravesite. There is a sense of inhabiting a world apart at Rungstedlund, even now, although Wilhelm's sister Alvide's adjacent home of Rungstedgaard has become the center of a sprawling hotel directly across the street from the shore with its blue horizon and popular dockside restaurants.

For a young man of thirty-five recently returned from the American wilderness, the purchase of Rungstedlund represented Wilhelm's desire to settle down and also to expand his horizons beyond his ancestral estate of Katholm in northern Jutland. The less remote province of Zealand felt ideal as it would, he correctly assumed, offer train service between Copenhagen and Helsingør by the end of the nineteenth century. My own train took about thirty minutes from Copenhagen to reach Rungsted Kyst, the coastal village where the Dinesen property remains a popular hub of activity on the (now paved) Strandvej. From the train stop, a short walk on a sidewalk leads to the Karen Blixen Museum, Bird Sanctuary, bookshop, and café that welcomes tourists and researchers who come to grasp whatever might remain of the subject's world. Though profoundly associated with Kenya through her famous memoir, Rungstedlund is the place where Karen Blixen was formed, to which she returned to fulfill her destiny as a writer, and also where she aged, died, and chose to be buried. It is, consequently, the place to begin a search for biographical context and the storyteller's sensibility that frames all of her work, including *Out of Africa.*

When the Dinesen children were small, there were stables and a groom for horses on the estate as well as two maids, a washerwoman, a gardener, and a cook, to say nothing of workers who lived on the acreage in small, thatched huts that blocked the road. Wilhelm loved the buzz of activity and family life as much as he loved sharing observations of the natural world with his favored child as they walked hand-in-hand through the woods behind the house. Within that house Ingeborg and a small staff managed the family home as a safe harbor of domestic efficiency from the nursery upstairs to the bustling kitchen in the basement. As soon as the children were old enough to sit still, they delighted in their mother's voice reading aloud from Hans Christian Andersen's fairy tales and Norse sagas on winter evenings. Through such stories lovingly told, Ingeborg nurtured her children's imaginative life with shape-shifting gods and goddesses, talking animals, witches, giants, fairies, and supernatural beings. By contrast, Wilhelm was an outdoorsman who instilled a restless curiosity and love of nature in his three inquisitive daughters and two small sons.

Tanne Dinesen was a gifted child who navigated her parents' divergent worlds and instinctively felt alienated from people less interesting than herself. Her mother's sphere was almost entirely domestic, although Ingeborg was active in her church and also in favor of voting rights for women. As for Wilhelm, the Danish writer and critic Georg Brandes described him as "a dreamer in broad daylight."[2] His good looks, energy, and cleverness were almost heroic, especially after he retreated from Europe to live among the Chippewa in the United States for three years. That dramatic rejection of European life was inspired by Denmark's tragic losses in the Dano-Prussian War (1864) and the revulsion he felt as a French Army captain in the bloody Paris Commune (1871).[3] To make matters worse, it was during that conflict that he learned of the death of his adored cousin of noble birth, Agnes Frijs, who died of typhoid fever in Naples while on vacation. In the wake of those years, Wilhelm Dinesen's reputation as a romantic legend was secured when he decided to write two books about his dramatic life experiences: *Paris under the Commune* and *Boganis: Letters from the Hunt,* which told of his adventures among the Chippewa.[4] Wilhelm eventually became a member of the Danish parliament, a role that marks him as a patriotic Dane. He was also a member of the Hørsholm Parish Council for ten years prior to his suicide in 1895, service that enhances his tragic image as a force in the community. In brief, in life and in death, Tanne's father was a complex personality whose multifaceted identity greatly appealed to his talented daughter.

Astute psychoanalyst and descendant of Ingeborg's family Anders Westenholz explains that "by identifying with her father, she [Karen Blixen] won not only the right but also the privilege of rebelling and liberating herself."[5] It was as if she felt a moral obligation to protect her innate alliance with Wilhelm in opposition to her mother's bourgeois view of the world to the extent that she eventually viewed a new life in Africa as her birthright. Unfortunately, while her African adventure brought her closer to her beloved father's memory, the loss of the farm and return to Denmark threatened to kill something of his spirit within her. In a veiled threat that reflected her suicidal depression in 1931, Blixen made her position clear to Thomas in one of her last letters from Africa: "I still feel that death is preferable to a bourgeois existence, and in death I will confess my faith in freedom."[6] Clearly, the meaning of suicide was not unfamiliar to Karen Blixen when she penned that reference to chosen death. Furthermore, her reference to "freedom" as an outcome of death conveys a deep, perhaps even instinctive, understanding of her father's predicament that was never explained to his children. For a long time, the unspoken "motive" was assumed to be syphilis—the same debilitating and disfiguring disease that Karen acquired from Bror Blixen in 1914, for which no reliable treatment or antibiotic cure existed until the mid-twentieth century. Had Wilhelm Dinesen been infected by a prostitute? Or did he feel hopelessly trapped between a passionate love affair and his "proper" marriage to the mother of his children? Neither financial woes nor legal matters seem to have played a part. For Tanne, at age ten, her father simply vanished.

The news of Wilhelm's death first broke as an announcement of illness when the Dinesen sisters were visiting Aunt Bess and their grandmother Mary Westenholz at nearby Folehave Farm.[7] Isak Dinesen's lifelong memory of this moment was inextricably linked to a deeply felt sensation of her father's footsteps pacing the floor "like a fox in a cage," although she could never be sure if the sound in her head was a memory of actual experience or a recurring dream.[8] She must have discussed it often with her longtime assistant Clara Svendsen, whose writings explain that "the children had been told that he was ill. When one of the aunts came into the room Tanne asked, 'How is father?' and was told that he had died." Shortly after this revelation, her older sister Ea spoke in a hushed voice to a room full of stunned adults when she said, "Tanne is trembling so." Svendsen also recalled an admonition that was, apparently, spoken that day and perhaps repeated through the years: "A widow's children must behave better than other children."[9] Thomas Dinesen, born in 1892, was too young to remember the drama of Wilhelm's death, although he was often taken to his father's grave at Hørsholm Cemetery with the other children and carefully taught to respect the man he barely knew. In his memoir written at age eighty-three, Thomas treats the suicide as a private matter beyond comprehension. "For some strange and, to us, quite unknown reason, he finally found life too difficult and in 1895 chose to take his own life at the age of forty-nine," he writes, adding that "he has always been a father to be proud of, a man we wished to emulate." The only judgment, if it can be read as such, occurs in his statement that Wilhelm's suicide "cast a shadow over Mother's life for many years."[10]

Eventually, Ingeborg came to terms with life as a widowed mother of five children between the ages of one and twelve at the time of her husband's death. Yet only in 1931 did she pen a reflection on the tragedy in a poignant letter to Thomas. Her words follow a sincere apology to her son for mistakenly opening a private letter addressed to him from his sister in Africa that *only he* was meant to read. Depressed and ill as she dismantles her life in Africa, Karen confesses in this letter that she cannot imagine returning to her mother's house as a permanent home because she would only feel "incarcerated" there. In fact, she states clearly that she would prefer death to the "bourgeois existence" that her mother had to offer. In Ingeborg's apologetic letter to Thomas, she expresses angst for all that she cannot do to help her daughter, even as she expresses respect for Tanne's true "nature." These thoughts of honoring a nature so different from her own naturally lead to thoughts of her husband's suicide, a topic triggered by Karen's frank mention of death in presumed confidence with her brother. Ingeborg opens her heart to Thomas with what amounts to a confirmation of syphilis, a disease then linked solely with sexual promiscuity, as the explanation for Wilhelm Dinesen's suicide in 1895: "To Father the thought of having to live as a sick and stricken man was intolerable, and when I felt,—especially during the initial painful period,—as if he had failed me, it immediately grew clear to me that it would have been impossible for him to live like that, and so he chose the only solution available to his nature."[11]

Ingeborg's revealing letter then turns to Karen, who is thousands of miles away in a desperate state of mind with no clear vision of the future. At this point, her troubled daughter and long-dead husband seem to merge as kindred spirits as Ingeborg struggles to understand them both:

> It must have been something in him that needed another side to life, perhaps during a period when he needed more peace and quiet after a stormy spell. I have no doubt that he was happy here in his home—happier than Tanne has ever been. . . . I know—and I know that you believe it to be true—that I will be able to give Tanne complete freedom to do what she thinks is best, for herself—I will not hold her back if she thinks life is too hard for her. . . . The sole consideration for me is that she should live according to her nature—I neither can nor will demand anything else of her.[12]

As a young widow in 1895, Ingeborg Dinesen's life, and that of her five children, became safely enclosed at the edge of a coastal village where life revolved around house, yard, stable, and farm. In this place, chosen by Wilhelm, they all felt protected—at least until the cottages blocking the road and view of the Sound collapsed in flames in the middle of a summer night on July 14, 1898. At the first sign of fire, Ingeborg dashed out of the house in her nightgown and ran toward the stable where she suffered a swift kick from a frantic horse. A farmhand was killed, as were pigs, hens, and the family's beloved Icelandic deerhound.[13] Suddenly, the yard was cloaked in ash, loss, and death while Ingeborg was confined to her bed for weeks, injured and shocked by a disaster that seemed to flow from the greater tragedy of her husband's suicide only three years earlier. As soon as she recovered, Thomas and Anders, at six and four years old, were moved to Folehave, where they would live with their grandmother and Aunt Bess for more than six months. And once the New Year's celebrations had passed, Ingeborg packed up her three adolescent daughters and invited their dear friend Else Bardenfleth to join them as they set off for Lausanne, Switzerland, where they all lived from January to July of 1899.

Lausanne opened the world for the Dinesen girls, who attended school for the first time in their lives—a French-speaking school called the École Benet. They were, in retrospect, the perfect ages (fifteen, thirteen, twelve) to delight in the city's steep streets and boat rides on Lake Leman before their final sojourn together on Isola Bella in northern Italy, just a few hours away by train. Understandably, the Dinesen sisters returned home as "young ladies" who could now claim a measure of sophistication in life as they settled into a "new normal" at Rungstedlund, where the rooms had been refurbished to eliminate the stench of smoke and the yard was now open to the endless blue of the Sound. A new tutor with competence in French, Miss Zøylner, was hired to maintain what they had learned in the French-speaking city of Lausanne. Even so, Tanne, more than the others, felt a longing for the wider world that neither cooking lessons (1901) nor Miss Sode's Drawing School (1903), nor painting lessons at the Royal Academy in Copenhagen (1903) could satisfy.

Fortunately, the Dinesen sisters gradually enjoyed more freedom to venture further from Rungstedlund. They accompanied their little brothers on outings to the deerpark in nearby Klampenborg, where they eventually attended horse races and fancy-dress balls whenever they were invited by aristocratic cousins. They also took the train to Copenhagen that had opened up the coastal "corridor," just as their father had predicted it would. The main attraction across the street on arrival in Copenhagen, then as now, was Tivoli Gardens Amusement Park with its eye-popping colors, fountains, gardens, and high-speed rides. Judith Thurman sums Tivoli up as "a great northern fantasy about southern life and love of pleasure, about Italian brilliance and temper, about Eastern luxury." In American terms it was, and is, a mixture of theater, circus, and county fair that invites people from all walks of life to step into a world of fantasy and excess. For Tanne Dinesen, the most fascinating part of Tivoli was the pantomime theater based on the Italian *commedia dell'arte* that fed her taste for symbolic characters as keys to the theater of life. As Thurman observes: "The tradition of virtuoso improvisation would help form Dinesen's sense of what it meant to be an artist, and the masquerade—the drawing of character in broad, mythic strokes—was an important element of her own art."[14] Still and forever, Tanne missed her father, even if the world that had formed him was within reach on the Dinesen family estate in Jutland. There at Katholm Castle, during a particularly long visit at age fifteen, she embraced her affinity with the rustic comfort of cluttered rooms, tangled woodlands, and marshes teeming with birdlife overlain with her father's spirit as a model of revolt against bourgeois conformity.

Although she was artistically motivated by fairy tales and sagas that offered magical solutions to real-world dilemmas, the puzzle of creating her own life at the dawn of a new century loomed large as Tanne Dinesen approached her twentieth birthday in April 1905. Many of her friends were accepting marriage proposals that settled all philosophical questions with romantic assumptions and Christian piety, yet her own life felt increasingly complicated. After the traumatic events of her father's death and the fire, she found it impossible to attribute pain and loss to "God's Will" or explain away evil as a consequence of the "Fall of Man." Why would a higher power punish her or anyone so severely? What ancestral guilt could account for the end of her walks to Ewald's Hill with Father or the death of an innocent dog in a raging fire? And if there was such a thing as the "Fall of Man" that required atonement, why shouldn't human intervention be possible to protect oneself against it?

Paradoxically, it was Tanne's mother, aunts, and grandmother who provided veiled answers to such questions by ensuring a relatively broad education at home. It was Ingeborg, after all, who had introduced her children to art, music, literature, and theater—that is, to imaginative reinventions of human experience that aspired to a higher level of human consciousness than the balm of "God's Will." Through the filter of such exposure to artistic creation Tanne, in particular, began to explore her own powers of imagination. In his 1978 memoir, Thomas recalls an unfinished "long drama" titled *Pride before Fall* written by Tanne at age eleven and another memory of an impressive "heroic poem of four long verses" performed for the family by his three sisters in 1897 to celebrate peaceful coexistence among Scandinavian nations.[15] A year later, at age thirteen, Tanne authored a play titled "Cassandra's Journey" to entertain the family as one of her "great dramas" in which she played the tragicomic servant Pierrot who hides his feelings behind a mask while her sisters acted out the romance of Harlequin and Columbine. The eighteenth-century plot would have been familiar to Tanne as it was popularized by the *commedia dell'arte* pantomimes performed at Tivoli in Copenhagen. There, as in her own production, the plot was neatly resolved in Columbine's declaration of love, although the thirteen-year-old author chose to add a statement of prophetic wisdom beyond her years: "Everybody's destiny is contradictory, and what you think will happen, never does."[16]

And so the depth and breadth of human imagination unfolded in the lives of Ea, Tanne, and Elle in multiple forms—from poetry and puppet shows to elaborate plays driven by comedy, irony, and tragedy. For despite the Victorian discipline of their matriarchal household, the girls were exposed to the classics of their era: Cervantes, Molière, and Shakespeare, to say nothing of real-life tales of Denmark's "mad King" Christian VII (r. 1766–1808). They were also taught to think and to reason in writing through ambitious essay assignments on topics as broad as "Matter and Spirit" or "Women in the French Revolution," although Tanne always found artistic invention preferable.[17] Among her projects at Miss Sode's Drawing School was a group of illustrations of Shakespeare's magical woodland scenery of *A Midsummer Night's Dream,* in which Elizabethan grandeur blended with the mystery of a nocturnal woodland.[18] Shakespearean scholar Anne Barton captures the essence of young Tanne's fascination when she writes that "it is in the nature of forests, both in literature and in life, not to be safe."[19] In this artistic phase of her young life, she also enjoyed a trip to the Netherlands to see Rembrandt's paintings, no doubt imagining herself as a great artist of darkness and light, and studied painting at the Royal Academy School in Copenhagen before she realized that her talent for painting was simply not remarkable enough. In the end, it was her literary talent that emerged from that world of verses, sonnets, stories, plays, puppet shows, and word games that she described as "the center of life" in her childhood home.[20]

By her early twenties, Tanne Dinesen was ready to turn from stories performed in the parlor at home to writing for publication. With the advantage of family connections, her stories appeared in the Danish magazine *Tilskueren* (The Spectator) under a pseudonym inspired by the heroic Seminole Indian "Osceola." These included "The Hermits" and "The Plowman" (1907), as well as "The DeCats Family" (1909), a drama set in the eighteenth century, originally conceived as a "comedy in two acts." In this early piece, we find elements developed years later in *Seven Gothic Tales,* most notably Blixen's aristocratic characters caught within twists and turns of a plot designed to expose secrets. The ever-elusive Truth emerges in "DeCats" as the author unmasks self-deception in a well-established family in Amsterdam whose members believed that "although . . . bourgeois, they surpassed all others in honesty and righteousness."[21] The ironic, comic tone with its allusions to colonization and slavery in distant lands might also be read as elements of an early glimpse of her interest in otherness, if not a nascent impulse to escape from Continental Europe as her father had done decades earlier. Finally, as the moment of reckoning in "DeCats" occurs in the intimate circle of a transformative dinner party, this early piece also serves as a prefiguration of *Babette's Feast,* another comic tale that would become popular a half century later, after its first publication in the American women's magazine *Ladies' Home Journal.*

Karen Blixen's impulse from an early age was to produce work of her own, even as the problems of Truth and Destiny remained unresolved in her mind. Until she could understand those looming questions, she could not take her work seriously. More to the point, she could not yet see herself as the writer she would become: "I really began writing before I went to Africa, but I never once wanted to be a writer. I published a few short stories in literary reviews in Denmark, when I was twenty years old, and the reviews encouraged me but I didn't go on—I don't know, I think I had an intuitive fear of being trapped."[22] Only gradually, in the mid-1920s, did she turn to writing tales at night as a kind of distraction from the burden of managing the indebted farm in Ngong. But she would have to wait until that first year after returning to Denmark in 1931 before she could "see the stork," to borrow a Dinesen-family metaphor eventually explained in *Out of Africa* with stick-figure drawings and a parable titled "Roads to Life." In this brief, illustrated story, avian body parts represent obstacles encountered by a man awakened in the night by a strange noise. He staggers out of the house in the dark in search of the cause but can't find it. He twists, turns, and falls into a ditch three times—but gets up and continues to stumble around in the dark until he finds the noisy leak and plugs it up. Only in the light of a day does he realize that his wanderings have made a clear, identifiable outline on his land that forms a picture—of a stork. Thus "seeing the stork" is equivalent to "seeing the whole," as opposed to the dark, disassociated fragments of a problem. In Karen Blixen's world, the fullness of Truth comes with dawn—an idea she returns to, again and again.[23]

Thanks to such puzzles, stories with symbolic characters, and Wilhelm Dinesen's fascination with the unknown, Tanne Dinesen reached adulthood prepared for the winding path her life would demand. She had absorbed the accumulated wisdom of pagan sagas, whimsical fairy tales, the *Arabian Nights,* Shakespeare, and the timeless model of Don Quixote's endless wandering. Furthermore, she welcomed magical figures as part of her own imaginary world, as we learn from Judith Thurman's summary of the contents of "a large bundle of Tanne's copybooks" dating to 1893 that include her first collected stories in which a "nisse" (gnome or elf) makes mischief in the spirit of a Hans-Christian Andersen.[24] Ultimately, the freedom to turn to the supernatural as a hidden power was always an option for Karen Blixen. Not surprisingly, we find it deployed in 1904 in her first wholly original work, "The Revenge of Truth—A Marionette Comedy." In this early masterpiece, a teenage Tanne Dinesen distilled everything she knew into one compelling plot propelled by a spectacular witch named Amiane whose flamboyant power expresses the young playwright's deep frustration with evil.

CHAPTER THREE

Truth and Revenge

The truth, my children, is that we are, all of us, acting in a marionette comedy.

—Amiane in "The Revenge of Truth," 1926

If *Out of Africa* is the flower in which the seeds of all of Blixen's previous works find expression, "The Revenge of Truth" is a first sign of germination. The drama revolves around a murderous innkeeper motivated by greed who is suddenly forced to confront a "good witch," Amiane, who casts a spell of Truth on his corrupt way of life. Not only did Tanne Dinesen create this character to entertain her family in 1904, when she played the role herself, she also created her first of many revealing self-portraits in this central and symbolic figure. In time, Blixen's body of work would be populated with witches and cunning old women described by Judith Thurman as "similarly infertile and capricious females who have more than made up for in power what they have lost in sex appeal."[1] As the moral conscience of "The Revenge of Truth," Amiane exists apart from sexual expression, just as Tanne did when she wrote the play. Yet more significantly, Amiane exists apart from limitations imposed by gender assumptions and social norms. In that sense, she is an early reflection of freedom expressed by those "new women" in modern society who were prepared to leave the Victorian era behind and claim, or earn, personal power in the new twentieth century. Young Tanne clearly wanted to be one of them.

It is no accident that in 1926, many of Karen Blixen's nights in Ngong were devoted to editing "Revenge" for publication in *Tilskueren* as a distraction from long, exhausting days of trying to save a doomed coffee farm. In the simplest terms, Amiane's feminized power expressed in her curse of Truth prefigures Blixen's acceptance of loss as the price paid for self-realization, an exchange she eventually enacted when she challenged herself to write a memoir of life in Africa as a work that would, above all, "tell the truth." It is no accident that Donald Hannah, the first translator of "Revenge," astutely described the witch Amiane as "the all-powerful God of Isak Dinesen."[2] As a literary persona and alter ego, the narrative voice of Isak Dinesen eventually shaped the author's confidence as this pseudonym became her most inventive mask of all. As a play written by a gifted young woman, "The Revenge of Truth—A Marionette Comedy" can be traced to the imaginary world of fairy tales, Norse sagas, and the tragic "split" between reality and dreams that marked Karen Blixen's childhood from the moment she learned of her father's death. The play also owes some debt to the nocturnal magic of Shakespeare's *Midsummer Night's Dream*, a play beloved by young Tanne, in which every character is trapped within an assigned role and the mix of roles converges to heighten comic tension. Framed by an inn, "Revenge" was first performed as a puppet show at the Dinesen family home, which had once been an inn, where the young playwright could easily imagine travelers pausing in the midst of their mysterious journeys. Her sharply drawn characters revive dark undertones of the age-old European tradition of moralistic tales published by the Brothers Grimm ("Hansel and Gretel," "Little Red-Riding Hood"). And finally, her invented lives draw on her exposure to the *commedia dell'arte*, first seen at Tivoli Gardens in Copenhagen. In a sense, "The Revenge of Truth" was Blixen's own "artful comedy" featuring familiar characters found in classic Italian Renaissance productions once performed by itinerant actors who were, not insignificantly, masked.

As her great-nephew Anders Westenholz reminds us, "Karen Blixen was fascinated by the puppet theater all her life, and she perceived since her return from Africa herself and her fellow human beings as puppets in the hands of Destiny."[3] Blixen's play is the first recorded sign of that fascination with its obligatory pair of young lovers—Sabine, the innkeeper's daughter, and Jan Bravida, who is just passing through. Their comic passion echoes the similar roles of Columbine and Harlequin that Tanne had assigned to her sisters in "Cassandra's Journey" in 1898, when she assumed the role of the tragicomic Pierrot. In keeping with the standard plot of a *commedia dell'arte* performance, the lovers in "Revenge" are thwarted by another familiar character—the miserly old man whose numerous versions include King Midas of Greek mythology, Shakespeare's Shylock in "The Merchant of Venice," and Dickens's infamous "Ebenezer Scrooge." In Blixen's creation, the miser happens to be the innkeeper as well as Sabine's father, Abraham (note the ironic biblical reference), who has become rich by murdering his guests and burying them in the garden as he pockets their money and steals their possessions.

Into this chaos steps the proverbial clever servant Mopsus, who predictably outwits his boss in order to redeem the underpaid servant class. It is a wild romp of a play in which good triumphs over evil with plenty of action and amusing "asides" spoken directly to the audience in the spirit of Tanne's beloved Shakespeare. The distinction from classical literature in "The Revenge of Truth" is, however, the matriarchal vision of a world in which magical power exists in the hands of a female character. Not only does Amiane embody Truth, she is also granted physical strength, as we see when she mounts a goat and dashes away after stating her terms to the evil innkeeper Abraham:

> Now, I am going to weave a spell, so listen carefully, for the whole point of the comedy lies in this. It is dark in the woods and in the meadows, the owls are hooting—can you hear them? I shall keep to darkness and to truth, for I guard the roots, and every living thing needs those two qualities for its own roots. You, you rich old miser, who do not recognize the truth when you see it, every lie told in your inn tonight shall be turned into truth before sunrise tomorrow morning. Only then will the spell be broken.[4]

Amiane thus resets the rules of the game as she implicitly appropriates the idea of "God's Will" as her own, a twist that Karen Blixen must have enjoyed. Meanwhile, the unscrupulous innkeeper represents the evil that must be overcome for balance to be restored "in the woods and in the meadows" teeming with life. As Amiane becomes the protector of life, Abraham and his ilk represent the specter of death with which so many age-old tales grapple. In a world where moral authority is reclaimed, the disgraced Abraham has met his match in Amiane, whose feminine powers include creativity, wit, and beauty—even if she is well beyond the game of seduction. Through Amiane, Blixen liberates herself at an early age to imagine herself as the one who "pulls the strings" of Destiny behind the scenes in order to choose her own life. Behind the mask of Amiane, the young author clearly refuses to become a mindless marionette.

Karen Blixen was feeling very much like a marionette in 1926 while writing "anecdotes" of African life and editing "Revenge" for *Tilskueren.* Based on that revision, Danish literary scholar Aage Henriksen wrote at length about Blixen's interest in marionettes as one of two dominant themes in her work, the other being the Fall of Man. In his astute reading, the 1926 version of the play "contains in essence the thoughts which later will receive much larger orchestration in her famous tales."[5] As he explains it, "The identifying characteristic of the central poetic figures in her tales is that they have appropriated all of the culture's religious and moral values, which they then use as a mask. With this mask as a means of social accommodation and external legitimation, they unleash a power that comes from a completely different source: the ancient, wild creative power that is utterly unconcerned with human order and morality."[6] This perspective, enriched by Donald Hannah's development of Blixen's "mask of Isak Dinesen," also offers a key to understanding *Out of Africa* as a battleground between Ngong's untamable environment in confrontation with the mask of the dominant social power awaiting her at Rungstedlund in the form of bourgeois propriety. Paradoxically, at least from

Blixen's perspective, it was the former that held the greatest potential of mythical harmony and therefore deserved to be idealized in her memoir.

In the true story of *Out of Africa,* the farm's chief investor and least sympathetic family member, Aage Westenholz, unknowingly plays the role of Abraham the innkeeper, especially after the pledge he imposed in 1922 redefined his niece's place in Ngong as a salaried employee, as opposed to an innately powerful and deserving family member. Clearly, her uncle's understanding of "human order and morality" exists in opposition to the "ancient, wild, creative force" that Amiane represents as a masked version of Karen Blixen. Though largely erased from the text of the memoir, this collision of incompatible worlds and worldviews, with its added twist of gender assumptions, inflamed Blixen's temper in ways that can be traced back to "The Revenge of Truth." Amiane is not simply powerful and wise, she is ferociously and rebelliously *moral* as she resets the terms of engagement in opposition to the greedy, patriarchal world of injustice that surrounds her. Insofar as Blixen was, in one way or another, always in dialogue with her previous inventions, "Revenge" articulated her conscious awareness of the gifts she possessed at an early age when she first began to work with themes of identity, illusion, feminized power, and idealized visions of a tragically unbalanced world.

When the time finally came in 1936 to write *Out of Africa,* Blixen had lived long enough and written enough to know that her book would have to demonstrate her fundamental resistance to living the dull life of a marionette. After befriending the aging Karen Blixen in the 1950s, Danish scholar Aage Henriksen wrote about her fear of living a "profound philosophical joke" as the Destiny she had dreaded most. He also resolved Blixen's essential conflict, albeit posthumously, by arguing that even when bad choices result in a dilemma, humans do not forfeit control because they *always* have a right to make bad choices and reject an existence in which "pure matter" and "pure spirit" might be perfectly coordinated. Henriksen's argument further affirmed the human spirit within the context of Blixen's work when he wrote that as a result of our uniquely human self-consciousness, "of all beings, only the human is capable of creating himself, of remaking himself according to his ideas."[7]

Henriksen's words written decades after her death would have delighted Blixen as a justification for her stubbornly independent stance during the best of her African years as well as later on when the creation of fictional characters helped her to reinvent herself through writing. She had struggled with the concept of Destiny vs. God's Will as a young girl in her early stories and brought her thoughts together in "The Revenge of Truth" at age nineteen. When she came back to the play to revise it for publication over a decade later, she surely saw her own reflection in Amiane, who forces a final reckoning with Truth in the form of a spell cast over those sleeping-walking through life in blissful ignorance. As Amiane attempts to converse with Abraham at the beginning of Scene Two, it is not difficult to hear the young Karen Blixen speaking to herself and also to the audience:

Abraham: I don't know who you are. Have you come to have supper at the inn, or have you come to beg?

Amiane: I have come to tell you the truth.

Abraham: The truth? I'm not afraid of your threats. Sit down then and tell it.

Amiane: (*sitting down*) You are one of the ideas of Nature and they are all wise. The woods where I come from are Nature's ideas as well, they are her deep thoughts, and the cows in the pastures are good and pretty fancies. Every individual member of the audience in the theater may be thought of as one of the ideas of Nature, although, considered as an audience, they aren't really, for there are limits to everything.

Abraham: Old woman, what egotism to demand that others should listen just because you want to speak.

Amiane: Some people do things they don't want to do, and they forget what they themselves really are. They upset the ideas of Nature, they make her clear wells muddy, beware of them![8]

The Revenge of Truth—a Marionette Comedy was first performed as a play at Rungstedlund at Christmastime in 1904.[9] But this was only the "first act" for a work that evolved well beyond "juvenilia" as Blixen continued to turn to it throughout her life. After editing it in Ngong for publication in 1926, she set it into "Roads around Pisa," the fourth of her *Seven Gothic Tales* (1934), as a nocturnal performance. Two years later, it was actually staged as a midnight performance at the Royal Theater in Copenhagen and went through further edits shortly before her death, when it became a stand-alone volume published in Denmark in 1960. Judith Thurman explains the ongoing revisions by noting that the play was "in fact, written and rewritten at the moments of Karen Blixen's life that were the most uncertain, formless, anguished, and full of the blind hope that things would turn out."[10] It was almost as if she were constantly testing herself against the ideal implied by Amiane's rebellious wisdom. In the wake of her death, "The Revenge of Truth" became a popular production in Scandinavian theaters and even had a run as a television series in Denmark. It is one of her most enduring works because it expresses her most enduring themes: greed, love, betrayal, and the power struggle that being true to oneself implies.

Karen Blixen's keen awareness of her personal power, and the price she paid for it, speak to the "mysterious, tragic nature of her character" so perceptively explained by her distant relation Anders Westenholz.[11] As a wise and powerful woman in search of Truth, Amiane prefigures the invented persona of Isak Dinesen, who becomes Karen Blixen's mask, mirror, and alter ego, as well as the calmly detached narrative voice of *Out of Africa.* Not unlike the invention of a magical witch more powerful than Tanne Dinesen felt herself to be, Karen Blixen's invention of Isak Dinesen resists the world of "marionettes" waiting for her in Denmark in 1931. In this way, Amiane reveals Blixen's essential dilemma of longing for a role apart from the conventional frames of bourgeois life represented by Ingeborg Dinesen: marriage, family, polite society, commitment to Christian duty. The only way to resolve this dilemma was to find a way to "pull the strings" of her own life, which she finally did with the great success of *Out of Africa.*

By 1937, Blixen had traveled far from the ambivalence so clearly expressed in one of her first letters from Africa to Aunt Bess that happens to mention her expectations for "Revenge" and of herself as a writer:

> With regard to "The Revenge of Truth," I don't want anything in it changed; but I imagine there is little chance of it ever being published. I don't think there is anything blasphemous in it, simply that it is written from an atheist's viewpoint. I believe that it would be impossible to write if one gave consideration to who is going to read one's work,—but for that matter I don't think I will be writing anything in the near future. On the whole, I don't think there is room for so many considerations in life, or the world.[12]

PART II

The Mythmaker's Art

CHAPTER FOUR

Metaphors of Truth

Equitare, Arcum tendere, Veritatem dicere.

—Karen Blixen's epigraph to *Out of Africa*

The Latin motto on the first page of *Out of Africa* draws on the ancient vocabulary of hunting on horseback, even as it announces the idealized quest of a modern woman. Its reference to riding with a bow and arrow to deliver the truth of life and death could be translated for our own era as "Move freely, Stretch yourself, Speak the truth." Blixen had grown up with horses as a means of transportation, attended horse races in Klampenborg, and learned to ride well enough to ride a horse around the farm in Ngong. She was also a person who wanted to be honest in her interactions with others. But when it comes to "telling the truth," things get complicated, as one Blixen biographer discovered when she asked Thomas Dinesen about the epigraph and got a blunt, literal interpretation: "Well, in fact," he replied, "my sister couldn't ride or shoot an arrow, and she never told the truth."[1]

The ideal of unvarnished truth as a liberating quest is, nevertheless, an essential feature of women's memoirs, even if Blixen's contribution to the genre stands apart from more recent bestsellers. *Out of Africa* is not confessional, in the spirit of Joan Didion's *The Year of Magical Thinking* (2007) or Tara Westover's *Educated* (2018). It does not chronicle the aftermath of tragedy as does Sonali Deraniyagala's *Wave* (2013) or trace an inspiring arc of success, such as millions have found in Michelle Obama's *Becoming* (2018). By contrast, Blixen shapes her surprisingly apolitical quest with the soft art of erasure when it comes to serious illness, psychic despair, marital conflict, and consequential visits from family members in the mid-1920s. Her emotional conflict with Bror Blixen is rationalized with magnanimity before she tucks it under the wing of nostalgia, while her sister's death, in the wake of delivering a stillborn baby, is too painful to mention at all—even though she and Thomas mourned that loss together in Ngong in 1922. In keeping with Sven Birkerts's insistence that all memoirs are "staged," Blixen's artful use of compression, understatement, erasure, distraction, and metaphor converts selective memory into a modern myth of exile and loss.

Out of Africa begins with nearly twenty pages of travelogue as the author recalls vistas of grassy plains, stately processions of animal migration, and tribal customs surrounding the farm in Ngong. Eventually, the narration returns to daily life when she zeroes in on the practicalities of coffee farming to evoke a symbolic self-portrait as she describes "plants set in the regular rows of holes in the wet ground where they are to grow, and then have them thickly shaded against the sun, with branches broken from the bush, since obscurity is the privilege of young things."[2] From this humble beginning, the book spreads out to encompass five "zones" of memory: I: Kamante and Lulu; II: A Shooting Accident on the Farm; III: Visitors to the Farm; IV: From an Immigrant's Notebook; and V: Farewell to the Farm. These parts are further divided into fifty-four incidents, anecdotes, parables, stories and portraits that seem to exist apart from the constraints of chronological—or historical—time. The memoir becomes a myth, in part, because "things happen" in a world where time is not "kept" or measured as we tend to do when we live by the clock. Though determined to "tell the truth," Blixen reveals a sense of truth that is primarily internal, personal, and reflective, not unlike the stream-of-consciousness approach to narrative associated with her famous contemporary Virginia Woolf.

Inevitably, *Out of Africa* raises essential questions about memoir and its uneasy relationship with truth. Is a memoir still a memoir when it treats memory like a dream of disconnected parts? Or does the impact of the whole—as Susan Tiberghien argues in *One Year to a Writing Life*—

constitute a deeper level of truth? On what basis can the memoirist be trusted with interpretations of emotional experience? And what about the author's perception of her own historic moment, which is likely to blur in the minds of readers within a generation or two? Blixen scholar Susan Hardy Aiken raises our awareness of all of this when she describes *Out of Africa* as a work "situated between the discourses of history and myth, fact and fiction, prose and poetry; partaking generically of forms as diverse as pastoral elegy, classical tragedy, autobiography, memoir, and travel tale; compounded of narrative, philosophical speculation, aphorism, parabolic reflection, and song."[3] It is almost as if Karen Blixen believed her experience to be so extraordinary that no particular genre could contain it, although one genre is deep enough and wide enough to contain everything on Aiken's list and that is *myth*. Yet because Blixen's myth is rooted in the familiar existential struggle of modern life, as opposed to playing out among ancient gods and goddesses, it takes a leap of altered expectations as well as an awareness of *OA*'s complexity to see it.

For readers willing to take such a leap, the questions posed above shift to make room for imagination, a release from chronological time, and the author's indulgence in self-mythology that makes a quasi-mythological figure of Karen Blixen herself in the pages of *Out of Africa*. The tone and tenor of her voice allow the narrator to present herself as a mere observer peering through a private window on the wonders and peculiarities of a place that she approaches as undiscovered, unknowable and, significantly, *timeless*. It is as if she has suddenly parachuted onto the African continent by accident with her vibrant claim to artistic freedom and authorial authority, both of which steer the reader toward a suspension of disbelief. In this interplay of voice, time, and storytelling, the narrator becomes a character in her own right whose idealized self in an idealized place observes a world that is "vital in its beauty, even as that beauty dissolves in a moving mirage." With these words, Blixen biographer Olga Pelensky captures something of how the internal/external quest embedded in *Out of Africa* is, ultimately, a quest for something that cannot be achieved as she writes of "the loss of Africa that is the Africa of the imagination."[4] Blixen herself seems to confirm this seismic shift in the final section of the memoir: "It was not I who was going away, I did not have it in my power to leave Africa, but it was the country that was slowly and gravely withdrawing from me, like the sea in ebb-tide."[5] At this point Blixen's ideals have been shattered as she concedes the territory of her own personal loss to a larger story. In this way, *Out of Africa* inscribes the narrator's particular loss as a metaphor for *all* losses everywhere.

Although a very different project from *Seven Gothic Tales,* the mythical mood of Blixen's memoir draws on her cultivated taste for long, intricate tales. Margaret Atwood has observed that age-old tales tend to evolve in the way of Scheherazade's *Arabian Nights* as a means of keeping death, and other terrifying consequences, at bay. In a similar way, writing a memoir reenacts life by giving the past a new life with new possibilities. At the end of "Deluge at Norderney," the opening tale in *SGT,* the spirit of Scheherazade is evoked through the voice of the indomitable Miss Malin, who, in a sense, dominates the tale. As Atwood reminds us, "Tales have tellers and listeners within them much more frequently than realistic stories do."[6]

The interaction of a variety of voices is especially common in journey tales in which mythical wisdom emerges from a group of strangers whose lives intersect in strange surroundings. In the case of "Deluge," the characters endure a stormy night of rising flood waters by telling tales, including some blatantly dishonest ones, until the first hint of light appears on the edge of the horizon. Just as dawn sheds the light of truth in "The Revenge of Truth," the first rays of morning sun signal survival in "Deluge" when "the old woman slowly drew her fingers out of the man's hand and placed one upon her lips." Miss Malin's narration then closes the tale in italicized French that reads like a whisper: "'*A ce moment de sa narration,*' she said, '*Scheherazade vit paraître le matin et, discrète, se tut.*'" ["*At this moment in her narrative,*" she said, "*Scheherazade saw dawn appear and, discreetly, became silent.*"][7] This reference at the end of the first tale in Blixen's first book announces her recognition of storytelling as a death-defying power that had, effectively, enabled her to overcome her devastating loss of self in 1931. In her exploration of the cultural "trope" of feminine death, which appears so often in western art and literature, literary critic Elisabeth Bronfen begins her provocative *Over Her Dead Body: Death, Femininity, and the Aesthetic* with an intriguing question: "Wherein does the power, the necessity, the fascination, and the inherent danger in the conjunction between femininity and death lie?"[8] Blixen would, no doubt, answer that question with one word: "storytelling," which is to say with a woman's voice speaking her truth as a means of survival. As Bronfen probes the depth of this idea that we encounter in Blixen's "Deluge," and in many other works, evocations of Scheherazade emerge.[9]

That said, the age-old image of Scheherazade seducing the once-betrayed Sultan with stories for 1001 nights—until he falls in love with her—has also "shape-shifted" throughout western culture as an image that represents a life of pleasure and privilege. As Susan Brantly notes, the origins of Scheherazade's presence in western literature are essentially aristocratic, as she finds when "the baroness in Goethe's *Conversations of German Emigrants* (1795) insists that stories should show they are being told 'in good society.' After all, Scheherazade's tales told to the court of the caliph and the storytellers of the *Decameron* were all noble ladies and gentlemen."[10] It is fitting, then, for Blixen to be reminded of Scheherazade in *Out of Africa* in the context of her relationship with the Somali women whose lives prepare them for a kind of aristocratic existence: "Sometimes, to entertain me, they would relate fairy tales in the style of the Arabian Nights, mostly in the comical genre, which treated love with much frankness."[11] It is also fitting for Blixen to evoke an image of herself as a seductive Scheherazade exercising her feminized "power" over the aristocratic Denys Finch Hatton: "In the evenings he [Denys] made himself comfortable, spreading cushions like a couch in front of the fire, and with me sitting on the floor, cross-legged like Scheherazade herself, he would listen, clear-eyed, to a long tale from when it began until it ended."[12] And finally, a similar association echoes as a bitter critique in Ngũgĩ wa Thiong'o's prison essay titled "Detained," in which he imagines how "every European was instantly transformed into a blue-blooded aristocrat" when he arrived in colonial Kenya and saw himself transported to "a vast valley garden of endless physical leisure and pleasure that he must have once read about in the *Arabian Nights* stories."[13]

One way to read *Out of Africa* is, most certainly, as a series of tales similar to Blixen's favored form of the "journey tale," which often begins by venturing out of familiar territory into new relationships. This calls for a boundary between the vanished past and problematic present such as we find in Blixen's deceptively simple first line: "I had a farm in Africa, at the foot of the Ngong Hills." Attentive readers tend to hear this as a wistful, confiding voice that lures the reader across a psychic threshold into an unknown past. This "signpost" invites readers to follow the narrator on a journey concocted of memory and nostalgia into a lost world that can only exist in the author's imagination now that many years have passed since the events she is about to recall—or invent—with her storyteller's voice, which is a kind of mask. Judith Lee writes persuasively of Blixen's consciously altered voices as she navigates and writes about her "three most important relationships—with the Africans, with other women, and with a man . . . by which she reconciles opposing values in a way that both valorizes and modifies her imagined autonomy." Blixen needed to do both as the writing of *OA* required her recreation of herself as a protagonist in a story or, as Judith Lee would say, "a representative individual," as opposed to the "private person she was in her letters.[14]

As we know, Blixen circumvented this duality by inventing an exotic, male pseudonym circa 1932. "Isak Dinesen" enlarged Blixen's storytelling powers as it conjoined the contradictory sensibilities of irony and comedy (Isak = Hebrew "one who laughs") with familial love and tragedy (Dinesen = her paternal family name). This name, now oddly familiar, evokes the image of Karen Blixen as the ever-present listener intent on learning something from her "other voice" that came from her less-restricted self in the masked persona of Isak Dinesen. Danish literary scholar Mads Bunch defines the "liberating mask" of Isak Dinesen as "an emblem of a particular voice, or worldview, that includes irony, the right to poke fun at everything, truth seeking, and complete artistic freedom both thematically and style-wise."[15] Susan Hardy Aiken puts it more simply, but no less profoundly, when she states that "Karen Blixen is and is not Isak Dinesen."[16] In *Out of Africa,* two "minds" and two voices coexist—and need to coexist in order for this story to be told.

In *Out of Africa*'s mythical tone and structure of multiple genres I read a writer's artistic method of replicating the kaleidoscopic interplay of truth and fiction that inevitably converges in the art of memoir. This offers the narrator a range of possibilities in her quest to reclaim a vision of Africa as place to which she once belonged in terms of emotion as well as acreage. It is, ultimately, the tension between loss and belonging that makes the narrator's exile relatable, since most of us long for a time or a place that can never be recovered. When Blixen's life in Africa becomes infused with loss, the metaphor of the "lost place" of lived experience in a vanished past is artfully evoked as a unifying metaphor in the Gikuyu custom of leaving a door open as a space through which the absent person might return—in body or in spirit, since both claim a kind of presence.[17]

Loss is woven into the fabric of *Out of Africa.* It links predominant themes of exile and possession and develops in the context of Blixen's encounter with Others who appear, at first glance, as shadows belonging to groups that naturally exclude her new identity of Baroness Blixen. She, who represents yet another white smudge of "otherness" to those who must now make a space for her, watches their movements and hears their voices in the landscape encompassing her new house, the Ngong Hills, and her yet-to-be discovered frame of personal experience. This "surround" includes wild animals such as Lulu, the fine-boned bushbuck who becomes an honored guest until she returns to the wild, ready to mate. There are also collective "characters" in the form of mysterious Masai warriors, "squatters" who live on her land, ever-present children (*totos*) too numerous to name, and an old Gikuyu women fascinated by this *msabu* (white woman). Yet another category of Others involves the individuals Blixen comes to depend upon: house servants Juma, Farah, and Kamante become known to readers of *Out of Africa* as personalities, as does the Gikuyu chief Kinanjui, played to perfection in the 1985 film by his grandson. These closer relationships eventually open her mind to listening and learning with self-deprecating humor as she begins to question her own otherness in their eyes. This capacity of Blixen to see herself through the eyes of people so unlike herself creates a mood of compassion in *Out of Africa,* even if many a postcolonial scholar "reads" her underlying motive as a self-serving image of benevolence.

Inevitably, Blixen relies on a language of metaphor to express and center herself. Lulu's freedom to roam as a wild creature is a metaphor for the freedom Karen Blixen desires. Farah's stoicism conveys a version of aristocracy she hoped to achieve through her marriage to Baron Bror von Blixen-Finecke. And the Gikuyu boy Kamante Gatura's status as an outsider is a reflection of her own marginal position in British colonial society, even as she struggles to comprehend him. As her close relationship with Kamante unfolds, she writes amusingly of his giftedness and his ways of working around her pointless rules, as he does when he learns how to cook for her despite his indifference to European food or cooking implements. "When I gave him a machine for beating eggs he set it aside to rust, and beat whites of egg with a weeding knife that I had had to weed the lawn with and his whites of egg towered up like light clouds."[18] Clearly, Kamante is adept at quietly, but firmly, resisting Blixen's attempts to train him when "training" involves too much departure from his own way of being. To her credit, she realizes this even if she cannot quite imagine his reality.

When Kamante suddenly appears in her room in the middle of the night with a hurricane lamp, he becomes a metaphor for her encounter with otherness and, in a sense, matches her power as he stands at her bedside "like a dark bat that had strayed into the room, with very big spreading ears."[19] In this riveting vignette, he urges her to get out of bed because he is obviously troubled by something he has seen. "I think that you had better get up. I think that God is coming," he says. She gets up and goes to the window with him where they stand shoulder-to-shoulder as he directs her attention to a strange grass fire on a distant hill. For her, it is identifiable as a fire on a hot night that will vanish with predictable rainfall. For him, it is a spiritual sign of God's presence. They stand side-by-side for a long moment, both fascinated and somehow connected at opposite ends of a mysterious, human continuum.

In this strangely intimate moment Blixen realizes that the boy who seems like such an oddity is actually endowed with valid ways of seeing and feeling the world that are simply inaccessible to her. This realization emerges out of utter darkness, like the faraway fire that becomes a perfect metaphor for all that is unknown. Blixen's narration allows us to see them there, two radically different people staring at something that is either a grass fire or God in a scene that encapsulates metaphors of darkness and truth-signifying light. The entirety of such moments becomes a metaphor for the creative potential of memory itself as Susan Hardy Aiken suggests when she writes that "if, out[side] of Africa, she imagined her existence as an exile, a living death, a 'dream,' by a great act of courage and imagination she also plunged into those depths, turning the space of that dream—the dislocations of that life—into the site of restorative creation."[20]

This vision of Karen Blixen sharing a visual, metaphorical, spiritual experience with Kamante circumvents the problem of language and brings them closer—for a moment. Yet it also reminds us of how elusive cultural understanding can be when the standard filter of English language and European culture is applied. The Kenyan novelist Ngũgĩ wa Thiong'o (1938–2025) zeroed in on the problematic nature of this when he explained that as one of twenty-eight children in a large, peasant family, "We spoke Gikuyu as we worked in the fields. We spoke Gikuyu in and outside the home. I can vividly recall those evenings of story-telling around the fireside. It was mostly the grown-ups telling the children, but everybody was interested and involved."[21] Oddly enough, his memory echoes Blixen's own childhood evenings of tales told at Rungstedlund, but here Ngũgĩ wa Thiong'o was interested in exploring the unique cultural memory that language represents and how English serves to appropriate and/or dilute the meaning of African lives. "Language, any language, has a dual character," he writes. "It is both a means of communication and a carrier of culture."[22]

Another dramatic lesson in *Out of Africa* avoids the issue of spoken language because it concerns animal life in a parable of possession titled "The Iguana."[23] This story is told in an unhurried voice that recounts a frank encounter with otherness in the form of a sparkling lizard whose death gives birth to Blixen's more authentic self. We do not know if this parable is based on factual memory or not, but this barely matters as Blixen cleverly demonstrates the limits of unentitled possession by confessing her instinctive need to possess the object of her desire.

She begins with a young woman's fascination with the iridescent skin that catches her eye, which Blixen translates into a purely European image of a stained-glass window: "They shine like a heap of precious stones or like a pane cut out of an old church window." But unlike the Christian "text" of tales told in stained glass, these African iguanas "swish" and move away in a "flash of azure, green, and purple over the stones" so that "the color seems to be standing behind them in the air like a comet's luminous tail." In the face of such natural beauty, the "immigrant"—an ironic word chosen to indicate the author's position as an outsider—is filled with a desire to possess a piece of this iridescence in order to make "some pretty things."[24] Here, the concepts of possession and desire for "pretty things" can be compared to her desire to both own and live off of the farm she is struggling to keep, as well as the vast world of Nature that constantly affirms her fragile sense of exile. Nevertheless, she acts instinctively as a person who has come to Africa to purchase and possess whatever she needs or wants when she shoots the iguana without thinking much about it.

To her surprise, and ours, she confesses regret almost immediately when she writes that "once I shot an Iguana." The flat simplicity of that statement echoes the memoir's opening line that divides past and present. With this boundary established, the narrator is now prepared to tell the tale of her frivolous desire, of her unjust claim to possession, and of her sense of shock as she approaches the dead animal that suddenly "faded and grew pale, all color died out of him as in one long sigh, and by the time that I touched him he was gray and dull like a lump of concrete."[25] In this moment, the iguana's soul is vanishing before the narrator's eyes and taking its sparkling life with it. As she observes the transformation,

Blixen is left with the painful realization that she cannot possess the dazzling beauty she craves because it is, or was, another being's beauty that only existed as part of the other being's life. Like Kamante's fear of God ignited by a grass fire that will soon be dampened, the dying iguana forces a reversal of the gaze in order for her to see the Other as a creature who should—like herself—be free to live or die quite literally in its own skin.

This parable glitters with meaning as the death/murder of a wild lizard becomes a metaphor of cultural appropriation, an idea central to Ngũgĩ wa Thiong'o's recurring critique of *Out of Africa.* As readers, we observe a young woman standing alone, confused, and bereft, still holding a gun when she seems to turn to the reader with a warning: "For the sake of your own eyes and heart, shoot not the Iguana." With those words, the narrator of this parable expresses a moment of double-consciousness—the deep realization of two subjectivities where she had previously been conscious of hers alone. It is too late, of course, but now she knows that another's life can be admired but never possessed and made into "pretty things" with which to adorn herself. *Don't even try it,* she seems to say, because any such act of possession is equivalent to death. In this way, the metaphor of a dying Iguana becomes an image of an unknown world that is not only Karen Blixen's farm in Ngong but of the world beyond the farm that belongs to itself, full of creatures who belong to themselves, in a world that exists beyond the will of colonial domination. In *Out of Africa,* Blixen/Dinesen's metaphors do what all metaphors must do: pierce the surface to reveal hidden truths. Truth is the origin of metaphor because there is no metaphor without truth.

CHAPTER FIVE

A Trace of Erasure

By thy mask I shall know thee.

—The Cardinal's valet, masquerading as the Cardinal, in "The Deluge at Norderney," 1934

Staging a memoir requires acts of erasure, large and small. Some clarify. Others omit. Still others function like an ancient palimpsest where the hand of time can be traced through earlier versions and distant visions. Once identified, the soft art of erasure becomes absorbed into the meaning of a text. Erasures occur throughout *Out of Africa* and encompass omissions of family visits, Blixen's syphilis diagnosis, financial details of the indebted farm, emotional meltdowns, and her deafening silence regarding the British Colonial Administration's exploitation of land and labor. As Simon Lewis argues, "Erasing the historically specific conditions of labor on which the cultural capital of book, film, and safari depend is both exploitative and exploitable."[1] This cannot be denied, yet how one act of "literary" erasure leads to other/larger inaccuracies in other/larger forms beyond the grave is not the focus here. Rather, I want to understand how Blixen's use of the art of erasure creates an illuminating absence—something like emptying a room of heavy, uncomfortable furniture—in order to fill that space with a lighter version of reality from a particular angle of vision.

Writing in a first-person voice that foregrounds inner life and avoids historical particularity, Blixen often turns to the natural world as if Nature exists to anesthetize—or aestheticize—pain. Robert Langbaum found a perfect word for this sleight of hand when he defined *Out of Africa* as a "pastoral" in the first literary study of Blixen's memoir: "It is because Africa figures as a paradise lost—both in Isak Dinesen's life and in the life of Europe—that *Out of Africa* is an authentic pastoral, perhaps the best pastoral of our time."[2] This statement hints at the deep layers of historical longing discussed earlier in Thomas R. Knipp's analysis of "triple nostalgia."[3] Yet even as the literary achievement of *Out of Africa* tapped into collective nostalgia, it could not conceal elements of colonialism that surface in the book. At the same time, references to Blixen's contradictions also reveal nuances of her relations with the African people who lived and worked on and near the farm who "lost a passionate advocate when Dinesen was forced to return to Denmark."[4]

An obvious example was her deep concern with the fate of the "squatters" (displaced people) who would be evicted once she sold the farm. To Blixen's credit, she worked hard to negotiate a place where all 2,000+ of them could live in the Dagoretti Forest Reserve because she felt a deep sense of personal responsibility that echoed her definition of *noblesse oblige*. In that scenario she also understood that their plight had been created by the absurdity of colonialism itself: "It is more than their land that you take away from the people, whose Native land you take. It is their past as well, their roots and their identity," she writes.[5] In happier times, she created a controversial school and established a clinic for non-Europeans on the terrace of her house where "my renown as a doctor had been spread by a few lucky cures, and had not been decreased by the catastrophic mistakes that I had made."[6]

Why, then, does so much of Blixen's memoir suggest an apparent desire to disassociate herself from the historical reality of colonialism in Kenya? One answer to that question is simply a matter of her literary voice, which is naturally selective in her desire to produce a storyteller's effect decidedly different than the reportage of daily life in her *Letters from Africa*. There, she felt free to explain and complain about things that she consciously decided not to bring into the narration of her "pastoral." Another reason might be that her position as a foreigner of Danish nationality living alone in colonial Kenya created a sense of separation from the dominant colonizing culture. As Brantly points out, "Dinesen was highly interested in Kenyan politics, but was doubly disenfranchised because she was not a man and not a British citizen."[7]

Ultimately, Blixen's acts of erasure are more personal than political and begin with the absence of her dysfunctional relationship with Bror Blixen. As Langbaum points out, "You would have to look hard to gather that she was married and divorced while in Africa."[8] A few years later, writer Jean Stafford quipped that "one could say that she eliminated the sour notes through the simple expedient of eliminating her husband . . . but there is more art to it than that."[9] In the same spirit, she accepts her difficult case of syphilis, most likely acquired from Bror in their first months of marriage, for which the only treatment at the time involved arsenic and mercury, both poisons known to ravage and sterilize the human body.[10] In the face of such erasure, even high-minded philosophers such as Hannah Arendt could not resist pointing out that "*Out of Africa,* which is often called autobiographical, is singularly reticent, and silent on almost all the issues her biographer would be bound to raise. It tells us nothing about the unhappy marriage and divorce, and only the careful reader will learn from it that Denys Finch Hatton was more than a regular visitor and friend."[11]

Another ordeal almost as painful as her marriage, divorce, poor health, and her ultimately tragic love affair with Finch Hatton was Blixen's ongoing struggle to cope with discouraging legal/financial matters. These involved the principal investors in the farm: her mother Ingeborg Dinesen and Uncle Aage Westenholz, as well as others in their wider family circle. After his personal visit to Ngong in 1921 as chairman of the board of the Karen Coffee Company, Uncle Aage gradually became Blixen's nemesis acting on behalf of his sister, the aging Ingeborg. By 1922, the acrimony reached a new level with Westenholz's blunt "pledge" that required Karen Blixen's signature and a change in her status in order to keep the farm afloat financially. In the memoir, all of this is told "slant" or simply not mentioned because "these did not fit the shape given to her experience in

Africa by the succession of catastrophes which finally separated her from what, in retrospect, figures as an unalloyedly golden time."[12]

Blixen's *Letters from Africa*, first published in Danish in 1978, and in English in 1981, are indispensable reading alongside her memoir because they illustrate her conscious technique of masking lived experience through omission, understatement, and self-absorption, all of which constitute acts of erasure designed to conceal uncomfortable truths. Regarding family pressure to divorce Bror Blixen, she eventually becomes so irritable with her mother that she suggests they cease to correspond. She even scolds Ingeborg Dinesen with a rare reference to the humiliation of Wilhelm Dinesen's sordid suicide by hanging in a Copenhagen hotel room and the gossip that it surely inspired. As 1921 draws to a close, Blixen writes that "you talk about the humiliation to which Bror has exposed me. But just once endeavor to compare seriously in your mind some humiliation that father might have imposed on you in your private relationship with the humiliation it would have been for instance, if Uncle Gex and Aunt Ulla, Ulf, and Uncle Alfred had been called to a meeting to discuss whether you should get divorced or not."[13]

By the end of November, Blixen's tone has become wistful as she ponders "if it would ever be possible to put on my tombstone, as on [Robert Louis] Stevenson's, 'Here he is, where he longed to be, home is the sailor, home from the sea, and the hunter home from the hill.'"[14] And early in 1922, she sends a particularly heartfelt letter to Ingeborg to "give you some sort of explanation of my relationship with Bror. . . . For I now think we are, in fact, going to be divorced, and there is no need for this to be kept secret, although I am reluctant to have it mentioned to outsiders."[15] Her letters to her mother were not always so open in the matter of personal relationships, but at this point she is eager to rationalize Bror's temperament as "completely different from mine" and to generously absorb the fault and failure of their relationship: "In many ways my relationship with Bror was a problematic task,—one that I believed to be the most important of my life,—and that I have been quite unable to fulfill. . . . Much of my youth has and my strength has gone into it, and I think something of my soul. I have cared indescribably much for Bror in spite of everything, and for many years he has been the person I was closest to in the world."[16]

Eventually, this letter gathers the strength to explain that should it all "come to nothing," she could never return home to Denmark because of her delight in the house and the garden and also in people she has become "attached to," people like Denys Finch Hatton, for example. "I have the feeling, which one seldom gets at home, that I have created this myself and that it is a part of me," she writes, before her desperate "addendum" addressed to "*Beloved Mother*": "So I beg of you all, and especially you, to help me by speaking well of me, and also thinking kindly about me; it is harder for me than you perhaps understand."[17] Alas, her feelings for Bror were never understood by her family, not even by her closest sibling, Thomas, who urged her to go through with the divorce that became final in 1925 and, like the others, found Bror to be a convenient scapegoat for the unprofitability of the farm. After all, his weakness and ineptitude as a husband masked Aage Westenholz's own lack of judgment in encouraging this privileged young couple to set off for the East African Protectorate in the first place.

After her erratic plea for understanding in January 1922, Blixen waited three months before writing again to her mother. In the interim, she was immersed in an unpleasant correspondence with Uncle Aage involving the legalistic pledge he drafted to keep the farm afloat with his niece as a salaried employee, albeit with the title of "general manager" (*fermière générale*). Despite its repugnant tone and far-reaching implications, Blixen reluctantly signed the new "terms of engagement" on February 2, 1922. Considering the significance of this document and her uncle's authority over her life throughout this period, the pledge is worth quoting here in full:

> Whereas engineer Aage Westenholz, chairman of the board for Karen Coffee Co. Ltd. A/S, has stated to the undersigned, Karen Christentze Blixen-Finecke, his wish that Baron Bror Blixen-Finecke, in the interest of the company, hereafter shall have nothing whatsoever to do with

> said company; not be consulted with respect to its affairs; not act in behalf of the company or by others presumed to have any authority in its behalf; not receive as compensation, gift, or any other way except as a shareholder in the company anything therefrom in terms of money, valuables, securities, or guaranties, or a promise of such, and not appear at or reside within the borders of the company's premises.
>
> I, the undersigned, pledge hereby that as long as I am in the service of the company, I will to the best of my ability strive to comply with the above-stated wishes in order that Baron Blixen-Finecke never with my knowledge and consent shall have anything to do with the affairs of the company, receive anything therefrom, or be found upon its premises as stated. If at any time it cannot be successfully managed to keep Baron Blixen out of the company's affairs and borders, I pledge to bring this to Engineer Westenholz's attention without delay as well as the extent to which, and the causes why, this happened.
>
> Should it be found that I, in the opinion of Engineer Westenholz, have not been able to comply with the above pledge, I declare myself ready to, upon his request, immediately resign from the service of the company and leave its premises against payment of my salary for the current month. (Signed Karen von Blixen)[18]

Uncle Aage's controlling impulse as "Engineer Westenholz" and denial of his niece's feelings were deeply offensive to "Karen von Blixen," who expressed as much in her response that accompanied her signature on the pledge: "The entire mode of thinking here is to me so incomprehensible that I would really rather not have anyone know that my family had been capable of putting together such a document," she wrote in a note sent back to Denmark with the signed pledge. To that, Aage Westenholz replied, "But I fail to see that this pledge is anything but a very moderate and sensible demand."[19]

Thomas was with Blixen in Africa and able to read these letters in real time, and so he began his own correspondence with Aage Westenholz in defense of his sister's struggle against Bror Blixen's "vicious lies" and incessant pleas for funds. In hopes of a truce, Thomas suggested that

Westenholz draft another document ensuring a potential benefit for Bror Blixen of 10 percent of the sale price, in the event that the farm might eventually be sold to cover debts. Uncle Aage promptly dismissed this idea as "unthinkable," adding that while he would regret Karen Blixen's departure: "The majority of the board wishes nothing better than that she should disappear. I, who for the most part represent a minority, would be sorry to see Tanne leave KC [Karen Coffee Co.], but I do not, on the other hand, believe that she is indispensable." He goes on to state in no uncertain terms that if Thomas's sister were to leave Ngong and the farm "collapse," at least the family would "quickly and easily be rid of this interminable drain which we to a great extent got a hold of and kept going for Tanne's sake."[20]

Clearly, Westenholz was a businessman disconnected from his niece's emotional life, which he interpreted as little more than stubborn resistance. He saw her as spoiled and impractical in the 1920s and because he died in 1935, never knew her as particularly successful at anything. He obviously could not know circa 1922 that she would become the best-known writer among "Kenya's literary ladies," as Thomas R. Knipp described the triumvirate of Karen Blixen, Beryl Markham, and Elspeth Huxley. Knipp's regrettably patronizing critique dwells on Blixen's bubble of self-mythology and apparent dehumanization of Black African people. Yet he is not incorrect when he describes *Out of Africa* as the "paradigmatic white African memoir" in which the author's mythmaking results in a "myth in which Africa plays a central structural role in a European story."[21] For Simon Lewis, Knipp's work loops back to "the question of pastoral and the erasure of economic considerations in presenting a benevolent lord of the manor—in Blixen's case, the benevolent 'literary lady' who had a farm."[22]

Nor could Uncle Aage have imagined that his niece would, one day, be described as one of three "notable figures" in the early years of Kenya's development who "owed their fame and socio-cultural capital in part to being semi-incorporated into tribal peoples but tacking back into the world of white privilege." This somewhat back-handed compliment from cultural anthropologist Janet McIntosh occurs in the context of her fascinating study of the descendants of early British settlers in colonial Kenya, which is one reason Karen Blixen is somewhat out of place here. For unlike her fellow "notables"—Lord Delamere and paleontologist Louis Leakey—Karen Blixen did not acquire land, build wealth, or bequeath fortunes made in colonial Kenya to descendants. In fact, she had no descendants at all. Rather, her inclusion here seems to be based on her reputation as a woman "whom many settlers saw as unnaturally respectful of Blacks." In any case, these three are notable for McIntosh because they "got to feel as though they belonged to Kenya and Kenya to them."[23] Yet much as Blixen might have liked to be short-listed with them, not least because the others are men, her feelings of belonging were tenuous at best. Ultimately, McIntosh's analysis demonstrates how hard Blixen is to categorize as a racist, land-grabbing colonialist.

Ultimately, Blixen's quarrel with Uncle Aage was about two, separate worldviews that could never be reconciled. Hers was that of a white, privileged woman who remained economically dependent on family until she published *Seven Gothic Tales* at age forty-nine. Meanwhile, Westenholz's identity rested on his role as a responsible, upright Dane who had made his fortune as a civil engineer and plantation owner in Thailand and Malaysia and was eager to share his wisdom with the next generation. His intuition faltered, however, when he encouraged the unreliable and ill-prepared Bror Blixen to dash off and buy a farm in a fertile region of Great Britain's East Africa Protectorate in 1913, a time when white Europeans in the region numbered no more than 1,300. Westenholz's calculation of opportunity was nevertheless correct since the development of land, technology, and government continued after World War I as the Crown Colony of Kenya entered its "sunbeam period."[24] It is difficult to imagine a century later that when the first conference of the East Africa Federation was convened by Lord Delamere in 1925 "not more than 20,000 non-official white Europeans were scattered over a territory one-third the size of the United States."[25]

As subsequent letters reveal, the farm would continue to take on debt throughout 1922 and into 1923 until it reached the brink of bankruptcy. At this point, Uncle Aage expressed his fear that the situation threatened to leave "poor Mother picked to the bone." This concern resulted in his proposal, floated at a board meeting of the Karen Coffee Company thousands of miles away in Denmark, that as *fermière générale* Blixen should agree to settle for a reduction of her salary of approximately $1,600 per month in 2023 values ($95 in 1923) to a new formula of 50 percent in cash and 50 percent in ownership shares in the farm. In rationalizing his idea, he explains to his niece in March 1923, "I am definitely of the opinion that you ought to bear this sacrifice."[26] Needless to say, this was yet another remark that triggered ill-will and deep despair, as Blixen took on a moral debate with her uncle over the meaning of "sacrifice" and wrote to her brother—now back in Denmark—that "since I received Uncle Aage's letter, the fragrance has gone out of the rose and the radiance from the full moon in my life here."[27]

In contrast to the text of *Out of Africa,* this brief summary of Karen Blixen's "real life" in colonial Kenya reveals the extent to which she was consumed with emotional turmoil, financial anxiety, and alienation from family in the early 1920s and, effectively, until her departure in 1931. Yet, the true extent of this ordeal never quite filters into the text of her memoir. Rather, the all-consuming problems touched upon here are compressed into poetic vignettes and reflections on Nature. Even as the fifth section of the book, titled "Farewell to the Farm," summarizes her struggles across five pages under the confessional rubric of "Hard Times," she artfully evokes the unpredictability of Nature rather than the angst she and the farm's investors endured: "My farm was a little too high up for growing coffee. It happened in the cold months that we would get frost on the lower land and in the morning the shoots of the coffee-trees, and the young coffee-berries on them, would be all brown and withered. The wind blew from the plains and even in good years we never got the same yield of coffee to the acre as the people in the lower districts of Thika and Kiambu, on four thousand feet."[28] Blixen also mentions being "short of rain" in Ngong, a stunning understatement that covers three droughts, each of which lasted a full year. She also attributes her rising debt to the global price of coffee in 1929 rather than to the soil and altitude well known to be less than ideal for growing coffee. None of her "excuses" are entirely dishonest, but she opts for the art of erasure time and time again as she describes the farm's inevitable failure as the result of "natural" events beyond human control. In fact, the actual cause of her failure at running a coffee farm in Ngong was a combination of poor judgment and the utter lack of experience she and Bror brought to their optimistic vision imagined from the comfort of family wealth back in Europe. As Elspeth Huxley put it, "The colonial farmer is optimistic to the point of folly."[29]

No one lived up to this statement as fully as Karen Blixen, although she was not alone in her assumption of success based on a home-grown sense of entitlement. Bror Blixen's safari skills, sexual appetites, and sheepish charm, memorably portrayed by Klaus Maria Brandauer in the 1985 film, have long since entered the "Happy Valley" legend of colonial Kenya as an elite society of endless parties, reckless adventures, and extramarital affairs.[30] Yet Karen Blixen's only slightly accusative tone in *Out of Africa* comes as she looks back on the fact that the capital available in the beginning "had all been spent in the old days before I took over the running of the farm." This, for Karen Blixen, explains why "radical improvements" were impossible as she "had to live from hand to mouth,—and this, in the last years, became our normal mode of living on the farm." On the same page, she manages to reduce years of debate, disagreement, pleading, and rancor with Uncle Aage Westenholz into a single sentence: "My people at home, who had shares in the farm, wrote out to me and told me that I would have to sell."[31] In the end, it was Farah who delivered the final blow when he informed her in Mombasa of the inadequate yield from the coffee-picking season when she returned from a visit to Denmark in 1929. Blixen had hoped for sixty tons, maybe more, and anxiously avoided the question for hours. When she gathered the strength to ask, Farah "half closed his eyes and laid back his head, swallowing his sorrow, when he said: Forty tons, Memsahib." Only then did the hopelessness of the farm become real. "I did not say anything more to Farah, and he did not speak again, but went away, the last friendly object in the world."[32]

As *Out of Africa* draws to a close, Blixen's fragmented existence seems to dissolve in a pool of nostalgia. Robert Langbaum describes this effect as "her own feeling that she was surrounded by a circle of adoration." If so, much of that feeling was rooted in Nature and often affirmed by friendly relationships with Black Africans and others of Arab descent who were willing to acknowledge her power. Some of these people became "characters" in her story as representations of the wild, natural world described in the opening pages of the book because they belonged to it all in ways she never could. In this way, Blixen's essential contradiction involves alternating layers of truth and fiction that call on memoir to unify the writer's trilogy of needs to comprehend the past, tell the truth, and yet live safely behind a mask. "She has achieved the main aim of romantic autobiography," writes Langbaum, "which is to pull the ideal out of the real by calling in as witness not the authority of traditional myths but one's own experience. The aim is to achieve a perfect union of fact and myth."[33]

Among Blixen's literary talents, she understood that facts, histories, agonies, and memories would have to be sacrificed to the goal of mythmaking. Yet something stalls in the final pages when a sense of self-inflicted purgatory invades the work. Her imminent departure linked to an accumulation of loss yearns for resolution, even as the book seems to keep the end of the story at bay. In a sense, *Out of Africa* ends with no ending at all because almost everything in the memoir remains unresolved through the filter of the narrator's emotions. The death of Denys Finch Hatton three months before her departure is as close as we come to any sense of closure in Karen Blixen's life in colonial Kenya. In Thomas Knipp's reading, Finch Hatton's death in 1931 and that of Berkeley Cole in 1925 combine to create a moment when "history defeats myth" as their passing marks "the end of the magic kingdom."[34] That kingdom would shudder again a few months after Blixen's returns to Denmark with the death of Lord Delamere in November 1931.

It is, perhaps, the elegiac mood of tragedy that rings false for Ngũgĩ wa Thiong'o when he sarcastically derides Karen Blixen as a "literary saint" in the eyes of western readers and "the best representative of the Africa of European fiction" because "she embodies the great racist myth at the heart of the Western bourgeois civilization."[35] That "great racist myth" was based on an ideology of white superiority that encompassed the perceived good intentions of colonization by elites who ultimately dehumanized people such as Ngũgĩ himself, a man who grew up in a large Gikuyu family with his father's four wives and their children.[36] Eventually referring to settlers in Kenya as "parasites in paradise," he understood all too well that white, privileged people like Karen Blixen, and others mentioned above, felt free to claim everything, including a romantic sense of tragedy that paled in comparison to the tragedy inflicted on his own people.[37]

Judith Lee's reading of the dénouement of Blixen's time in Ngong, as told in *OA,* is as a time that "implicitly justifies her creation of a mask that obscures as much as it reveals."[38] It is, in other words, the perfect time for invention. In the last, staged "scene" of *Out of Africa* the Ngong Hills look small from the train station in Nairobi. Hours later, in the port of Mombasa, Farah's silhouette becomes indistinct in Blixen's eyes as her ship drifts away from a land she will never see again. As a storyteller looking back through a haze of years, Blixen's desired sense of finality searches with mixed results for Langbaum's "perfect union of fact and myth" as her ultimate achievement. If *Out of Africa* finds a delicate balance, it is because the author has erased sharp fragments and fundamental facts of a vanished world where kindness, cruelty, and tragedy itself were determined by race and class. The vast, incomprehensible past has been settled and softened by Blixen's need to make it so with a trace of erasure that leaves its mark like a scratch on the wall.

CHAPTER SIX

In Search of Vanished Time

The kitchen door was flung back as if Death, after having rushed in, had rushed out again.

—"The Shooting Accident," *Out of Africa*

The art of memoir requires more than a consciousness of a personal past. The memoirist must also have a consciousness of "vanished time," which enfolds a consciousness of death that releases the writer from temporal concerns. Few twenty-first-century memoirs balance on this precipice as effectively as Philippe Lançon's *Disturbance: Surviving Charlie Hebdo,* a book written in the aftermath of the author's hard-fought survival of a brutal terrorist attack in Paris that killed twelve of his colleagues during an editorial meeting of the irreverent tabloid *Charlie Hebdo.*[1] During long months of hospitalization and quasi-isolation, as his face and his life were being reconstructed, time "splits" into distinct dimensions of Before and After. For Lançon, recovery becomes an empty word since very little can be "recovered" in the sense of returning to normal life, including the pleasure of anonymity after winning the prestigious 2018 Prix Renaudot for his gripping survival memoir.

Karen Blixen's *Out of Africa* also looks back on life-altering loss as the author resets the clock from the opening sentence that nudges the reader *through time* and across a threshold that leaves the familiar world behind: "I had a farm in Africa, at the foot of the Ngong Hills."[2] Less well-known are the final lines of the book from the section titled "Farewell to the

Farm" in which the narrator looks back at the same hills for the last time from the platform of the train station in Nairobi: "From there, to the Southwest, I saw the Ngong Hills. The noble wave of the mountain rose above the surrounding flat land, all air-blue. But it was so far away that the four peaks looked trifling, hardly distinguishable, and different from the way they looked from the farm. The outline of the mountain was slowly smoothed and all leveled out by the hand of distance."[3] These words bring the reader full circle as the "hand of distance" draws a new boundary around a space that is temporal as well as geographical. Furthermore, the only way to return to that point of departure will be through fragments of reconfigured memory as a book imbued with a sense of "time regained," to borrow a term from Marcel Proust (1871–1922),who was a famous French contemporary of Karen Blixen. Primarily written post-WWI, his *In Search of Lost Time* offers invaluable insights to the process of writing as a means of reclaiming the past.

Not unlike Proust's narrator, Blixen seeks to infuse memory with meaning through prolonged reflections and entwined themes, each of which develops at its own pace. As we know, Karen Blixen was driven by a desire to write about Africa for over a decade before she was able to do it. In Proust's work, both the writer and the reader experience a similarly interminable gestation period that requires three thousand pages across seven volumes to reach the narrator's reflections on death in the final pages. Only then does he explain why it took him so long. It is intriguing to note that both Proust and Blixen evoke Scheherazade's storytelling powers in their work. In Proust's case, the reference comes up when he first ponders "the ingenuity of Scheherazade" and again as he reflects on when and how he will write the book he has in mind:

> If I worked, it would only be at night. But I would need a good number of nights, perhaps a hundred, perhaps a thousand. And I would be living with the anxiety of not knowing whether the Master of my destiny, less indulgent than the Sultan Shahriyar, when I broke off my story each morning, would stay my death sentence, and permit me to take

> up the continuation again the following evening. Not that I was claiming in any way to be rewriting the *Arabian Nights*. . . . It would be a book as long as the *Arabian Nights* perhaps, but quite different.[4]

For Blixen, whose time in Africa coincided with the publication of Proust's multivolume masterpiece (1913–27), it comes as no surprise that her library in Rungstedlund contains her own edition of Proust's second volume, *A l'ombre des jeunes filles en fleurs* (*In the Shadow of Young Girls in Flower*), which won the Prix Goncourt in 1919.[5] In addition to the habit of writing at night and a shared literary culture in the wake of World War I, Blixen and Proust also shared a presumption of truth hidden in the redeeming potential of memory. For even if Proust is considered to be a novelist, *In Search of Lost Time* could just as easily be approached as a "fictional memoir" that exists to explore the evolution of self, conquer the ravages of time, and keep death at bay—just as *Out of Africa* attempts to do. Proust's narrator queries himself on this question as he immerses himself in his project: "Was not the recreation through memory of impressions, which then needed to be investigated, illuminated, and transformed into intellectual equivalents, one of the preconditions, almost the very essence, of the work as I had conceived it just now in the library?"[6]

Ultimately, both works achieve a sense of "time regained," although Blixen outperforms Proust in her talent for nostalgia. If we think of nostalgia as a symbolic language liberated from an objectively accurate vision of the past, its usefulness becomes obvious. In that half-imaginary world we claim the right to dwell on fragments as we distill, erase, or omit all but the most appealing flickers of experience. Nostalgia is also a distraction, as Blixen realizes when she bathes in long, poetic passages devoted to Nature that seem to clear the clutter of daily life and banish unpleasant emotions. Rain often features in her memories—rain that ends as a kind of "new world" washed clean: "The great vault over our heads was gradually filled with clarity like a glass with wine. Suddenly, gently, the summits of the hill caught the first sunlight and blushed. And slowly, as the earth leaned towards the sun, the grassy slopes at the foot of the mountain turned a delicate gold, and the Masai woods lower down. And now, the tops of the tall trees in the forest, on our side of the river, blushed like copper."[7]

This humanized "blushing" of a hilltop not only dismisses dark skies and heavy rain; it *eradicates the memory* of dark skies and heavy rain as it brings the world back into the harmony of Karen Blixen's idealized world that never existed "with clarity." Such moments also occur when something equivalent to a beautiful sky overhead forces her to turn toward the same old world with "new eyes" and radiant colors. It is no accident that generations of Proust aficionados have relied on the following quote to explain the import of such moments in a quotable nutshell: "The only real journey, the only Fountain of Youth, would be to travel not toward new landscapes but with new eyes, to see the universe through the eyes of another, of a hundred others, to see the hundred universes that each of them can see, or can be."[8]

When Karen Blixen lifts her eyes to the distance while waiting for her last train out of Ngong, the Ngong Hills suddenly look "different from the way they looked from the farm." The ethereal beauty of vanished time has rushed in to replace the feeling of being bound to the "local time" of clocks and train schedules. As she gazes on a lost world with "new eyes," Karen Blixen's life in Africa becomes the vanished past and her long process of looking back can now begin.

Memoir is rooted in life-altering moments of transformation—large and small, not unlike myths and tales, including those that have been modernized for new generations. My children loved the idea of passing through the wardrobe in C. S. Lewis's *Chronicles of Narnia* at bedtime, and for my son, the imagined experience of soaring through star-studded space in a *Star Wars* spaceship occupied countless hours of his childhood long before he became the professional aviator he is today. Popular novels, including graphic novels, are popular because they take the reader out of daily life through visual frames. Meanwhile, travel literature offers a sense of safe discovery in an increasingly dangerous world. With displacements of time and place in mind, Karen Blixen's journey to the familiar village and dunes of Skagen in 1936 not only cleared a space for recollection of the past, it also made it possible for her to *feel* the past at a safe distance from daughterly duties and the bourgeois bustle of life at Rungstedlund. For Proust, a similar effect was achieved in his Paris apartment overlooking a busy avenue, safely shuttered within a cork-paneled room to blot out the noise of the world below.

The hand of "distance" and strategic isolation in Skagen may also account for the reader's impression in the pages of *Out of Africa* that Blixen is rediscovering colonial Kenya as a mythical space of her own making. The critical point, however, is that a distance of time and space allows her to rediscover the past with "new eyes" through which she envisions an idealized younger self, despite the highly visible race and class divisions of colonial Kenya. As Simon Lewis explains, "Her life in Kenya is presented not so much as life in another place as life in another time, and this temporal displacement allows her to appear to endorse the modern anthropologist's belief in the plurality of civilizations without denting her faith in the transcendence of European culture."[9] This keen observation reminds us that however "new" our vision of the past may be, we remain embedded in a specific historical moment to the extent that it cannot easily be altered by the stories we tell or the voices we use to tell them. The old maxim that a man who cannot change his ways is a "man of his time" contains a stubborn kernel of truth. However much the memoirist attempts to reinvent time on the page, as Karen Blixen did, remnants of the past persist within the habits of storytelling language. Karen Blixen may have reinvented herself in *Out of Africa,* but she had no power at all to reinvent the world around her.

Denial of oneself as a creature embedded within the group dynamic of culture is a common feature of European writers of Blixen's ilk and era. Thomas Knipp explains how typical she was when he points out that "the concept of cultural time [was] a concept used by many Europeans writing about Africa, including Joseph Conrad, André Gide, and Graham Greene. Like them, Dinesen places Africa at the beginning of a cultural time continuum—or even earlier in the inchoate world before culture."[10] In other words, the "cultural time" of *Out of Africa* assumes two thousand years of ever-evolving European civilization as a creation of a superior "race," for lack of a better word, in confrontation with an unknown culture that constitutes a blank page as far as privileged Europeans of Blixen's era were concerned. Even if she does not consciously express faith in "the transcendence of European culture," and soundly rejects the idea of cultural superiority throughout her *Letters from Africa,* Blixen's phrase for pre-Europeanized Africa remains "primitive time" for the obvious reason that her presence assumes and therefore "proves" African culture(s) to be backward.

Karen Blixen nevertheless remains dazzled by the "timeless" world evoked by her "African invention," to borrow a term from Simon Lewis, in part because of her taste for aristocratic nostalgia and in part because "timeless time" exists in opposition to the "historical time" of European culture in which human beings are pinned to a particular place on the map like captured butterflies. European culture also defines time within frames of sociopolitical reality while "timeless time" releases the mind and body from such constraints. In the tension between these two "time zones," the idea of belonging to a place *in time* collides with Blixen's desire to *suspend time* in her memoir by erasing the frame of colonization. Ultimately, her narrative voice creates a unique time effect that is neither time-less nor time-conscious as she attempts to slip through the net of historical reality. She also, as we have seen, erases personal conflict, financial insecurity, and agonizing details of her emotional life as she "edits out" dates, travel schedules, and the chronological unraveling of events found in her letters. All along, she knows where she stands in "historical time" as a privileged, white, European woman free to choose her tenuous membership in colonial society out of greed, ignorance, fascination, and naïveté. On her return to Denmark as a middle-aged, unemployed, spinster reduced to living with her mother, she manages to get a book of stories published by age fifty and goes on to write a bestselling memoir. Ultimately, Karen Blixen's life is a remarkable example of *time regained.*

Time navigation in *Out of Africa* works well because it is almost imperceptible to the reader. Blixen allows time to blur and blend across the long arc of seventeen years in a place where the clock is always ticking in the form of an amusing cuckoo clock that excites the *totos* (African children). This scene, recreated in the film, delights the reader who is "in on the joke," stuck as we are in local time with its relentless obligations that often feel like the startling "whoo-hoo" of a cuckoo bird. Yet even as the days are "clocked" within the construct of "real time," *Out of Africa* claims a space for the gentle backward glance of memory as well as moments of "vanished time" engulfed in the sacred space of Nature. Within this flexible frame, multiple genres and episodic storylines emerge that take time to unwind. As these stories move forward, we are only slightly aware of a natural suspense moving toward the critical moment when the loss of the farm announced in the first line will become the narrator's moment of departure. This underlying suspense has been there all along like a swirling funnel on the distant horizon as the calm narrative voice prepares us for the inevitability of loss as a kind of fugue of recurring themes that J. S. Bach would appreciate. In a text woven through with the force of Nature, we have also grown accustomed to Nature's ferocity that brings another "storyline" of storms, droughts, dust, and infestations of grasshoppers.

In time, Blixen's controlled narration delivers the long-awaited shock of human weakness and violent death that hints at the vulnerability of even the most innocent or privileged of people. As we wait patiently for this inevitable moment, Blixen's narrator assumes the position of the omniscient eye of pure observation. There is no bitterness or resentment as the narrator looks back dispassionately on a time lived apart from a keenly felt consciousness of time. There is, rather, a feeling of hard-earned detachment, enchantment, and gratitude for *what is* and *what was* at every turn in the road. As we read *Out of Africa* in the twenty-first century, these feelings are all the more precious—even with the postcolonial critique in mind—because everything in the book is now beyond living memory. There is no one alive in "our time" who sat on the veranda with Karen Blixen at Mbogani House or bid her farewell from the train station in Nairobi. All we have are books, letters, scholarship, photographs, and the annals of history to guide us into an accurate vision of her now-vanished life.

Karen Blixen, writing as Isak Dinesen, manipulates time in *Out of Africa* through dynamic zones of reflection, separation, and transition that mimic the process of memory itself. An illuminating example of this is "The Shooting Accident," the first of five chapters in the lengthy section of *Out of Africa* titled Part II: A Shooting Accident on the Farm.[11] The tragic incident recounts the accidental death of two African children at the hands of a third African child and encompasses the aftermath of these events within the Gikuyu community. In terms of "plot," insofar as memoir contains a "plot," the destabilizing events of this story allow the narrator to reflect on distinctly different social and judicial systems of British colonial Kenya as Blixen demonstrates her observant eye. Yet her intentions go far beyond a linear reportage of external events. Like all good titles, "The Shooting Accident" makes a promise that piques the interest of the reader as it calls on the art of time navigation, which inevitably involves time manipulation. In Blixen's telling of the tale, the reader is taken on a magic-carpet ride that lifts our eyes above the earth and deep into the mythical past then back down to earth again as she moves through *multiple dimensions of time*. The passages below, from the opening paragraphs of "The Shooting Accident," offer a valuable opportunity to trace her skill at thinking and writing her way through an array of "time zones" to enhance the reader's experience. Note that Karen Blixen's words are italicized, while my annotations appear in bold.

A Closer Look at Blixen's Art of Time Navigation in "The Shooting Accident"

On the evening of the nineteenth of December, I walked out of my house before going to bed, to see if there was any rain coming. Many farmers in the highlands were, I believe, doing the same thing at that hour. Sometimes, in a lucky year, we would get a few heavy showers just round Christmas, and it was a great thing for the young coffee, which has set on the trees after the flowering in the short rains of October. This night there was no sign of rain. The sky was serene and silently triumphant, resplendent with stars. (*OA*, 89)

Unlike most chapters in *Out of Africa*, "The Shooting Accident" begins with a specific time and date, which creates suspense as it enhances the quietly ominous mood established by the chapter title. This beginning also locates the earthbound narrator in time and place before she turns our attention upward to Astrological Time.

The Stellar heaven of the Equator is richer than that of the North, and you see it more because you are out more at night. In Northern Europe, winter nights are too cold to allow one much pleasure in the contemplation of the stars, and in summer one hardly distinguishes them within the clear night sky, that is as pale as a dog-violet. (*OA*, 89)

This brief paragraph begins to feel like a distraction designed to prolong suspense. What about the urgent promise of the title that drew the reader into the narrative in the first place?

The tropical night has the companionability of a Roman Catholic Cathedral compared to the Protestant Churches of the North, which let you in on business only. Here in the great room everybody comes and goes, this is the place where things are going on. To Arabia and Africa, where the sun of the midday kills you, night is the time for traveling and enterprise. The stars have been named here. They have been guides to human beings for centuries, drawing them in long lines across the desert-sands and the Sea, one towards the East, another to the West or the North and South. Cars run well at night, and it is pleasant to motor under the stars, you get into the habit of fixing visits to friends up-country by the time of the next full moon. You start Safaris by the new moon, to have the benefit of the whole row of moonlight nights. It is then strange, when back on a visit to Europe, to find your friends of the towns living out of touch with the moves of the moon and almost in ignorance of them. The young moon was the sign of action to Khadija's camel man, whose Caravan was to start off when she appeared in the sky. With his face toward her he was one of the "Philosophers who spin out of moonlight systems of the Universe." He must have looked at her [sic] much, that he made her his sign in which to conquer. (OA, 90)

The narrator's thoughts expand in a long paragraph with the suggestion of a journey through time and space that must begin at night. Her knowledge of Astrological Time connects to the reality of human technology signaled by her mention of cars and safari life. She is, in effect, weaving a tale with threads of time as she blends heaven and earth's fluctuations between disparate "time zones." The overall effect is a deliberate connection between her readers in their cozy chairs and a vast, timeless universe in which she centralizes herself as a knowledgeable participant.

As the paragraph reaches its denouement, she references the ancient Islamic world and the powerful woman (Khadija) who was the first wife of the Prophet Mohammed. In this way, we are reminded of a distant but datable past on earth that operated with astrological time envisioned by lunar calendars once used for earthly navigation. This analepsis ("flashback") actually reaches back to mythological time, which exists in Blixen's present as a source of human wisdom.

I had got a name amongst the Natives, because a number of times I happened to be, on the farm, the first to see the new moon like a thin, silver bow in the sunset; particularly because, two or three years running, I had been the first to catch sight of the new moon of the month of Ramadan, the Mohammedan's Holy Month. (OA, 90)

And now, a short paragraph brings us back to earth as the narrator further centralizes herself with claims of uniqueness, expertise, and friendly relations with Africans ("Natives"), all of which assert her sense of femininized power that echoes in her reference to Khadija.

The farmer slowly turns his eyes all around the Horizon. First to the East, for from the East, if it comes, comes the rain, and there stands clear Spica in the Virgin.[1] *Then South, to greet the Southern Cross, door-keeper of the great world, faithful to travellers and beloved by them, and higher up, under the luminous streak of the Milky Way, Alpha and Beta in the Centaur. To the South West sparkles Sirius, great in heaven, and the thoughtful Canopus, and to the West above the faint outline of the Ngong Hills, now nearly unbroken, the radiant diamond ornament, Rigel, Betelgeuze, and Bellatrix.*[2] *He turns to the North last, for to the North we go back in the end, and there he runs upon the Great Bear himself, only he is now calmly standing on his head on account of the heavenly perspective, and that has all the air of a bearish joke, that cheers the heart of the Nordic emigrant.*[3] (*OA*, 90–91)

Having shifted the rhythm with long and short paragraphs and drawn our attention back to human experience, the narrator continues to weave her vision of harmony into the vast universe. She begins here by linking the Local and Seasonal Time of agricultural production on earth to Astrological Time with its star formations, of which she has a navigator's understanding that enables her to make connections with her own existence.

And yet by now, dear reader, we have lost track of the promise of the chapter title that raised our expectations of a story about a shooting accident. The narrator—ironically self-defined as an outsider ("Nordic emigrant") at the end of this passage—also seems to have lost track of her theme as her wandering mind, now focused on the night sky, leads to a lengthy commentary on dreams in the next paragraph . . .

---

[1] Spica is one of the twenty brightest stars in the night sky. The name derives from the Latin *spīca virginis,* which means "the virgin's ear of [wheat] grain." This explains its association with agriculture and Demeter, Greek goddess of the harvest.

[2] The three brightest stars in the constellation of Orion among fifty-seven stars used in navigation are Rigel, a blue star, the biggest and brightest; supergiant Betelgeuze, which is visible from Earth as orange-red; and Bellatrix, meaning "goddess of war." The intriguing aspect of this foray into astronomy is how familiar Karen Blixen seems to be with the night sky.

[3] The Ursa Major (Great Bear) constellation resembles the profile of a lumbering bear and contains a few dozen identifiable stars.

People who dream when they sleep at night know of a special kind of happiness which the world of the day holds not, a placid ecstasy, and ease of heart, that are like honey on the tongue. They also know that the real glory of dreams lies in their atmosphere of unlimited freedom. It is not the freedom of the dictator, who enforces his own will on the world, but the freedom of the artist who has no will, who is free of will. The pleasure of the true dreamer does not lie in the substance of the dream, but in this: that there things happen without any interference from his side, and altogether outside his control. Great landscapes create themselves, long splendid views, rich and delicate colors, roads, houses, which he has never seen or heard of. Strangers appear and are friends or enemies, although the person who dreams has never done anything about them. The ideas of flight and pursuit are recurrent in dreams and are equally enrapturing. Excellent witty things are said by everybody. It is true that if remembered in the daytime they will fade and lose their sense, because they belong to a different plane, . . . (OA, 91)

The overarching theme of this paragraph is freedom or, as she writes, the "unlimited freedom of dreams." The absence of interference is the absence of Time with a capital "T" or, more to the point, the absence of a consciousness of Time passing.

It is also significant that she links a dreamer's sense of freedom with "the freedom of the artist who has no will, who is free of will." The role of the artist on a journey through the world is a favorite theme of Karen Blixen, who considered herself to be an artist from an early age.

It is when one begins to lose the consciousness of freedom, and when the idea of necessity enters the world at all, when there is any hurry or strain anywhere, a letter to be written or a train to catch, when you have got to work, to make the horses of the dream gallop, or to make the rifles go off, that the dream is declining, and turning into the nightmare, which belongs to the poorest and most vulgar class of dreams. (OA, 92)

After further imaginative visions that flow from the passage quoted above in which the narrator considers how dreams "fade in daytime" and the "feeling of immense freedom" gradually vanishes, she seems to awaken in real time. Her entry into that other world includes an array of stressful thoughts among which is the loud, crackling sound when "rifles go off." This, clearly, brings us back to earth—with a bang!

As Blixen returns to the sights and sounds of nightfall that include bats "cruising as noiselessly as cars upon the asphalt" and small hares springing onto the road, she writes that "The Cicada sings an endless song in the long grass, smells run along the earth and falling stars run over the sky, like tears running over a cheek."[12] This image of tears on a cheek is a startling, transitional image that may appear as a first warning related to the theme of "A Shooting Accident," although it follows a sense of impending tragedy expressed in descriptions of nocturnal happiness "which the day holds not" and the narrator's subsequent awareness of when "the dream is declining and turning into a nightmare." In any case, the image of "tears running over a cheek" jolts the reader into the human world after those passages that read as odes to Nature and astrology, if not a soliloquy. The narrator has, in brief, cast a wide net of subtle foreshadowing to prepare the reader for the turning point in the text that follows her reflections through multiple dimensions of time. Those deliberately "time-consuming" passages that seem to exhaust the reader's patience actually enhance the contrast that inevitably occurs when a dream does, in fact, become a nightmare:

> As I was standing before my house a shot fell, not far off. One shot. Then again the stillness of the night closed on all sides. After a while, as if they had been pausing to listen and were now taking it up once more, I heard the Cicada chiming their monotonous little song in the grass. . . . There is something strangely determinate and fatal about a single shot in the night. It is as if someone had cried a message to you in one word and would not repeat it. I stood for some time wondering what it had meant. Nobody could aim at anything at this hour, and, to scare away something, a person would fire two shots or more.[13]

In this example of Blixen's talent for time navigation, the reader's journey through time ends with a jarring return to the material reality that existed before the dreamer—whose dreams are remarkably similar to storytelling—awakens to a shot in the dark. Like the narrator, we have been temporarily released from time in these passages and granted the illusion of being neutral observers of an eternity that we can never know in our mortal lives. At this point, it is fitting that death interrupts the narrator's dream as it slams the door on her sense of boundless freedom, because *death always stops time* before a new story begins again.

Judith Lee's insightful analysis of this "shot in the dark" links the event to the larger theme of self-discovery when she compares it to Blixen's mention of it in a letter to her mother in which she writes that "I was in my bath before dinner when I heard a shot,—which I always hate to hear, especially at night, but I thought it was one of the white people shooting at a hyena."[14] Blixen's repurposing of the sound and timing of the shot confirms its conscious importance as a time-navigation device that, as Lee reads it, represents a "moment of awakening" as the narrator realizes that the "central problem is to negotiate her need to be both autonomous and responsive."[15] Susan Hardy Aiken also interprets this "shot in the dark" within the larger frame of the book when she writes that "that shot—fired, tellingly by an African child who 'had acted the part of a white man' by borrowing 'his master's gun'—shatters the atemporal, dreamlike idyll of Africa even as it shatters the bodies of Gikuyu children Wamai or Wanyangerri, or as colonialism has shattered the lives of the African peoples: 'Death . . . rushed in . . . and left the place in dire devastation.'"[16]

If there is a lesson here for writers of memoir, it has something to do with the ways in which Karen Blixen's nonlinear writing allows for a sense of movement as she starts and stops, pauses and prolongs, then restarts the essential thread of her story in order to move it forward. The reader naturally follows the tempo that, not unlike music, is carefully orchestrated. Yet the essence of movement "on the page" does not necessarily rest on the pace of the narrative, but on the fact that the pace changes *within the narration.* Only when something changes does the reader sense that something is happening—or did happen—*in real time.* Both Judith Lee's and Susan Hardy Aiken's astute observations of just how much that "single shot in the night" moves the plot along as it echoes and expands the larger meaning is a memorable illustration of the way interconnected meaning(s) resonate throughout Blixen's prose.

In *Out of Africa,* the narrator's ability to shift from one time dimension to another replicates the fragments of our timebound existence and even more significantly, of inner life, which encompasses internal release from time in the forms of dreams, sleep, memory, and imaginative writing. Such shifts could be conveyed with techniques as simple as alternating long and short sentences to establish authorial control of how a text will be read. A passage might feel prolonged or off-point, as several do in the passages quoted above, yet this will not matter if the overall effect is a sense of anticipation followed by movement. Patient prolongation can also express a sense of time passing, as it does across Proust's three thousand pages that begin with the narrator's bedtime in childhood and end with his reflections on death. In Blixen's passage above, prolongation is mercifully deployed to a much more manageable extent when the narrator gives herself to the distraction of the night sky and all that it holds before coming back to the sentence that moves the story forward: "As I was standing before my house a shot fell, not far off." The sentence continues with a staccato rhythm: "One shot." And then as if to close the thought with a deep breath: "Then again the stillness of the night closed in on all sides."

This ticking movement of the prose emulates the "stop-restart" of a new beginning that the reader naturally feels and needs at this point. The clock is, in a sense, rewound when Blixen's manipulation of time allows the reader to step out of time with the narrator as a trusted guide. However, depending on the reader's sensibilities, such time-effects can be problematic, especially when her literary reinventions interpret colonial society in Kenya with a brushstroke of peace and abundance. There is also a danger in reading *Out of Africa* as a distinctly dated example of European manners that clings to the voice of Blixen's reinvented self.

And so we stumble into her contested legacy, not only expressed in her life choices and aristocratic attitudes but also within the very fabric of her prose.

Susan Horton summarizes this essential dilemma in her study of Isak Dinesen and Olive Schreiner aptly titled *Difficult Women, Artful Lives:* "In 1914 Dinesen went to what Europeans of her time thought of as the past—to Africa—to construct a past for herself and to make herself a future more exciting than she found her present to be. Returning to Denmark seventeen years later, in composing a memoir of her time in Africa she created her experience of Africa retrospectively. In doing so she simultaneously brought her self into her performance of Africa and transformed her performance of Africa into her self."[17] Simon Lewis takes a similar view when he writes that Blixen's "nostalgic invention of the farm . . . produces racialized models of culture and civilization that simultaneously valorize both the apparent timeless authenticity of the Masai and Denys Finch Hatton's ancient English lineage." Ultimately, he writes, "her life in Kenya is presented not so much as life in another place as life in another time," which explains why she chooses to relieve her mind of political reality. Instead, she prefers to imagine a timeless existence lived at the heart of a peaceable kingdom where mostly male, aristocratic friends meet to enjoy her hospitality made possible by exploited African servants. As Lewis points out, her reality "is not white-settler 'culture' (which she largely scorns), but the culture of an earlier age and distant place."[18]

Blixen's reinvented self, conveniently relocated in the soothing "time zone" of selective memory, thus becomes an inherently conflicted figure whose consciousness of time bends to harmonize contradictions of past and present. For those readers who want to somehow save her from emotional chaos and the inevitable loss of separation, it's important to keep in mind that her performance as Baroness Blixen in *OA* is a self-portrait of her own making. It is, perhaps, her "near-miss" of an idealized Destiny that feeds her readers' hunger for nostalgia and the wondrous sensation of *time regained* that comes with realizing that despite years of chaos and uncertainty, she managed to write a magical memoir. After all, one of the pleasures of reading *Out of Africa* is the feeling that Denys and Tania are together again, living day-to-day beneath a golden sky, sipping drinks on the veranda, and settling down at nightfall for storytelling by the fire.

PART III
Contested Legacies

CHAPTER SEVEN

Otherness as Revelation

One loses a good deal of racial superiority out here; it seems obvious to me that the natives surpass us in many ways.

—Karen Blixen to Thomas Dinesen, April 22, 1914

Karen Blixen's encounter with otherness is a major theme of *Out of Africa* that appears throughout the memoir and inspires her thoughts in the wake of its publication. Episodes such as "The Iguana," in which the life of a wild creature is unjustly sacrificed to the narrator's desire for its glittering skin, and Kamante's interpretation of distant grass fire as the coming of God mark symbolic moments of double-consciousness that the narrator experiences for the first time in Ngong. Cultural anthropologist Janet McIntosh explores double-consciousness in her extensive work on the twenty-first-century lives of descendants of colonial Kenya and finds that "among former settlers and their descendants, their nascent double consciousness stems from an unsettling of the colonialist notion that whites are paragons of humanity, and a realization that to some, they and their history represent injustice. But when they experience the shock of seeing their community being seen, they see themselves 'othered,' that is, refracted through essentialist stereotypes that portray them as part of an undesirable, alien social mass."[1] Unlike many of those descendants, Blixen felt herself to be "alien" from the beginning and was honest enough about it to be curious about the contradiction her presence created.

As the only Danish woman living among an estimated 1,300 white settlers in 1914, she dealt with her own sense of "otherness" by forging friendly relations with those Africans who lived and worked on and around the farm.[2] However self-serving this might have been, the practicality of it required interactions that many other settlers, especially British women, avoided. Blixen's letters are consequently threaded through-and-through with observations of and admiration for African people that include her frustration with racial injustice. The text of *Out of Africa* itself delves into a few extreme situations concerning race and justice such as "The Shooting Accident" that occurs on the farm in which the gun used by a Black child to kill or wound three other children happens to belong to a white man. Because of the location of the shooting and its circumstances, Blixen is drawn into an assembly of Gikuyu elders (a *Kyama*) in which a fair number of sheep must be negotiated as compensation to the families. Another matter involves the relocation of "squatters" forced to leave the farm as a result of her own departure in 1931. In both instances, she accepts a leadership role and with regard to "my" squatters, takes full responsibility for working out a resolution that keeps them all together.

Yet even as an active participant, Blixen repeatedly finds herself in a curious but politically powerless position. As Farah's brother, a judge, eventually wrote, "The Baroness felt that all were equal and that justice and fairness were everyone's right. In those days, racial discrimination in that multiracial country was similar to a war in which there was no actual field combat. The Baroness always pretended that racial discrimination was non-existent. She knew it existed, but at the same time she knew she could do nothing to remedy the situation."[3] Rather, her strategy was to keep silent publicly, at least until she no longer lived in colonial Kenya and until she had published a book that gave her the credibility of experience on the subject.

As a European woman raised in a privileged layer of Danish society, Karen Blixen arrived in Africa in 1914 with a deeply ingrained sense of white superiority as the standard against which Others should "naturally" be judged. She also arrived with her sense of aristocratic social organization reaching back to medieval Europe intact and a "house" vs. "country" orientation to place and people. In 1914, her fellow "settlers" were initially members of the English upper crust who had come for adventure and cheap land in the guise of a self-congratulatory "civilizing mission." She also valued their antecedents, those "noble pioneers" who had ventured out to the African continent even before the Uganda Railroad connected Mombasa to Nairobi in 1899. As rightful heirs, her closest friends were no less noble in her eyes and included Berkeley Cole, an expert on the Masai, and Denys Finch Hatton, who first arrived in Nairobi on March 18, 1911, after months in South Africa, where he found the anti-Black policies troublesome.[4] These men, Blixen believed, recognized racial injustice in the larger frame of global culture as few people did at the time: "The particular, instinctive attachment which all Natives of Africa felt toward Berkeley and Denys, and towards few other people of their kind, made me reflect that perhaps the white men of the past, indeed in any past, would have been better in understanding and sympathy with the colored races than we, of our Industrial age, shall ever be. When the first steam engine was constructed, the roads of the races of the world parted, and we have never found one another since."[5]

The recognition of insurmountable difference and the futility of protest implied in these words expresses what we might view as Phase 1—of three, distinct phases—in Karen Blixen's approach to otherness that has left her open to accusations of racism in our postcolonial world. In the first phase, her thoughts are private and her opinions voiced only within the realm of letters sent home to Denmark and, we can surmise, in conversations with people who share her views, such as Denys Finch Hatton. Rarely, if ever, does she raise objections to racial injustice in public in Ngong, even when she tries to make life better by offering medical care on her veranda or in driving Kamante to the hospital at the "Scotch Mission," which keeps him for three months as he recovers from an infection. Meanwhile, the overuse of possessive pronouns and animal metaphors, to say nothing of the self-mythology embedded in *Out of Africa,* do little to convince critics like Ngũgĩ wa Thiong'o that her book is anything other than the embodiment of "the great racist myth at the heart of the Western bourgeois civilization."[6] After all, isn't the invisibility of racial tension and absence of meaningful protest in Blixen's memoir a reflection of the ways in which white people in Kenya, and elsewhere, have felt free to choose how and when to interact with "others" through the filter of white privilege?

The standard that evolved in the late twentieth century has set the bar higher with expectations of critical self-observation such as women's studies scholar Peggy McIntosh modeled in her groundbreaking 1989 paper "White Privilege: Unpacking the Invisible Knapsack." Indeed, this work was "groundbreaking" because it seemed very few had bothered to reverse the gaze of "White Privilege" as she did. In that seminal work, published four years after *Out of Africa* onscreen swept the Academy Awards, McIntosh began by approaching white privilege as parallel to male privilege in American society: "I have come to see white privilege as an invisible package of unearned assets which I can count on cashing in each day, but about which I was meant to remain oblivious. White privilege is like an invisible weightless knapsack of special provisions, maps, passports, codebooks, visas, clothes, tools, and blank checks."[7] Her language was persuasive and her idea revealing in the way it suddenly shifted responsibility to those in possession of "unearned assets." More recently, Robin DiAngelo ignited a controversy in the United States when she attempted to explain "why it's so hard for white people to talk about racism" through the lens of *White Fragility.*[8] National Book Award winner Ibram X. Kendi has since become the moderator of a national conversation by redefining the terms of engagement from a Black perspective, beginning with two, simplified definitions that echo through Karen Blixen's strategies of silence, invisibility, and selective kindness. Kendi's measure in the current century comes down to the hard evidence of action vs. inaction: "RACIST: One who is supporting racist policy through their actions or inaction or expressing a racist idea. ANTIRACIST: One who is supporting an antiracist policy through their actions or expressing an antiracist idea."[9]

If we apply Kendi's terms of engagement to *Out of Africa*, Blixen represents a racist figure in Phase 1 of her encounter with otherness in Ngong when she acts to help the few others with whom she feels safe while expressing her antiracist thoughts within primarily private—and white—relationships. It is the scale of her action focused on finding a dignified place large enough to keep over two thousand squatters together, and the moral determination it took for her to do it, that alter how we should begin to think about Blixen at the end of her long sojourn in Ngong. It is also worth noting that as the process of writing *Out of Africa* draws her into deep reflection, she uses her skill as a writer to develop a form of action and expression that defines Phase 2 of her prolonged education in otherness. In this important phase, it is her experience—and her reflection on that experience—that redefines her relationship to Black African people and the world as she writes of herself not necessarily as she was, but as she wanted to be portrayed in memory. *Out of Africa*, as we know, amplified her voice as it reached tens of thousands within the first year of publication in 1937. Indeed, it is only because of *Out of Africa* that she was invited to speak publicly about her evolution vis-à-vis race relations in a little-known speech delivered to Swedish students in 1938. Her new persona as a popular writer and thinker constitutes Phase 3, a phase that qualifies as antiracism in Ibram Kendi's lexicon. Ultimately, the Karen Blixen who spoke publicly on otherness as a "revelation" was not the same Karen Blixen who arrived in Ngong in 1914. Given her nineteenth-century beginnings and the sociocultural era in which she came of age, it should come as no surprise that it took time for her to locate herself in the matter of global race relations.

Rob Nixon speaks for many postcolonial critics when he describes Blixen's relationship with Black Africans as "a species of philanthropic feudalism, with her at the center exercising *noblesse oblige* and anticipating a deferential loyalty in return."[10] Without denying the power imbalance, Susan Brantly clarifies the meaning of *noblesse oblige* when she focuses on Blixen's own understanding of the term as she explained it in a Danish anthology of interviews.

> The only really reliable principle in the relationship between parties where one is technologically and economically superior to such a fantastic degree must be 'Noblesse oblige.' . . . Yes, if society was so democratic that white people could recognize the blacks as equals, a modus vivendi might possibly be found. But it is my experience that the longer

> one comes into a white democratic society, the stronger the whites feel and insist upon their race's superiority. . . . Noblesse: It is nothing else or less [*sic*] than this: to keep one's word. It is to take responsibility for what one says and does.[11]

Blixen held herself to that standard with people of every imaginable age, social rank, race, gender, nationality, and/or tribal affiliation and yet even Blixen's biographer Judith Thurman, whose 1982 book is somewhat dated in its mild critique of colonialism, writes that "her [Karen Blixen's] situation, as one of the greatest feudal overlords in the country, was a paradox, as was the fact that her own *noblesse oblige* in the role gave her such pleasure."[12] Here, we stumble from the otherness of race to the clarity of Blixen's class-consciousness that, inevitably, colors and underpins her assumptions and interactions with others of all kinds.

Since the 1980s, many critics have called out *Out of Africa* as racist from within due to Blixen's persistent use of possessive pronouns, as Ngũgĩ emphasized when he brazenly titled his 1980 talk at the Danish Royal Library's seventy-fifth anniversary in Copenhagen as "Her Cook, Her Dog: Karen Blixen's Africa." Others have combed the text of the memoir for animal metaphors that perform zoomorphic transformations on Black African people with imagery such as "The old dark clear-eyed Native of Africa, and the old dark clear-eyed Elephant, they are alike."[13] And then there is Lulu, the anthropomorphized gazelle who "came to my house from the woods as Kamante had come from the plains."[14] In this description Kamante becomes a crossover symbol between wildness and the "civilizing mission" of British colonialism, a role pointedly deconstructed by Simon Lewis when he writes, "He [Kamante] was not a stray wild animal like Lulu but a Gikuyu whose connection with the land of Blixen's farm was not to a mythic, asocial Africa but . . . to a political history of ancestral inheritance and a political present of dispossession."[15]

Context matters here, as Blixen scholar and environmental humanist Peter Mortensen makes clear when he writes that "using animal epithets to characterize other humans in a context of unequal power relations is inherently controversial and problematic."[16] He nevertheless proposes a dispassionate analysis since they are, as Susan Brantly points out, "legion throughout all of her works," which include numerous tales in which Europeans are given animal characteristics.[17] Zoomorphism and anthropomorphism also exist in ancient myths such as we find in Crete's mythical minotaur, in whom human and animal traits blur into one magical character, as well as in age-old tales where we encounter a "big, bad wolf" speaking gently from grandmother's bed or a very clever cat called "Puss in Boots" or the sly fox of the medieval cycle of *Roman de Renart* (Tales of the Cunning Fox). Animals who talk and demonstrate moral wisdom form the cast of characters in Jean de la Fontaine's seventeenth-century fables and seem perfectly natural in A. A. Milne's stories of Winnie-the-Pooh, first published at Christmastime in 1925 when Blixen was in Ngong. Indeed, our attitudes turn on how such transformations are deployed and to what purpose, not that they appear throughout human history or in a memoir written by a woman who tends to think in metaphorical imagery. In her "Mottoes of My Life," Blixen writes about the commonplace practice among Africans of bestowing animal names on white people that, clearly, tend to express admiration—including her own nickname "Lioness," which pleased her very much:

> I have been out on safari, a hundred miles from another white person, with native companions only, and have become one with my surroundings, with the landscape, animals, and human beings and with the hours of day and night. This feeling was enhanced by the natives giving us white people native names, characterizing us in words of their own language. Most of these were animals' names, although there were exceptions to this rule. . . . My husband and I were *wauhauga*, the wild geese. Later, when I was alone on the farm, my old Somali gunbearer, after returning to his own country, wrote me a letter addressed to 'Li-

oness Blixen' and beginning 'Honorable Lioness,' which resulted in all my friends in the colony calling me "Lioness."[18]

In *Out of Africa*'s longest section, "From an Immigrant's Notebook," anecdotes and parables based on the metaphorical wisdom of animals abound and include the iguana, whose dazzling beauty holds an important warning against unentitled possession, and the stork with its birds-eye-view of a problem. In *Out of Africa*'s lexicon of humanized animal characters, oxen are particularly expressive of endurance, hermaphroditic hyenas represent harmony, and exotic birds—nightingales, and cranes—mirror the natural flow of time. As for Scottish deerhounds, they "have acquired a human sense of humor," which the author illustrates with a brief story about one of her own beloved hounds who mistook a black cat in a tree for a wild, spotted feline then placed his feet on her shoulders to share a good laugh.[19]

Peter Mortensen's interest in how Blixen's work relates to the natural world has brought a fresh perspective to our reading of anthropomorphism and zoomorphism in *Out of Africa*. In his 2018 article titled "'Both Men and Beasts'—Rereading Karen Blixen's Anthropomorphisms," Mortensen responds to Ngũgĩ's biting critique exemplified by an essay in which he writes that "as if in compensation for unfulfilled desires and longings, the baroness turned Kenya into a vast erotic dreamland in which her several white lovers appeared as young gods and her servants as usable curs and animals."[20] Setting aside the inaccuracy of "several" lovers, this direct attack on Blixen's zoomorphism invites the sort of reinterpretation that Mortensen offers within the frame of ecocriticism, which has become one of the intellectual currents of our time. Within this rubric, Mortensen addresses the skewed impact of the human-animal "binary" as he proposes a shift in outlook that includes the useful term "humanimal" from a Dutch source.[21] Mortensen's central concern is with our longstanding idea that philosophical humanism elevates the human mind and body to the pinnacle of all forms of life without recognizing the multiple forms of wisdom and intelligence that surround us in the animal world, which Karen Blixen respected instinctively.

In *Out of Africa*, animals are everywhere as part of Blixen's vision of an idealized natural world—just as they were everywhere in her idyllic early childhood at Rungstedlund, where dogs, horses, and birds were ever-present. And when she engages in safari life prior to 1921, she does so with recognition of the strategic survival instinct that makes hunting lion and cheetah an equal match for the skilled human hunter. Ultimately, in Mortensen's view, the established distaste for Blixen's animal metaphors signals assumptions of human superiority and animal inferiority that many people today would like to overcome as we attempt—however unsuccessfully—to adapt more intelligently to our environment. In other words, Mortensen flips Ngũgĩ's critique on its head when he writes that "engaging with a broader and more representative range of characterizations, I argue, makes Blixen less a 'racist' preserver of essential hierarchical differences and more of a 'proto-posthumanist' critic of entrenched human/animal distinctions."[22] This perspective acknowledges Blixen's codebreaker instincts as it advocates her respect for ecosystems, her connection with a wide range of species, and her interactions with animal life in all its forms as part of human life itself.

Since the turn of the century Tanne Dinesen had longed for an outward change that would set her apart from all those ordinary, bourgeois lives humming along in Denmark. Suddenly, in January 1914, she arrived in the East Africa Protectorate and found herself surrounded by Others of many kinds. Writing of the "conversion experience" that often accompanies fascination with otherness—and often in the form of sexual possession—bell hooks explains that within the forcefield of opposites, the more powerful figure's expectation is to "be changed in some way by the encounter."[23] Yet as she drills down into the roots of this desire, hooks arrives at a surprising twist when she states that "the desire is not to make the Other over in one's image but to *become* the Other."[24]

This idea of becoming someone new and different is an aspect of the hoped-for transformation Blixen embodied from her first moment on arrival in Ngong, even if she may have underestimated how British colonialism would ultimately shape her experience. In a letter to Ingeborg Dinesen written four months after arrival, she included her first mention of the sociopolitical reality of Black African people: "All the white people out here are pressing the government to raise the 'Hut Tax,' the tax on natives, from 3 rupees to £1, in order to make them work." Her letter goes on to lament the "sorry idea" of "forcing an entire nation, that is now rich, into poverty in such a way, but on the other hand I don't think the natives can go on living in their present fashion." As for the end of tribal warfare achieved by British reconfiguration of land into tribal Reserves, Blixen could see that African men had much less to do and, consequently, "do absolutely nothing" while women worked constantly, as before. Blixen expresses empathy in this letter, especially for African women, as her remarks reveal her newfound awareness of the ways in which the European vision of Africa works against centuries of tribal life. "As a whole, I don't think black and white can live together in one country; the black will be destroyed," she adds.[25]

In another early letter written to Aunt Bess, with whom Blixen often debated social issues, she expresses her feelings for the "natives" and describes the British as "narrow-minded," even as she represents what would be described today as a passively racist worldview that echoes Farah's brother quoted earlier: "With a little understanding and interest, this society is in many respects ideal: social problems don't exist here,—and they will not arise providing there is no mixing of the races; but I think the races differ too much for any intermixture to take place. . . . When I observe the various races here, I feel that superiority of the white race is an illusion."[26] A decade later, Blixen was most likely to confide in her brother Thomas when it came to her disgust with British mistreatment of Africans because "I dare not talk to any of the English, I think my influence here as a woman and a foreigner must be strictly confined to being an example; if I start to preach I shall lose my power, which must be won through being a hostess and a friend . . . but the 'example' takes effect so slowly, and sometimes one feels like firing off a broadside right in their silly faces, when that typical English stupidity starts braying too loudly!"[27]

These brief quotes trace Blixen's true feelings shared privately with family members that never get past the critique of "inaction" that characterizes Ibram Kendi's definition of racism. Nevertheless, as Brantly points out, "One of the challenges Blixen poses to postcolonial criticism is her own brand of multiculturalism."[28] This statement recognizes Blixen's unique "place" in colonial society as that of a foreign woman most often living alone and yet subject to approval by the English men and women with whom she shared a European consciousness of racial and class superiority. Her friendly relations with Black Africans raised eyebrows, but may have been little more than a coping strategy at first as she learned to negotiate her multiple identities in new surroundings. Yet even if we eventually come to the same conclusion as Brantly does regarding Blixen's "central paradox" of being "still the oppressor as well as the oppressed," the problem of precisely where to locate Blixen in the annals of British colonialism involves an overlay of nationality, race, class, marital status, and "first world" gender discrimination.[29] In brief, Blixen embodied multiple forms of otherness throughout her time in Ngong.

Women postcolonial scholars tend to be feminist scholars likely to understand these nuances because they understand the weight of patriarchy in their own lives and family histories as they seek to locate Karen Blixen in colonial Kenya. They are, consequently, more able to read Blixen's acts and words through a lens that accommodates that complexity. Susan Horton, for example, suggests that Blixen's waves of double-consciousness regarding race might have been related to her own "oscillations between identity with and alterity from East Africans . . . determined by which groups and which gender she was representing."[30] Toggling between her various representations as colonist, immigrant, baroness, farmer, humanist, foreigner, lover, and storyteller, she no doubt brought an instinctive understanding to the "oscillations" of those she met—Black or white. Blixen's position in colonial Kenya often comes back to her essential reality as a woman alone, dependent on family money (as she approached age forty), and running a farm in a misogynistic culture. After all, the only power she possessed on arrival was her whiteness, which ultimately served as a "blank page" on which her experience of otherness would eventually be written in the second phase of her evolution as the author of *Out of Africa*.

When World War I broke out in August 1914, Bror Blixen, Swedish by birth, volunteered to join Lord Delamere at the border of German-controlled Tanganyika, which has since become the independent nation of Tanzania. In his absence, Karen Blixen refused to be placed in a camp with British women as a safety measure and, instead, took it upon herself to relocate to Kijabe, where she worked as a telegraph operator. It was in that role that Blixen received Bror's request for supplies that she personally delivered in the fall of 1914. This incident is carefully retold in the book in the section titled "Part IV: From an Immigrant's Notebook."[31] There, we learn that the three-month expedition involved four wagons, each with sixteen oxen, and a team of seventeen young African boys. Significantly, however, Blixen's deepest memories of the journey were not marked with the triumph of safely reaching Bror or in finding him amorous, as he is depicted in *Out of Africa* onscreen. Rather, she delighted in the sense of freedom she experienced through miles of wide-open Nature, accompanied by young, Black African men: "The air of the African Highlands went to my head like wine; I was all the time slightly drunk with it, and the joy of these months was indescribable. I had been out on a shooting safari before, but I had not till now been out alone with Africans."[32] The same experience retold in a letter to her mother had even more to say: "I am absolutely convinced that the natives are the *best class* out here," she wrote. "I find it impossible to take any interest at all in the English middle class, but the boys are absolute gentlemen."[33]

In a similar way, Blixen expresses fascination for the circle of young Somali (Islamic) women she comes to know through Farah, her Somali servant. In keeping with her openness to Africans of various tribes and origins, she becomes a chauffeur to these women at times, which exposes her to their charms, their dignity, their expectations of marriage, and their distance from her European point of view. In them she sees the influence of their powerful tutor, a woman whose appearance and placidity Blixen compares to that of an elephant. It is this woman who instructs them into a "great noble conspiracy into which her pupils were by privilege admitted" as they develop a keen sense of their own moral and economic value as brides.[34] Ultimately, they reverse Blixen's gaze when they ask her if it could possibly be true "that some nations in Europe gave away their maidens to their husbands for nothing."[35] Blixen's openness to these women evolves out of her unique relationship with them—as an admiring observer and object of their curiosity that involves unexpected interactions including her almost inadvertent role of introducing them to the mysteries of Christianity.

In Judith Lee's reading, the Somali women are one of three "most important" relationships Blixen experiences in Ngong that lead to "self-discovery and her awareness of her own limits." (The others are Denys Finch Hatton and "Africans" in a generalized sense that rightfully includes the expedition to Tanganyika.)[36] In such associations, primarily with young people, Blixen's early encounter with otherness is imbued with fascination and a sense of freedom that leads to the experience of *shared otherness* as a significant marker in this phase of Blixen's evolution of double-consciousness. The Somali women clearly allow her to feel less strange as her inquisitiveness—and theirs—is satisfied. It is interesting to note that with regard to this familiar pattern in the sociology of otherness, bell hooks adds a note of caution, "Difference can seduce precisely because the mainstream of sameness is a provocation that terrorizes."[37] Yet for Karen Blixen, the recognition of difference leads to a lessening of social boundaries and the enriching, new reality of code switching in her daily life as she discovers her capacity to appreciate a variety of cultures.

She was, in the end, able to "oscillate" as needed and live with layers of "duplicity" explored in Susan Hardy Aiken's work on Blixen's narrative voice. This involved a cunning ability to negotiate various levels of otherness while turning the proverbial "blind eye" when a blind eye was useful. In the mid-1920s, for example, her letters express frustration when the British poll taxes on Black Africans increased from 20 shillings to 150 shillings per year. "If only people at home could get to know about it, but this country is so amazingly outside the bounds of law and justice. The upper classes haven't improved in the least since the [French] revolution; when they are not *afraid* of the lower classes, they are without shame," she writes.[38] Even Lord Delamere, a man much admired and considered to be the de facto leader of the colony, fell into the crosshairs of her opinions: "Lord Delamere has just had a dinner in Nakuru for 250 people, where they consumed 600 bottles [of Champagne], and they have *no* idea; the [British] women here are quite capable of asking why, when they [Africans] cannot get *posho,* they don't eat wheat or rice, just like Marie Antoinette asked why the poor didn't eat cake if they had no bread."[39] Yet, as with the poll tax, her anger is more comfortably focused on the excesses of the upper class in the colony than it is on the existence of a colony in the first place. Later that year, a reflection emerges with new confidence in her correspondence with Thomas Dinesen: "I have realized the fact, which is in itself very strange . . . that the greatest passion of my life has become my love for my black brother, and apart from the fact that he causes me a great deal of trouble and worry, there is still huge satisfaction and enormous enjoyment involved."[40]

Among the examples of "trouble and worry" that reveal Blixen's interest in otherness is the one she writes of in *Out of Africa* as "Kitosch's Story" and returns to later in a 1938 speech delivered to (male) students in Lund and Stockholm, Sweden, titled "Blacks and Whites in Africa."[41] As a lens through which to trace Karen Blixen across time in the context of otherness and racial justice, there is hardly a better example than Kitosch, a Gikuyu boy who dies after being flogged, tied to a post by his white "master," and left to die—in part because it was determined by a colonial court of justice that he "willed" his own death—all for a minor disobedience. The incident is also referenced in a letter from Blixen to her Norwegian friend Gustav Mohr, who was still living in the colony of Kenya in the summer of 1936 as she worked on *Out of Africa* in Denmark. And lastly, "Kitosch's Story" emerges in a vociferous critique by Ngũgĩ wa Thiong'o titled "Detained: A Writer's Prison Diary," in which he rejects Blixen's "total acceptance of the hideous [will-to-die] theory and her attempts to draw from it aesthetic conclusions meant to have universal relevance and validity."[42] These layered perspectives invite a reading of "Kitosch's Story" in which we find both clarity and contradiction in Blixen's attitudes toward her "black brother."

Ngũgĩ does not, actually, contest Blixen's facts in her telling of "Kitosch's Story" found in Part IV of *Out of Africa* as one of thirty-two anecdotes, observations, fables, and parables. Like all of these texts, this one draws the reader in with a clear, descriptive opening paragraph:

> Kitosch was a young Native in the service of a young, white settler of Molo. One Wednesday in June, the settler lent his brown mare to a friend, to ride to the station on. He sent Kitosch there to bring back the mare, and told him not to ride her, but to lead her. Kitosch jumped on to the mare, and rode her back, and on Saturday the settler, his master, was told of the offense by a man who had seen it. In punishment the settler, on Sunday afternoon, had Kitosch flogged, and afterwards tied up in his store, and here late on Sunday night Kitosch died.[43]

Note that the flogging was likely carried out by another "young Native" with a whip, called a *sjambok,* made from the tail of a hippopotamus. In any case, Blixen explains in *Out of Africa* that "upon the matter the High Court was set in Nakuru, in the Railway Institute, on the 1st of August" where it reached its conclusion with a verdict of "Guilty of Grievous Hurt" on the settler, who received a sentence of "two years R.I." (house arrest) while a lesser sentence of one day each was given to the "Natives" who carried out the flogging because "as they had acted under the orders of their master, a European, it would be an injustice to imprison them."[44]

Any twenty-first-century thinker with a modicum of postcolonial understanding will agree that Kitosch's punishment was a violent overreach by the settler named Abraham, as Blixen later recalls in her letter to Gustav Mohr that requests his help in finding copies of newspaper reports to refresh her memory on the incident, since Mohr is still living near Nairobi in 1936. In her letter, Blixen clarifies that she would like to have some clippings "not for the sake of propaganda, from which I'll refrain, but for the sake of a few reflections—as you know, the doctor Jex Blake had given an explanation of this matter, that amounted to saying that the *natives* could, in a certain sense, decide to die and that this, effectively, allowed them to die."[45] Ngũgĩ's sharp critique seizes on this bizarre idea when he writes decades later that "the outcome of the High Court at Nakuru turned to rest solely on the intentions of the victim," quickly adding that "in Anglo-Saxonland, it seems colonized natives have a fiendish desire for suicide that absolves white murderers."[46]

Meanwhile, Blixen's approach to writing this "story" into her memoir shines a light on the essential question of intent, beginning with the judge's reminder to the jury of white men that the case would be decided based on the intentions of the "persons concerned, and not upon the results." With this in mind, Blixen asks. "What then had been the intentions, and the attitude of mind, of the persons concerned in the Kitosch case?" In an effort to determine the answer for herself, she summarizes the facts of the case, which have never been in dispute.

> Kitosch had not much opportunity for expressing his intentions. He was locked up in the store, his message, therefore comes very simply, and in a single gesture. The night watch states that he cried all night. But it was not so, for at one o'clock he talked with the Toto, who was in the store with him. He indicated to the child that he must shout to him, because the flogging had made him deaf. But at one o'clock he asked the Toto to loosen his feet, and explained that in any case, he could not run away. When the Toto had done as he asked him, Kitosch said to him that he wanted to die. A little while after, he rocked himself from side to side, [and] cried: "I am dead!" and died.

Ngũgĩ quotes this passage in his 1981 essay, although he omits the details that Blixen takes time to explain in *Out of Africa* when she clarifies that the cause of death was pronounced by the district surgeon to be "due to the injuries and wounds that he had found on the body." Yet two other physicians, who had come to Nakuru from Nairobi, differed in their combined opinion, and the older of the two, who had been in the region for twenty-five years, insisted that neither the flogging nor starvation was enough to cause death. As the younger doctor then conceded to his colleague's authority, "An important factor came into the matter, not to be ignored: that was the will to die." A negotiation to reduce the settler's guilt then ensued in which a mysterious, unscientific cause of death became entwined with medically verifiable causes.[47]

Ultimately, the High Court relented and inscribed "the-wish-to-die theory" into the verdict that ultimately stated the cause of death as flogging, starvation, and the victim's wish to die, "the latter being the subject of special emphasis." As Blixen reflected on the case while writing "Kitosch's Story" in Part IV of *Out of Africa,* she came to her own "verdict" that comprehends a desire for death as a human response to a brutally unjust situation yet also dares to imagine a "wish to die" among people as mysterious as Kitosch was to her as a wish so powerful that death might actually occur—at will. Her closing paragraph of "Kitosch's Story" consequently becomes the essence of Ngũgĩ wa Thiong'o's critique as Blixen turns to poetic prose to rationalize a troubling incident and, furthermore, deploys a metaphor with reference to "wild things." Unfortunately, her words are simply too literary for the facts of this story to bear. Her flaw is her attempt to memorialize a boy who had not been dead long enough and should have lived much longer: "By this strong sense in him of what is right and decorous, the figure Kitosch, with his firm will to die, although now removed from us by many years, stands out with a beauty of his own. In it is embodied what is fugitive of the wild things who are, in the hour of need, conscious of a refuge somewhere in existence; who go when they like; of whom we can never get hold."[48]

This last sentence is, perhaps, the most tone-deaf of Blixen's memoir, for she must have known what everyone has since come to know, thanks to David M. Anderson's research in the history of East Africa. In a particularly relevant article, he writes that "by the 1920s, Kenya's reputation for excess in respect of corporal punishment [of workers by settlers] was unrivalled anywhere in the British colonies." In the same article, he notes that the Indian Penal Code in force in colonial Kenya "contributed to the passing of lenient sentences in several notorious courts" despite "perceived 'injustices' in a series of flogging cases that culminated in the rewriting of the Penal Codes by 1930."[49]

A year after the first publication of *Out of Africa* in the U.K. and some months before her 1938 speech to Swedish students on the topic of "Blacks and Whites in Africa," in which she speaks of Kitosch as "a young Gikuyu who was punished by his white employer and died from it," Karen Blixen received a letter from a man she had never met. This man had read her book and wanted to clarify something regarding the outcome of the High Court proceeding on Kitosch's death, since he had been the third—and youngest—of the three physicians who studied the body of Kitosch to determine his cause of death. Over a decade later, he wanted Blixen to know that he had—indeed—been partial to the white man. "But," he explained, "I did it for [my] love of the prestige of the white race." As Blixen explains to the students gathered to hear her talk in Lund and Stockholm, Sweden, she interprets this letter as "courageous" and states that she believes his "good intentions," even as she believes his outlook had been "short-sighted." For, as she tells the students, "he had not served the prestige of the Whites. The Blacks knew perfectly well what was going on. One would have, I believe, scored a point for the prestige of Whites if the White man had been judged as if he had killed a White man. The Blacks would have then seen, to their astonishment, that we were capable of seriously considering the things of which we speak: justice, equality before the law, fault, and responsibility."[50]

In its clarity and open-heartedness, "Blacks and Whites in Africa" establishes Phase 3 in Karen Blixen's evolution of understanding otherness as it constitutes Blixen's first public act of "antiracism." The talk begins with her dramatized description of the vast terrain of the East Africa Protectorate, which actually encompassed five territories in East Africa at the time—Uganda, Kenya, Tanganyika, Belgian Congo, and northern Rhodesia. She falters somewhat when she expresses how this land "extends beyond view, as it has for a thousand years, without a trace of human passage, not even a path" [because] "the people who pass by still follow the trails of animals." As she muses on the arrival of airplanes described as "the twentieth century landing in the Stone Age," we get a sense of her talent for startling, if inaccurate, imagery before she emphasizes that the place she is speaking of is not actually "uninhabited," as was so often said. Rather, it is "the place of most significant meeting, for it is there that I met indigenous Africans."[51]

In a confiding tone, she explains how her confrontation with the Other involved a process of recognizing a foreign *subjectivity* that felt similar to her own and, furthermore, how this became an important experience in her life as a person and as a writer. As she speaks to young Swedes, she deploys a musical metaphor to express how "the entire world and life were enlarged for me, a solidarity, a common action was established that made new melodies possible."[52] A critical feature of this "music" was the element of the unexpected, for she had not anticipated that getting to know them as individuals would "enlarge" her world: "We had not mutually searched for each other. I had not come to this land to study Blacks, and they had seen to it that we did not do it. But confronted with destiny, we found each other as we went about our daily life. We were human beings living in the same conditions; if rain was slow in coming to us Whites, the situation was heavy with troubles for Blacks as well; if we ran out of water on safari, we were thirsty together."[53]

As we read these words through the filter of time, it's not difficult to see why she became the object of postcolonial critique in the 1980s, especially after the 1985 film reduced her to a romantic heroine. Yet in her willingness to expose herself in 1938 with what sounded *at the time* like a kind of confession, if not an apology, she models the possibility of respectful coexistence. When Blixen explains how one "gets rid of one's social and intellectual way of being, piece by piece," she introduces a new perspective into her own superficial accoutrements of power. "Who am I, when I am no longer the person I was supposed to be until now?" she asks. The only answer available to her is the reality of being a human being and this, she suggests, is the only place where a real connection is possible, even if her word choice would be edited out today: "It is as a human being, unique and singular, that you will meet in primitive beings with dark skin."[54]

A significant moment in this well-organized speech arrives with her prescient warning to her audience of young men poised to become world travelers, upper-class Swedes, and mid-century success stories: "You will change, in your own eyes, so much that in the end you will wonder: 'Who am I? How do I look to them?'"[55] In this sense, Blixen's 1938 speech guides these young men in the complex process of reversing the gaze to interrogate notions of race and power and, effectively, to question the morality of colonial domination. Here, she emphasizes the importance of "what one assumes and means or represents" apart from titles, professional accomplishments, and culture-specific markers of status. She then goes on to pose a critical question: "What do we have, besides our own personal power, and how could the conquered peoples whose land we took find hope in anything we would have meant?"[56]

As her thoughts wade into the dehumanization of colonialism, with "Kitosch's Story" lingering in the air, Blixen deploys the deceptively clever metaphor of a child's toy boat that would have been familiar to every young man in her audience. She builds on that image to speak of larger vessels, such as the enormous steamers full of complex machinery and powerful people that had so often carried her and her fellow passengers across the Mediterranean Sea and through the Suez Canal to the African coast. Yet she reminds the audience that travelers like her were inevitably "transporting an invisible cargo"—that is, their own worldview, learned values, and innate belief in white European superiority.[57] When she turns away from this "invisible cargo" to look back at Europe from her perspective developed through her years in Ngong, she says, "Of course, they find us capable and [believe] that we know how to do many things, and yet they find this disconcerting; for they have a hard time, in their hearts, sharing a position with us because they think we lack wisdom."[58] With her "they" and "us"—a linguistic dichotomy barely perceptible at the time—she notes that technical virtuosity means very little to people who have their own, time-tested techniques for navigating their own environment. In the end, she interrogates herself and her generation with a critical question, "What had *we* brought to *them,* apart from the losses of their liberty and higher taxes?"[59]

This little-known speech travels a long way from her private frustrations expressed in early letters to family to a bestseller that gave her a public forum and justified a new persona that feels perfectly natural to Karen Blixen in 1938. As she concludes her talk, she does so as a respected Danish writer with an international reputation and the unusual credibility of a woman who has lived among Black Africans: "For me, this experience was a sort of revelation not only of the world, but also of myself. And I can say that it was a great joy and liberation. . . . It was a place where all laws of gravity were left behind. . . . It required courage to go there, but it was intoxicating, splendid—one more step in this direction, I thought, and I will be face-to-face with God."[60]

CHAPTER EIGHT

Karen Blixen's Closet

At present I nearly always wear long khaki trousers and a kind of blouse reaching to the knee, and bare legs and clogs.

—Karen Blixen to Ingeborg Dinesen from Ngong, May 28, 1923

Clothing is a critical signifier of economic status, sexual availability, class, and culture—even when it displays disdain for economic status, sexual availability, class, and culture. As a child of a quasi-aristocratic family, Karen Blixen learned the codes of European dress at an early age. Hats and sweaters, skirts and blouses, stockings, boots, woolen coats, and fur-trimmed accessories were lifelong attributes of her Danish persona, initially mirrored in her sisters' identical outfits. As she came of age in a new century, Tanne adopted the corseted silhouette of a "Gibson Girl" as defined by the popular ink drawings of Charles Gibson. This called for voluminous blouses with leg-of-mutton sleeves tapered at the wrist, flared skirts, and long hair piled high under a hat resembling a flowerpot. As for "fancy dress," she needed some of that when she joined her aristocratic cousins at parties and events including the horse races at Klampenborg near Copenhagen. Her longtime assistant Clara Svendsen once explained that as a young woman, "Tanne, exuberant and ready to savor all that life had to offer, loved to go to the races and desperately wanted to wear elegant clothes that were just right for these occasions, despite Aunt Bess's disapproval of such activities."[1] An early portrait from 1907 gives a hint of why Aunt Bess might have been a little nervous with her niece's display of skin that stops just short of seduction (see photo gallery following this chapter, fig. 1).

Among the "elegant clothes" that can only be imagined is the outfit Karen Blixen wore on her wedding day in Mombasa on January 15, 1914, when she married her Swedish cousin Baron Bror von Blixen-Finecke after three weeks at sea. We have a sense of her ensemble, however, since she described it in a note to her mother from Ngong: "In reply to your question, this is to tell you that for my wedding day I wore a shantung silk suit and a helmet and one of the blouses we bought in Naples." Written from her sickbed with an illness she assumed to be malaria, the same letter explains that her day-to-day style had barely changed: "For everyday wear here I use exactly the same clothes as at home, a blouse and short skirt, often a divided skirt, brown boots, always a double-layered felt hat or a helmet."[2] Clothes were clearly on her mind as she added an ominous note for Aunt Bess: "Malaria makes you feel so miserable that . . . the whole world disgusts you like an ill-fitting dress."[3]

As we can see in the photographic record, Blixen's African years (1914–31) read like a runway show of dresses for work and play, suits, ruffled dressing gowns, shawls, hats, and shoes (with buckles, pointed toes, and ostrich feathers in the bedroom); she was, by this time in her life, a multifaceted modern woman with fashion on her mind. And so, she naturally accepted the brand-new necessity of "safari style" for which she remains best known a century later and is often erroneously considered the origin. As such, she seems to become a kind of romantic emblem for the feminine use of khaki, as seen in photos of her first safari under Bror's tutelage in the summer of 1914. Yet "safari style" was actually created by and for European men at the turn of the century and prolonged by movie stars, fashion designers, and clever marketing campaigns long after Karen Blixen returned to Denmark in 1931—never to don a khaki jacket again. Furthermore, as the six-thousand-acre farm began to dominate her days after Bror's departure in 1921, she gradually gave up the "sport" of killing wildlife and the clothes that went with it. "Before I took over management of the farm, I had been keen on many Safaris. But when I became a farmer, I put away my rifles."[4]

In truth, she never ceased to enjoy a good hunt and the social whirl that it entailed. After meeting Denys Finch Hatton at a dinner party in 1918, and especially after Bror spent less and less time at the farm, safari life with Denys became a pleasure, partly because he was good at it and largely because she was in love with him.[5] She also answered the call of the Masai who came to her house from time to time to ask that she "come out and shoot a certain lion or lioness which was killing off their cattle," a plea that led to memorable safaris with Farah at her side.[6] Eventually, however, Karen Blixen traded her khaki shirts and militaristic double-breasted suits for airy dusters and flared jackets suited to riding a horse around the farm, as well as shapeless smocks and trousers that constituted her "work clothes." It is surely her post-safari life in the 1920s that accounts for costume designer Milena Canonero's observation when tasked with outfitting Meryl Streep for the 1985 film: "Double-breasted didn't suit the shape of Meryl so we did a different jacket. And Karen Blixen was a bit frumpy. We didn't want to make Meryl frumpy." Apropos, Canonero took the liberty of replacing the layered cotton dresses Blixen actually wore with simpler, lighter styles in white linen for Streep.[7]

Frumpy or not, by movie-star standards, Blixen's preference for white blouses and cotton dresses becomes as much of a "text" to be interpreted as her safari clothing. A particularly iconic picture shows her in a full-length "portrait" in 1922, in which she seems to cradle a bouquet of long-stemmed lilies from her carefully cultivated garden (fig. 2). This look conveys feminine leisure, ladylike cleanliness, beauty, and abundant growth—all as an expression of self and place that illustrates Thomas Knipp's critique of Karen Blixen and her world: "It is in the poise with which the European maintains and exercises power in this counterpointed world of garden and wilderness—farm and safari—that he (or she) perfects his (or her) character," he writes.[8] Ultimately, Blixen's tiered white dress with white shoes and stockings becomes a "costume" as she assumes the leading role of a play—not unlike like those plays she created in Rungstedlund years earlier. Consequently, while the "lady of the manor" is only one of Blixen's many personas, it represents her preferred title throughout the 1920s of "Baroness Blixen." Ultimately, a juxtaposition of the lovely lady with an armful of lilies and the weary hunter in sweaty khakis reveals a sense of Blixen's contradictions.

Karen (called "Tania" in Africa) set off on her first safari in June 1914 with her husband of five months from their first house on Mbagathi Estate. This involved a caravan of mule wagons, African porters, skilled servants (including a cook and a kitchen boy), curious dogs, rifles, a canvas tent, folding chairs, portable bedding, and clothes made for what she described to her family as "change of air" prescribed by her doctor since "it is not so easy to regain one's strength after malaria."[9] This remark becomes poignant as we realize that her illness in 1914 was not malaria at all, but a first sign of the life-altering syphilis of the spine that would eventually settle in her gastrointestinal system and ravage her body. But in 1914, the safari that lasted a month, and encompassed relaxing pauses at a health resort near the Masai Reserve, allowed her confidence to grow as she learned new skills in the bush from Bror. Together, they celebrated the challenge of killing an astonishing array of animals, which she described in a letter to her mother: "It was a tremendously successful safari, six big lions, four leopards, one cheetah. As well as the usual kinds of game, eland, impala, gnu, boar, jackal, marabou—I shot one big lion and one big leopard. Bror has taught me to shoot and says that I shoot well."[10]

This letter cannot be read in the twenty-first century without thoughts of animal rights, endangered species, illegal poaching, and damage done to Kenya's ecosystems. For all of these reasons, hunting wildlife in Kenya was banned in 1977, yet such concerns were far from the minds of "great white hunters" a century ago who enjoyed celebrity status when guided safaris became a lucrative aspect of elite tourism in East Africa. Teddy Roosevelt led the way at the end of his presidential term in 1909 when a privately funded expedition sponsored by the Smithsonian Institute "bagged" over five hundred animals with the assistance of two hundred porters and the legendary Philip Percival as guide.[11] Percival later teamed up with Bror Blixen and also with Karen Blixen's beloved Denys Finch

Hatton before serving as mentor to the adventure symbol of the day, Ernest Hemingway.[12] Thomas Dinesen also enjoyed safari life during his 1921–22 visit to Ngong and shared his sister's enthusiasm conveyed in her earliest correspondence in *Letters from Africa,* beginning with the long missive written in the autumn of 1914. This amounts to a detailed essay on the safari that took place "90 miles from civilization" in the Masai Reserve:

> I have spent four weeks in the happy hunting grounds and have just emerged from the depths of the great wide open spaces, from the life of prehistoric times, today just as it was a thousand years ago, from meeting with the great beasts of prey, which enthrall one, which obsess one so that one feels that lions are all that one lives for—strengthened by the air of the high mountain region, tanned by its sun, filled with its wild, free, magnificent beauty of heat-dazzling days, in great clear moonlit nights.[13]

Blixen's exhilaration at having touched "prehistoric times" is evident in the photographs from this first of many safaris where she poses smiling in the grass with two dead lions (fig. 3). In keeping with the classic code of the safari portrait established by Teddy Roosevelt, she appears with her rifle displayed and exudes the triumphant demeanor of those who can rest now, having conquered Nature's threat. She wears a dark khaki camp shirt and pants, a pair of binoculars, and what appear to be two sun hats. This was obviously a happy moment for Karen Blixen, even if she is less fashionable here than she has ever been in her life, at least according to the dress codes for European ladies. The joy of these moments would not last forever, but the photos from the summer of 1914 hold important clues to the psyche of Tania Blixen, who describes the great expanse of landscape she sees as a kind of endless "Africa" in her letters home, as if she inhabits the entire continent. Not only is she clearly comfortable in her new clothes, but they allow her to experience what we would recognize as the ultimate freedom of "unisex" clothing as she passes the critical test of taming the wild. In other photos from the same safari, she stands next to Bror in almost identical dress as she becomes a contented codebreaker in comparison to the gender-specific clothing worn by women of her class back home in Denmark. With cotton twill the color of dust and wide-brimmed hats to block the sun, Blixen quickly slips into her new, adventurous persona of skilled hunter.

Among her "new pieces," we often see her in the close-fitting felt hat, or wide-brimmed sun hat, as opposed to the hard-shell pith helmet so often worn by Bror and other men. That ingenious invention, featuring an air space between the top of the head and the top of the hat, was developed in British colonial India circa 1850 and favored by thousands of men throughout colonial Africa, including Dr. Albert Schweitzer of Lambarene and his staff, as the best protection against sunstroke. Blixen must have experienced mild sunstroke—at least once—because she described the maddening sensation to her mother in 1923: "as if the Sun God had hurled his rays of anger on to one's topknot."[14] In any case, in the postcolonial world, the pith helmet has become a symbol of the violent excesses of colonialism, from land grabs to detention, torture, and murder. No wonder Melania Trump was widely criticized when she wore a pith helmet as a fashion accessory during her 2018 visit to Kenya, one of several poor choices that inspired Al Jazeera journalist Elliot Ross to explain the problem: "No country in the West has adequately reckoned with the historical reality of colonialism. Until such a reckoning takes place through broad-based education and memorialization, it is difficult to see how Western societies can ever move beyond the powerful investment in whiteness that so disfigures our common political, social and spiritual life. Like Melania Trump, too many in the West look at today's world not as it really is, but through a veil of racial and colonial delusions."[15]

Karen Blixen has also been accused of such delusions, although she wore safari clothes for safari life as the most practical and comfortable way to "dress for the occasion." Her preferred head covering was a snug fedora with a flattering brim, sometimes embellished with a white feather, called a hackle. Historically, this feature might imply any number of achievements from a safari "kill" to the divine protection of an angel.[16] Meanwhile, the ubiquitous leather boots worn in Africa protected men and women from snake bites and other venomous creatures, just as they did—

and do—in the American West. At its fundamental level, safari "style" was not a style at all but a utilitarian way of dressing in a particular environment. Karen Blixen would, no doubt, be surprised to learn that it became a popular fashion movement in the late twentieth century and even more surprised to learn that it was largely attributed to her.

It would be more appropriate to assign the origin of safari style to movies that appeared in her lifetime such as *Trader Horn* (1931), filmed in colonial Kenya, *The Snows of Kilimanjaro* (1952), or *Mogambo* (1953), in which box-office stars Clark Gable and Grace Kelly wear khaki with panache, thanks to legendary costume designer Helen Rose. Had she loved her "huntress" persona more than her personal body image, Blixen might have worn khaki throughout her Africa years, and beyond. Yet as she wrote to her mother in 1923: "As nobody wears corsets out here you can really move as a man's equal. If it suited me I would wear trousers here, *shorts* as so many ladies do; but alas, alas, I do not have the legs—or the moral courage—for that."[17] Her gender awareness of safari clothing tucked into this comment hints at its underlying meaning for Blixen herself and generations of women to come.

The essentially desexualized vocabulary of cotton pants, relaxed jackets, boots, belts, ammunition pouches, vests, and jaunty hats responds to a significant question for modern women in the colonial era: *How do we dress now to express power?* This question may explain part of the appeal of safari style for women born into a tidal wave of feminism in the last decades of the twentieth century. By the 1970s, clothing had changed to fit the new concept of a "liberated woman" as a new interest in the lives of accomplished women got underway, along with the popularity of pantsuits and business bags. These feminist forces account, in part, for the development of Blixen's literary fame that culminated—albeit posthumously—in new editions of her books, the publication of her *Letters from Africa* (1981), Judith Thurman's deeply researched biography (1983), and the wildly successful film of *Out of Africa* that premiered in her centennial year (1985). These developments delivered a newfound heroine to the women's movement whose difficult life and hard-won achievements were softened by a romantic spirit and an intriguing wardrobe.

Though never a self-declared feminist, Blixen had proven fifty years earlier that white women, like white men, could follow a guide, trek through the bush, live out of a tent, and learn to pull a trigger—especially with a skilled entourage of Black service personnel nearby. If Blixen understood safari clothes as a kind of "cosplay," or means of slipping into a borrowed identity, she did so with a consciousness of what she was doing and why. In her own words, she had no particular affection for safari style as we know it, as she expressed in a 1914 letter to her sister Elle when she described her distaste at the fashion sense of British women:

> The English ladies are particularly dreadful. Quite apart from the decidedly commercial flirting that all the English ladies indulge in—I doubt if there are ten decent women in this country—they have such appalling taste, always appearing in khaki down to the knees, with cartridge cases, and below the knee sheer silk stockings and high-heeled suede shoes, they are over made-up, screech frightfully, and laugh hysterically, scold their workmen like fishwives, are furious about everything in this country and all have to look like girls of 17.[18]

Embedded in this stinging commentary is Blixen's ever-present awareness of a feminine ideal defined by class, culture, and fashion against which she measured herself. As she discovered the rational reasons to add safari clothing to her repertoire, she realized that the khaki cloth linked to hunting—so readily available in Nairobi—expressed a significant connection to the feminized power acquired by marriage to Baron von Blixen. Though distasteful as worn by loud, British women, the ease of khaki cloth signaled a new kind of power—power *earned* as a woman able to compete in an aristocratic sport dominated by men. Ultimately, it was this new persona, not the costume that could be put on or taken off at will, that mattered.

And yet, as ever, Blixen was always happy to don a mask. In her clothing, as in her life, Karen Blixen adopted a repertoire of personas around herself in Ngong that, when "read" carefully and collectively, express her complex identity. Some were essential aspects of "country life" that mimicked codes of English aristocracy astutely analyzed by Simon Lewis when he writes that "the interest in hunting is bound up with class snobbery and self-aggrandizement." Safari life is, after all, centered on the lion that appears in heraldic family crests, marks the threshold of gates to private estates, and growls silently above the roaring fire of great rooms as the ultimate prize. Lewis extends his analysis to the colonial expression of racial codes that determine who can hunt and how and who might be permitted to eat the feast.[19] This etiquette of "the hunt" in colonial Kenya clearly formed a vast gentlemen's club without walls, a snippet of which we see in the opening scenes of *Out of Africa* onscreen that reaffirm the social structure controlled by men that young Tania has gotten herself into. In that society, male power was asserted in many ways, including the act of killing, possessing, and consuming wildlife.

Furthermore, insofar as the space for "country life" is located in opposition to the city, the seemingly limitless space for safari further delineates the boundaries of the colonial world of "colony" vs. "metropole," each of which constructs genderized dress codes within a matrix of social customs that call for a mingling of ladylike propriety, farm management authority, and adventurous days in the bush. In some images of Blixen in Africa, her deerhounds become props symbolizing her skill at taming Nature as they point to wildlife beyond the lawn well-kept by Black African servants. Meanwhile, the light fabric and roomy cut of tiered cotton dresses and voluminous blouses allow her to find a comfort zone for movement in the corset-free life of the colony. It was, in a sense, out of necessity that the more durable khaki twill associated with safari life merges "seamlessly" with the dress codes of feminized power found in equestrian, military, and aristocratic conventions of European society.

Paradoxically, Blixen's association with late twentieth-century "safari chic," in which products and materials linked to colonial life become signifiers of glamour and social status, raises a number of questions. Is there a link between Blixen's life in Ngong and the graphic configuration of zebra skin woven into a silk scarf by Hermès or the talisman of an animal horn handle attached to the Yves Saint Laurent "Mombasa bag"? I wonder if she would have taken such objects as an opportunity for a philosophical essay on the absurdity of clothing displaced from its natural surroundings, or simply laughed. I also wonder if she could have understood the social reality of a globalized consumer society in which anyone can "grab" a piece of status off the rack—or online—without the slightest awareness of its origin, original purpose, or impact on climates and societies near and far. In *Out of Africa,* Karen Blixen has little to say about safari style, nor does she interpret safari clothing as a "style," due to her direct relationship with it as utilitarian. Yet as the photographic record of her life in Africa illustrates, she is comfortable with herself as a woman whose sense of power can be made visible though whatever she has tucked away in her closet.

Anders Westenholz has analyzed his great-aunt's African years as the time when she began to feel her personal power expand. Yet he adds a dark note when he writes of her struggle "to keep the Power under control and live harmoniously with it."[20] This hints at the arc of her memoir which, as we have seen, required the invention of a mythical version of her past when she sat down to write *Out of Africa* in 1936. This psychic need explains her longing for experience in the first place as well as her self-aggrandizement reflected in her vision of Africa's vast, spacious landscape as a kind of "stage" where she might enact a new life through a new persona. In a sense, her enthusiasm for the life vs. death endeavor of safari life described in her long letter to Thomas in 1914 echoes her reward won not only through a confrontation of "man against Nature," but also one of "man against woman" in the "man's world" of colonial Kenya. This new, emboldened self evokes the mythical Diana (aka Goddess of the Hunt) discussed by Susan Brantly as one of Blixen's favored types in her tales.[21] Indeed, a Diana-like sense of power is felt in *Out of Africa* as the narrator *authorizes herself* to claim the authority required to tell her own story. Though serene in tone and often understated, Blixen's memoir tells a tale of evolving power prior to the mid-1920s followed by a precipitous loss of power by 1931.

As we trace that rise and fall of her personal power, it is easy to see how safari life—and its dress code—plays a role in her self-mythology. In an emblematic 1914 photograph, she appears "fixed" in place like a mannequin in a shop window dressed head-to-toe in a safari "ensemble" and surrounded with its accoutrements of tent, portable furniture, slumbering dogs, and servants (fig. 4). Yet it is her casual confidence with its touch of *coquetterie* that makes this a picture of the myth she wishes to inhabit. The subtext of the photograph is the presence of an inauthentic self who attempts to compensate for what is missing as she strikes a pose in a neatly pressed, double-breasted khaki jacket worn over jodhpurs and leather boots. She also wears a kerchief gathered around her neck to catch perspiration, although this photograph emphasizes upper-class, sweat-free aspects of safari life that include shade trees, a lounge chair, and Black African servants dealing with supplies. This photo reveals Baroness Blixen as we rarely see her in these early years in Ngong: effectively performing the image she desires because, when it comes to fashion, imitation is always part of the game. Ultimately, the power of "fashion," at its best, allows us to transform ourselves in a particular mood or context, as if wearing a mask. It is, ultimately, a form of expression.

In contrast to this image, in which we detect something of Karen Blixen's personality, there exists a full-length profile of her aiming a gun in the yard of Mbagathi House that was so meaningful to Bror that he glued it in the middle of the first page of his safari diary. He was clearly proud of her correct form with a rifle, since he had taught her how to track animals and shoot with precision. Yet when a rifle is the *only* element that cues the world of "safari," her image becomes hollow and devoid of her own "experience" of the moment. It is as if Bror had simply put a prop in her hands and said, "Aim the rifle and be still as I showed you how to do, my dear. I want to take a picture." Such images remain noteworthy for what they exclude, which, in this case, is Karen Blixen's personal expression of personal power through her fashion choices. There is nothing particularly colonial about her clothing in Bror's "rifle picture," for example. She is wearing a suit and polished shoes, as if setting off for town. There is no conquered animal carcass to celebrate; no wilderness or Black people; no markers of "White Man's Country," as Elspeth Huxley called it on the cover of her 1935 biography of Lord Delamere. In Bror's eyes, Karen Blixen's myth is lost in the shadows of a passionless marriage, as is her face.

As time passes, Karen Blixen's body thickens and her attire becomes increasingly workaday as she slogs about in boots and dresses or comfortable skirts and cotton blouses, as she does during Uncle Aage's 1921 visit devoted to negotiating new loans for the deeply indebted farm. Her snapshots, apart from pictures with Thomas in Ngong (1921–22) or during her mother's visits a few years later (1924, 1927), are likely to catch the baroness in a drab work smock and sun-shielding hat as she works alongside her Black employees in fields and jungles. It is in this era that a group of Gikuyu chiefs accustomed to seeing her in work clothes remarked that "we all think that here, every day on the farm, you are terribly badly dressed." This amusing comment arises in her final book, *Shadows on the Grass,* in the context of a local chief's admiration of "the nicest frock" worn among white people who came out for the African celebration to welcome Prince Edward VIII in 1928. Thirty years later, Blixen explained that her "robe de style" with "a hooped skirt of great fullness, in silver brocade" had been ordered from Paris, even though she claimed a certain indifference to fashion in Ngong: "Generally on the farm I wore old khaki slacks stained with oil, mud, and fouling."[22]

In the photographic record of Karen Blixen's closet, a critical question emerges that relates to her influence as a fashion icon: Considering how briefly she wore safari clothes—mainly from 1914 to 1921—how has Blixen come to represent a fashion trend that began sixty years after she "put away" her rifles? The simple answer for a biographer would be that biographical facts are often manipulated to suit the aims, arguments, and unfounded assumptions of others. Yet even if this blunt explanation fails to take Blixen's own myth into account—with its selective acts of erasure, omission, irony, performance, mask, and understatement—it boggles the mind to realize how exploitable her image became in the 1980s when "consuming Isak Dinesen" took shape as a line of feminist inquiry as well as a national pastime.[23]

One of the leaders of that wave of fascination was Ralph Lauren, who cleverly tapped into a cultural mood for feminine power in the 1980s in a way that conveniently preserved his masculine vision of feminine beauty and earthy sexuality as well as his own devotion to nostalgia: "I never went to Africa. But if I had I might never have done the clothes that I did. They were about romantic Africa, what I though a safari was like. The authenticity of the old surplus safari jacket I had worn since I was a teenager was part of it. And so was a little picture of Isak Dinesen in a romantic straw hat and boots. Sometimes it takes just one thing to excite a whole sensibility about a world."[24] From this pretense of "authenticity" attached to a discarded jacket we eventually get to seductive photographic spreads of beautiful young white people striking pensive poses within reach of cuddly lion cubs or a child perched on a zebra. Such mythical imagery carries the assumption of harmony—the proverbial "peaceable kingdom" described by Isaiah in the Bible. And yet, as we know, such versions of material and spiritual perfection can only be achieved in a world indifferent to historical reality.

Clearly, Ralph Lauren fulfilled his own mythical vision with his first "safari chic" ads in 1982, even if the first representatives—anonymous models supposedly inspired by Isak Dinesen—are astonishingly idle women whose clean hair and flawless skin glow above khaki skirts and white linen blouses. In this way, he associates the author of *Out of Africa* with his own private dreamscape: "I build a collection out of a dream. I'm making a movie," he writes.[25] In this statement, we confront Ralph Lauren's willingness to appropriate a woman's life into his imaginative world where everything that rests on the white privilege of being clean and cared for becomes a metaphor of colonialism itself. Not surprisingly, his signature fragrance named "Safari," created in 1990, sits glittering like liquid gold in a crystalline, cut-glass bottle. Safari life is coated in dust and blood, but everything in the world of Ralph Lauren's "safari chic" is pristine.

Karen Blixen wore khaki, the Persian word for "dust," because it was comfortable, affordable, and available in Nairobi, thanks to cotton fields throughout the British Empire. If it carried a sense of power rooted in its military associations, it also conveyed a blurring of gender restrictions that appealed to her in those years of coming of age as an adventurous modern woman. Only later, when African wars of independence coincided with the era of Blixen's last years, would the "British colonial look" be connected to exploitive military adventures, land grabs, torture, terror, and violent conflicts in the face of resistance.[26] Like all emblematic clothing, its symbolism evolves, which has as much to do with the story woven into a garment as with the people who wear it and make fashion trends fashionable. In its historical context, khaki was not a "guilt-free" fabric until it became ubiquitous. Once popularized, the military spirit of khaki shorts and shirts, multipocketed vests, utility jackets, and leather accessories gave way to associations of leisure, global travel, and an air of casual adventure. In a similar way, unisex denim jeans acquired a hint of "working class" sympathy in the 1960s among young people who wished to display their rejection of class and gender distinctions.

When Blixen left Africa in the summer of 1931, she left her safari clothes behind, even if she retained her taste for the uses of animal skin and fur. In particular, a leopard-skin stole traveled back to Denmark with her as a symbol of her deeply felt connection to animal life, paradoxically ennobled through her experience of safari life and, perhaps, as a reminder of the visitors she had welcomed: "In turn for the goods of civilization, the wayfarers brought me trophies from their hunts: Leopard and Cheetah skins, to be made into fur coats in Paris, snake and lizard skins for shoes, and marabout feathers."[27] Such materials signal her attachment to Nature and Robert Langbaum's famous designation of *Out of Africa* as "an authentic pastoral, perhaps the best pastoral of our time."[28] This does not, however, mean that Blixen was a sentimental "Nature lover." As Peter Mortensen has suggested as recently as 2020, it is her deep connection to

Nature that forms the "stage" of *Out of Africa* on which a world of unpredictable life represents yet another way to understand Blixen's memoir.

In an essay whose title is drawn from *Out of Africa,* Mortensen explains that he aims to articulate an "ecocritical approach" to the memoir within the constellation of "cyborg studies, human-animal studies, critical plant studies, and posthumanist thinking." "'The Grass Was Me . . . the Distant Invisible Mountains Were Me, the Tired Oxen Were Me': Greening Karen Blixen" thus becomes part of Mortensen's "reflection on humanism" intended to cast a new kind of light on the way(s) humanism has been understood since the Enlightenment of the eighteenth-century, which resulted in "a particular mode of liberal personhood."[29] By this, he means a sense of human superiority that has, as we know, inflicted consequences on animals, plants, ecosystems, and on our planet. Mortensen's reference points are widespread and include the work of Blixen's intimate post-WWII friend Thorkild Bjørnvig, who—as an "environmental activist, ecopoet, and ecocritic *avant la lettre*"—was the first to study Blixen's work from the perspective of an environmentalist in 1982. Among other things, Bjørnvig references Blixen's public activism in opposition to animal vivisection, although Mortensen's larger point is aimed at Blixen's unusual affinity for the natural world.[30]

Oddly enough, Mortensen's intriguing work lends itself to a discussion of Blixen's fashion choices when he argues convincingly for an understanding that "humans are no longer—and probably never were—wholly self-possessed and distinct from other beings." In this context, he turns to *Out of Africa* as "a powerful aid in helping us think [through] the borders of the human." His focus here emphasizes "key episodes, characterizations, and images to recover the imaginative, disruptive, de-centering, hybridizing, boundary-blurring and dichotomy-defying power of Blixen's writing." Insofar as these effects involve gender-blurring and persona-creation through the ever-changing fabrics, fashions, styles, and materials—such as animal fur and skin—that Blixen adopted throughout her life, it is not difficult to read her clothing as not only an indicator of her ever-shifting identity and/or provocation, but also as a way in which she lived *within* the world of Nature. In an effort to demonstrate this, Mortensen seeks to "pick up critical traces" that allow him to read *Out of Africa*'s relevance and "so far unacknowledged affinity" with a way of being described by his colleague Heather Sullivan as "ecological humanism."[31]

Mortensen's discussion of "prosthesis machines," for example, demonstrates human dependency on technology such as we find in *Out of Africa* when Wanyangerri survives a gunshot wound thanks to a reconstructed jaw made possible by WWI surgical techniques. Similarly, Blixen's typewriter "gives material form to her thoughts and allows her human voice to carry across oceans and continents."[32] There is also the relatively new Uganda Railroad, Denys Finch Hatton's "Gypsy-Moth" airplane, and "the introduction of automobility in East Africa" that account for Blixen's sense of freedom as well as the audible imagery of "bats cruising noiselessly on asphalt."[33] Equally relevant here to the material world of her closet is the plant and animal overlay represented by the "second skin" of clothing made of khaki and its link to cotton fields, leather boots that echo the clop-clop of horses, felted sheep's wool that formed her preferred hats, and, as Mortensen points out, "the mostly overlooked protagonist" of all in *Out of Africa,* the coffee plant against which Blixen struggles as she "finds that her own life and self are altered by her plants—that she is in some sense produced by coffee trees as much as she produces them."[34] Through Mortensen's reading, we realize that Karen Blixen was not only a keen observer of Nature but totally immersed in it and, literally, sheathed in it by every natural fiber available.

Today, we are keenly aware of our own globalized dependence on Indian cotton, Chinese silkworms, and herds of cashmere goats that seem to fly around the world daily to meet the insatiable habits of convenient consumption in the western world. Meanwhile, back in Kenya Anna Trzebinski, once described as "the wealthy daughter of Kenya's white elite," has evolved past her controversial marriage to a Masai Sumburu warrior to become a source for "Made in Kenya" luxury fashion that is also "Made of Kenya."[35] Trzebinski's "Inspired, Handmade" online shop relies on local labor and locally sourced materials including sisal, baobab fiber, ostrich feathers, suede, and animal horn. At $350, her "Handwoven Large Kikapu Bag" is the least expensive item to be found at annatrzebinski.com, while a cashmere shawl with a dangling feathered fringe or a Tuareg messenger bag made from recycled camel saddle bags exceed $2,000.[36]

If "safari chic" evokes a feeling, it also signals our disconnection from Nature, which has been reduced to economic value in so many ways. Does it matter who—or where or of which race or class—wears a beautiful shawl? To what extent does an article named "Kikapu Bag" (a woven, market bag with handles) preserve its link to a culture of origin that most of us have never observed much less understood? Perhaps it is easier, for the majority, to embrace the charm of shawls and shopping bags than to be confronted with antique rickshaws once operated by Black Africans in 1914 to make life in Nairobi less strenuous for colonists. Or even to confront the cultural distance of current-day Kenya. As cultural anthropologist Janet McIntosh observes, "Though white Kenyans enjoy friendly relationships with plenty of black Kenyans, whites have lost political sovereignty, epistemological credibility, and control over the plotline of Kenya and the narration of its colonial past. . . . They also know that some black Kenyans reject them as cultural citizens, on mingled grounds of race, class, and history."[37] Perhaps clothing, as a universal need offers a "way in" to cross-cultural communication even if "fashion" and "style" tend to preserve the mythical nostalgia that allows people to disassociate from reality and inhabit a desired persona.

After Blixen's years in Ngong, her life evolved into an unexpected career as the international literary phenomenon named "Isak Dinesen" that lasted thirty years beyond her return to Denmark. This persona, like all others, called for a new wardrobe. Apropos, her memorable "coming out" image was published in the United States in 1934 to introduce the mysterious new author of *Seven Gothic Tales* to her readers in the United States. For this, she commissioned a full-length studio portrait by the Danish photographer Reimert Kehlet (fig. 5). Here, her lithe figure sheathed in diaphanous white chiffon strikes a curious posture with an indirect gaze. This unusual portrait has been analyzed by Judith Thurman as an expression that "could be irony or *hauteur* or simply contemplation—and which, like the look of kings in their official portraits, does not acknowledge an obligation to please the viewer."[38] Susan Horton digs deeper as she reads the destabilizing angles of the picture plane within the context of early twentieth-century Cubism and finds it "so ethereal that her corporeal presence casts barely half a shadow."[39] In Horton's analysis, this is a portrait of ever-changing personas that might be seen as a visualization of Pellegrina Leoni, Blixen's ideal female character who first appears in "The Dreamers" and refuses to be limited to one identity.

In her later years, Blixen rekindled her interest in clothes as she enjoyed the elegant lines made fashionable by Coco Chanel worn with cloche hats and neat jackets. In 1956, she was described in the prelude to her *Paris Review* interview as "slim, straight, chic . . . dressed in black with long black gloves and a black Parisian hat that comes forward to shadow her remarkable eyes that are lighter in color at the top than at the bottom."[40] At some point, her image shifted to a flamboyant performance of fame marked with an eccentric sense of style as syphilis settled in her digestive system and a limited diet altered her appearance. In the 1950s, her pale body seemed to shrivel into a stick figure wearing a tight mask of thin skin in which sunken eyes were magnified with kohl. As Pulitzer Prize winner Jean Stafford observed, "She looked, and chose to look, like a witch," a comment that Blixen would have enjoyed, since it carries a faint memory of Amiane from *The Revenge of Truth,* the first among the witch-like women who populate Blixen's tales.[41] As she explained late in life, "There was a woman who, long before 'emancipation of women' came into use, existed independently of a man and had her own center of gravity. She was the witch."[42]

In any case, as she entered that provocative persona in the 1950s, Blixen was above all a well-dressed witch who could be counted on to appear in wool and silk suits draped with a swag of silver fox or leopard skin (fig. 6), turbans or hats made in Paris, and, on her trip to the United States in 1959, a bearskin coat that gave her the appearance of a fragile bird peering out of a nest.[43] She nevertheless liked to dress for every occasion and craved attention because she felt, down deep in her bones, that she had earned her individuality. As she said in her 1953 speech, "A woman's clothes are for her an extension of her own being."[44] In the case of Karen Blixen's "being," this point of view required a very large closet full of memorable clothes to fit the personas she inhabited throughout the seasons of her life: sheer blouses and flared skirts, suits and dresses, long and short, as well as sweaters, gowns, jackets, embroidered helmets, pointed shoes, and filthy smocks to shed at the end of a long day's work on the farm. Far in back of the wardrobe, there was also the memory of dusty boots and blood-stained khaki, not because it was something she thought of as "safari chic," or even a "style," but because it belonged to a time in her life that would never be forgotten.

FIG. 1. Karen Blixen as a young woman, 1907.
Danish Royal Library Digital Collections/Alamy.

FIG. 2. Karen Blixen in Kenya, c. 1922.
Courtesy of the Karen Blixen Museum, Denmark, Rungstedlund Collection.

FIG. 3. Karen Blixen's first safari, 1914. Photo by Bror Blixen.
Courtesy of Danish Royal Library Digital Collections.

FIG. 4. Safari life, 1914. Karen Blixen poses for the camera.
Danish Royal Library Digital Collections/Alamy.

FIG. 5. Karen Blixen's studio portrait by Reimert Kehlet, 1934. This photograph introduced Isak Dinesen to American readers. *Courtesy of the Karen Blixen Museum, Denmark, Rungstedlund Collection.*

FIG. 6. Karen Blixen in 1958, wearing a leopard stole from Africa.
Courtesy of the Karen Blixen Museum, Denmark, Rungstedlund Collection.

Numerous additional images of Karen Blixen can be found online.

CHAPTER NINE

On the Question of Feminism

In speaking about feminism I must begin by saying it is a matter which I do not understand, and which I have never concerned myself with of my own volition.

—Karen Blixen, "Oration at a Bonfire, Fourteen Years Late," 1953

Karen Blixen expressed herself at length on the question of feminism at age sixty-seven when she delivered a lecture at a Danish teachers' college founded in the nineteenth century.[1] The original invitation to speak at the Conference of the International Women's Suffrage Alliance in Copenhagen had come in 1939 at a time when she was booked elsewhere. "Oration at a Bonfire, Fourteen Years Late" was delivered in person in October 1952 and subsequently repeated in 1953 as a radio broadcast, as a magazine essay, and as a stand-alone pamphlet. In the post–World War II era that seemed to hold promise for the women's movement, Blixen's words fanned the flames of controversy and left a bad taste of Blixen's ambivalence lingering among Danish feminists. Among them was their leader, Estrid Hein, who had expected more solidarity from her famous neighbor, whose journey from a nineteenth-century childhood to the unexpected status of international literary star suggested a feminist sensibility. When Blixen finally spoke, however, her talk drew on well-worn nostalgia for "the way women used to be" as managers of the domestic sphere content to leave the world outside the home to men.

As Blixen spoke of two, separate worlds with women more or less excluded from professional achievement, her "Bonfire Oration" quickly became a hurdle to be surmounted by her contemporaries. Not the least of these was Hein herself, whose illustrious career as an ophthalmologist included her own clinic in Copenhagen. But Estrid Hein was only one among many who found Blixen's speech insulting when the speaker claimed not to understand the matter of feminism *at all.* Blixen further muddied the water when she set women writers apart as a special group that made them somehow less loveable: "I think that, as far as I'm concerned, were I a man, it would be out of the question for me to fall in love with a woman writer; indeed, I think that if I had met and felt myself powerfully attracted to a woman, the information that she is a writer would cool my ardor."[2]

It comes as no surprise that the speech has challenged feminist scholars in the late twentieth century, whose early works often focused on women artists and writers as keys to the hidden reality of women's lives. A short list of classics from the 1970s includes *Why Have There Been No Great Women Artists?* by Linda Nochlin (1971), *From the Center: Feminist Essays on Women's Art* by Lucy Lippard (1976), *A Literature of Their Own* by Elaine Showalter (1977), *The Madwoman in the Attic: The Woman Writer and the Nineteenth-Century Literary Imagination* by Sandra M. Gilbert and Susan Gubar (1979), and *The Obstacle Race: The Fortunes of Women Painters and Their Work* by Germaine Greer (1979). This short list of trailblazers explains why Blixen's "Oration" was published in *Daguerreotypes and Other Essays* with an introduction by Hannah Arendt in 1979. Biographer Judith Thurman, then working on *Isak Dinesen: The Life of a Storyteller,* read the "Oration" as evidence that Karen Blixen's views on feminism "had grown considerably more conservative since her letters on the subject to Aunt Bess . . . [in the mid-1920s]."[3]

Thurman's interpretation rests on Blixen's 1926 correspondence with her favorite aunt, Mary Bess Westenholz (1858–1947), who was a proud member of Denmark's Women's Citizens Society (Dansk Kvinndesanfund) and an early suffragette. In the give and take of their letters, Blixen states firmly that the women's movement "should probably be regarded as one of the most significant movements of the nineteenth century," even if "the upheavals it has caused are far from 'done with' at the present moment."[4] This profeminist statement gives us pause in light of her words in that 1953 appeal for understanding that a woman "possesses her power as a result of what she *is*" (that is, not what she *does*).[5] Nevertheless, the "Oration" need not be read as a rejection of Blixen's evolving feminist consciousness first awakened during her years in colonial Kenya. As a twentieth-century woman born in the nineteenth century and raised in a matriarchal family, she had an ingrained awareness of women as responsible, active people in possession of their own kind of power and expected nothing less of herself.

In her early years in Ngong, prior to meeting Denys Finch Hatton in 1918, Blixen was eager to prove herself and lend support to her husband, just as women in her family had always done. Yet when she became separated from Bror Blixen and immersed in her first experience of "free love" with Denys, her position in colonial society shifted from a "settler's wife" to that of an unusual woman living alone—unless her peripatetic lover happened to be sharing her bed in Ngong. Scholars of Scandinavian literature tend to approach Karen Blixen's sociocultural position in Africa with refreshing insights and compassion toward Blixen's evolution of feminism. As the most thorough scholar of the infamous "Oration" to date, Marianne Stecher-Hansen relativizes Blixen's urge to distance herself by suggesting that "the women's movement must have represented for Blixen another one of the dogmatic ideologies of the modern age that threatened to confine her artistically and philosophically."[6] This is supported by what we know of Blixen's inquisitive mind and eccentric personality with its fierce devotion to individual freedom—at least to her own individual freedom.

Susan Brantly comes to a similar conclusion in the larger context of postcolonial criticism, which inherently incorporates feminist demands for equity and power sharing. Furthermore, the women's movement looks different from the Danish perspective when compared to its British or American counterparts, in part because Danish women achieved the right to vote in 1915, two years behind Norway (1913) but well ahead of many other western nations, including the United States (1920) and the United Kingdom (1928).[7] As Brantly writes, "Blixen's Danishness, especially with regard to *Out of Africa,* becomes invisible or irrelevant to many who read her in a postcolonial context."[8] And yet for Brantly, Blixen's "invisibility" leads to an invaluable perspective of her position during her African years as a "cultural hybrid, negotiating the expectations of Denmark, Africa, and Britain."[9] That is—as a unique individual who deserves to be located within her particular cultural reality as well as her historic time and place. This leaves us with an appreciation of Brantly's description of Blixen's "own brand of multiculturalism," explored above in the context of otherness, that also operates as *her own brand* of feminism. As readers alert to the restrictive identity politics of our own era, these ideas challenge us to approach issues of race, religion, age, class, nation, and a host of historical factors in a holistic way when we discuss the global movement that feminism has become. As a unique individual resistant to labels, assumptions, or dogma—including the labels of "suffragette" or "feminist"—Blixen challenges us to rethink the resounding question that so often emerges at the heart of these conversations: *Was she a feminist?*

No one has negotiated this territory as effectively as Susan Hardy Aiken, whose provocative 1985 article titled "The Uses of Duplicity" focuses on Isak Dinesen's narrative voice as fundamentally serene on the surface while coded with feminist irony in its deeper layers of meaning.[10] Blixen herself dwells on the idea of duplicity in her "Oration" when she takes the example of Shakespeare's Portia, from *The Merchant of Venice,* as a woman who embodies "fearless heresy" even as she "pretends deep respect for the paragraphs of the law." As Blixen writes, "her magic lies precisely in her duplicity."[11] With such "magic" in mind, Aiken clears a feminist space for Blixen with her groundbreaking *Isak Dinesen and the Engendering of Narrative* (1990), in which she models the art of reading between the lines. Aiken's work demonstrates that, not unlike Portia, women in general and particularly Karen Blixen tend to create a language of their own if/when the system in which they live has no language to represent them. In response to Judith Thurman's suggestion that Blixen "ultimately rejected 'feminism,'" Aiken rightly asks "Which feminism?" And when she turns her attention to the "Oration," as all feminist scholars of Karen Blixen must do, Aiken notes that "though generally taken at face value, her remarks are actually worded with such deliberate ambiguity that they openly invite an ironic reading."[12]

As we have seen, Blixen's tales express a feminist sense of freedom through symbolic use of character, imagination, and comic intent, all of which allow her to see what she sees in a subtly subversive way. She also delights in provocation by making herself central, a sleight of hand that serves as a diversion from her fragmented self. Aiken's close attention to how the "Oration" is constructed echoes her awareness of *Out of Africa* as a text similarly constructed through a filter of identity formation. All of this leads to a list of questions inevitably more nuanced than "Was she a feminist?" The alternatives are many and include "What choices exist for feminists throughout the world today?" Or we might zero in by focusing on questions of time and place in order to ask "What choices exist for feminists in (fill in blank)?" Or the question could be colored with a historical perspective that asks, "What did a feminist represent in the world of past generations?" And in the context of *Out of Africa* itself, often interpreted through tropes of a lost paradise and/or European romanticism, we might ask "How does the making of a memoir authorize a woman writer's intention to become a creative force in her own life?" If nothing else, these questions should get us past superficial identity "tags" when it comes to the question of feminism.

Out of Africa is a feminist text because it grapples with the fundamental contradiction of a Danish woman struggling to survive within the patriarchal, militaristic project of British imperialism. Susan Hardy Aiken acknowledges this premise when she writes that "one of the gravest difficulties facing a contemporary reader [of *Out of Africa*] is the conflict one must negotiate *between* the sheer lyric beauty of this book and the disconcerting knowledge of the historical circumstances that formed its conditions of possibility."[13] This deceptively simple statement alerts us to an awareness of the historical angle of vision to which Karen Blixen was, herself, largely indifferent. It also acknowledges *Out of Africa* as a work of literature *authorized* by an individual whose inner life was the open terrain of her philosophical explorations, even if she has since become a kind of literary zombie wandering in our postcolonial era. And finally, it underscores the necessity of at least trying to "negotiate between" the two frames Aiken identifies—literary value and sociopolitical reality—that give shape to the essential contradiction of *Out of Africa*, and the woman who wrote it. As a memoir of inner life, Blixen's journey of awakening might have occurred anywhere yet happens to have occurred in colonial Kenya, which changes everything—and nothing.

The essential problem inherent in postcolonial critiques of *Out of Africa* focused strictly on historical facts is that they are willfully incomplete if and when they dismiss the author's inner life. When Aiken writes that "while Dinesen did indeed participate in the colonialist project as both immigrant and author, she also remained remarkably free, given her historical circumstances, of typical imperialistic attitudes," she relocates Blixen as a woman who marked herself as free and emotionally untethered to the social mores of British colonialism.[14] This is but one of Aiken's comments that shed light on how "tropes of place and displacement in *Out of Africa* are inseparable from questions of sexual difference." In modeling a feminist reading of *Out of Africa* through the prisms of history, individuality, and gender assumptions, Aiken notes that "Dinesen both evokes and unsettles imperial plots."[15]

The "Bonfire Oration" is important to an understanding of Blixen's pleasure in provocation, as well as to the evolution of her feminism. Yet an earlier essay, begun in 1923, must also be brought into this discussion. "On Modern Marriage and Other Observations," first published posthumously in 1977, is a twelve-part, seventy-page essay that represents Blixen's first effort to resolve the contradictions of modernity that she felt to be embedded in her life. By contrasting and interrogating "free love" and legally sanctified marriage through a historical perspective, the essay attempts to redefine both as its author searches for a new identity as a modern woman. This essay was very likely written at night, beginning around Christmastime in 1923. The timing of the work is part of its context, for Denys Finch Hatton, then living at the farm, had left in October for an extended stay in England to tend to his ailing mother. As Judith Thurman observes, the essay is written in a voice that "has an elegance, a dry formal intelligence for which there was little precedent" and which "seems to reflect the voice, the style, the disciplined self she had begun to perfect for Denys."[16]

Another motivation for committing herself to the tedious work of a rigorous essay on marriage was that Karen Blixen's divorce from Bror Blixen was in the negotiating stage at the time, which naturally made her chosen theme a personal challenge. Furthermore, she felt ambivalent about the divorce and, therefore, frustrated with her family's urge to see her divorce "done and dusted" and Bror Blixen dismissed once and for all. In other words, the author of "On Modern Marriage and Other Observations" was legally married to Bror and simultaneously immersed in a life-altering experience of "free love" with Denys Finch Hatton when she took up her pen. At the same time, her brother Thomas Dinesen was much on her mind as he, at age thirty-one, was emotionally occupied with his own internal conflicts as he stood on the brink of two major decisions: whether or not to follow a career that would lock him into a bourgeois life in Denmark and whether or not to marry. (Both of which he did by 1926.)

Thomas was the first to read "Modern Marriage," sent in two segments with letters from Ngong in May and June after his sister's first mention of her writing project in a letter dated April 27, 1924. Her passing reference comes in the context of many "shauries" (worries) and assorted mentions of Thomas's "flirtations" that Karen has obviously discussed with their mother, who "cannot understand that the tragedy of my marriage has been a greater sorrow to me than [her sister] Ea's death." As usual, Blixen shares her thoughts freely with Thomas when she writes that Ingeborg Dinesen's concern that her son might marry "a girl who is not worthy of us" exhibits a "frightful arrogance." Yet as the theme of marriage dominates this letter, Blixen confirms her loyalty to her brother: "It is really not right that she [Mother] should think of your wife primarily in relation to Mother herself, Rungstedlund, Folehave, Mitten, and me. If this point of view were carried through, it could become a formidable obstacle to your marriage as a whole, and for your married *happiness.*" Many other issues interrupt the theme of marriage in this letter—Bror's illness in Uganda, Denys's departure for England, Karen's financial worries, and the idea of "a small flat in Paris" that she and "Tommy" might share—before she adds that "I am writing a monograph on marriage."[17] Her next letter, in August, makes it clear that he, like she, remains focused on the pros and cons of marriage and his future role in society: "You write as if there were nothing else in the world besides traveling, studying,—and 'the eight hour's office chair' and bourgeois marriage." At the end of this letter, she adds that "regarding my paper on marriage, which you write so kindly about, you are welcome to show it to anyone especially interested, if you wish, but it was really written for you only."[18] Eventually realizing the importance of his sister's most ambitious writing project completed in Ngong, Thomas had a typescript done of the handwritten essay, which has since entered the Karen Blixen Archives at the Royal Library in Copenhagen, where it is filed under the title "Ideal og Natur" (Ideal and Nature).[19]

These various motivations, relations, and epistolary conversations contextualize Karen Blixen's state of mind in the mid-1920s. As "Modern Marriage and Other Observations" deconstructs the inherent conflict between "free love" and the uncertain outcome of legal, sanctified marriage, Blixen narrows the focus to a prolonged analysis as marriage as morally hypocritical in the twentieth century. Her examples used to illustrate her controversial point include "modern monarchy," which she is certain would be unrecognizable to Louis XIV, and to the debate surrounding "ladies' corsetless dresses." On the latter, she elaborates: "True enough, there were those who agreed that corsets could be somewhat shorter and looser, but it was impossible for a lady to have a well-dressed appearance without corsets, for how could a dress be made, and how could it fit properly without them? No one was able to answer this question, and corsets grew longer and longer."[20] And so it is, she reasoned, with love and marriage, since "love" is a higher value than legality or sanctification.

"What is it that changes a relationship between a man and a woman from immoral to a moral relationship? In ninety-nine out of one hundred cases, the answer would be: 'Love.'"[21] Her tone changes, however, when she turns to the idea of marriage as a kind of "unity" worthy of existence: "The love relationship between a man and a woman becomes a marriage when it enters into in the recognition that the personal feelings of both partners—no matter how much they had based upon them—must be subordinate to, and serve, an idea that for both of them is higher than love itself, the kind of idea that as a rule exacts the lifetime of both, and whose demands may reach even further."[22] Here, we sense that this is precisely the sort of unity Blixen imagined was possible with Denys Finch Hatton and wished for her brother and his bride in 1926. But what, if anything, does it tell us about her rapidly evolving feminism in the mid-1920s?

The answer, of course, is found "between the lines," which can be read as the work of a culture critic and/or as an example of Blixen's self-analysis. Yet because it was not written as a purely intellectual treatise, this essay should not be read or strictly judged as such. In the context of where and when it was written, Blixen was clearly experimenting with her power of reasoning in "Modern Marriage" as a useful power in and of itself. Yet over time, and despite her capacity for reason, her work on the imaginative world of tales clarified her preference for behavioral analysis and the challenge of puzzling through love and marriage as separate states of being. As one among many examples, "The Young Man with a Carnation" in *Winter's Tales* traces the thoughts of Charlie, a famous-but-restless writer who experiences "a strange optical illusion" regarding his wife: "When he was away from her, his wife took on all the appearance of a guardian angel, unfailing in sympathy and support. But when again he met her face to face, she was a stranger, and he found his road paved with difficulties."[23] He almost abandons her after a mysterious night of storytelling with sailors in a seaside bar before he realizes that he cannot leave her because "she is like a lighthouse, the firm, majestic lighthouse that sends out its kindly light."[24]

The true value of Blixen's entertaining essay on love and marriage is that it represents her awakening to the complexity of life as a modern woman. It also matters as an illustration of her commitment to writing as a coping mechanism, which can be called upon when she feels destabilized by events or relationships, even when there is no definitive solution in sight. This makes a kind of confession of "Modern Marriage" that forces her to locate herself in the shifting sands of her era as well as within her two, most significant "experiments" of love and marriage—Bror and Denys. The work also highlights her ability to question the social norms she has inherited as well as think freely for herself as a sexual being—an attitude that is essentially feminist. As she imagines the acceptance of "free love" in the future, she settles for the unknown: "It may well be that where love itself and the position of love relationships in society are concerned, free love affairs will be tolerated as long as they do not burden the race with undesirable specimens."[25] As Else Cederborg writes in her introduction to *On Modern Marriage and Other Observations,* "It may surprise those who took at face value Karen Blixen's statement, in 'Oration at a Bonfire, Fourteen Years Late,' that she had never been interested in feminism. Now that we have more keys with which to open up the secrets of her writings, we can see that it was crucial to her throughout her life, and, it follows, throughout her work."[26]

In 1924, Karen Blixen was, in a sense, a "feminist-in-training" as she held a prolonged debate inside her head that has since played out in the court of public opinion, to say nothing of novels, films, and murder trials. By 1926, her edits to *The Revenge of Truth* were on her desk and her first "anecdotes" about life in Africa constituted a tentative validation of her experience, even as a cloud of anxiety hovered over her daily life. What if she could not keep the farm? What would she do? Where would she go? At times, her only solace was the reliability of the Black African people who worked and lived on the farm: "They came into my life as a kind of answer to some call in my own nature, to dreams of childhood perhaps, or to poetry read and cherished long ago, or to emotions and instincts deep down in the mind, for I have always felt that I resembled the natives more than did other white people in the Protectorate."[27]

Meanwhile, she was filled with feelings of inadequacy that she could only express to her brother Thomas:

> There are of course such terribly great, almost insuperable difficulties in getting me into any kind of profession or any sort of "job," because there is nothing whatsoever I can do.
>
> But isn't it frightful that honorable people can allow someone to grow up,—merely because they belong to the female sex,—without learning *anything at all*? I believe that I was of above average intelligence as a child and I was *eager to learn,* mathematics, for instance, I really think I had talent for that; but while my family was eager to teach me moral conduct and unselfishness it never occurred to them to have me taught more arithmetic than Miss Zøylner could manage! Mama and Miss Zøylner were my teachers, and from the time we returned from Switzerland,—where we had learned nothing at all,—and I was fourteen, I learned absolutely nothing.[28]

A month later, Blixen wrote a long letter to Aunt Bess that represents an important step in her evolving sense of self:

> A subject that I have been thinking about and would very much like the chance of discussing with you again is the old one of "feminism," in its present-day form, which has come to mean something very different from what was signified by the term when it first evolved three-quarters of a century ago. I think one can see now that those who were at the time filled with horror at the thought of women being made eligible to take the student examination and thought that that would bring the collapse of the whole existing state of things,—and who were laughed at by others for it, in fact showed clear-sightedness and foresight. They were right, it did collapse and took very much more with it than they had thought possible; and that is what always happens

> whenever the very possibility of criticism and radical change in an area previously considered to be raised above it, or immune from it, enters the consciousness.
>
> . . . I consider [then] that "feminism" or, if you will, the phenomena that were the basic cause of it have had far more effect on and have far more radically divided the old society that was in existence when it arose,—that on the whole it should probably be regarded as the most significant movement of the nineteenth century, and that the upheavals it has caused are far from "done with" at the present moment."[29]

For obvious reasons, this letter has often been quoted to illustrate Blixen's support of feminism and, therefore, enters Marianne Stecher-Hansen's understanding of the "Bonfire Oration" when she writes that "thus, already in the 1920s, Blixen's reflections articulate a keen awareness of women's issues and an understanding of the phases of development within the women's movement; her early letters reflect a consciousness that remained central to her literary work and thinking throughout a lifetime." Karen Blixen's letter also conveys a particular understanding of the feminist movement as it played out in Denmark during her African years. Yet with national movements in mind, it is also important to be mindful of the nuances of translation when we use the word "feminism." Because the English word carries generations of cultural and political baggage, it is not a perfect translation of the Danish word used by Blixen in her "Bonfire Oration." Stecher-Hansen also notes that "*Kvindesagen* translates literally as 'Women's Cause' and equally well as 'Women's Movement,'" either of which sound slightly less "radical" than the feminist activism seen in the United States throughout the last half-century.[30] How Blixen might interpret women marching in public with pink hats and banners is hinted at in a 1928 letter to her sister Elle that informs our understanding of her "Bonfire Oration" delivered twenty-five years later: "I think that there has been another great change, that perhaps people are still not conscious of, in that the idea, so to speak has disappeared from 'womanliness,' of what it means to be a woman. I think that the women of the old days, as especially the best of them, felt themselves to be representative of something great and sacred, by virtue of which they possessed importance outside themselves and could feel great pride and dignity, and toward which they had an almost weighty responsibility."[31]

She was, of course, writing and thinking of women of a certain class, the same class that typically populates her tales, which are full of nineteenth-century "types" encountered in the society of Karen Blixen's youth. As Susan Brantly explains in the larger context of Blixen's tales that often informs a reading of *Out of Africa,* the strong, young *caryatids* support tradition while sexual *blossoms* represent beauty and procreation, in keeping with bourgeois and aristocratic values. Diana-types and witches are fearless and subversive, ever-ready to oppose or ignore the dominant patriarchal order. As a sporty, masculine type, Diana can easily be linked to Blixen's safari life, while the category of witches whose sexuality translates as dignity or mystery is clearly seen in Blixen's performance of late-in-life fame. As Brantly writes, "These designations are rather fluid and can sometimes represent different stages of a woman's life."[32] Blixen's concern for the loss of "womanliness" will also remind readers of her description of the Somali women, which leaves many options open. "There was no ignorance in their innocence," she writes, because a Somali man is "abstinent by nature, indifferent to food and drink and to personal comfort, hard and spare as the country he comes from: woman is his luxury."[33] To many of us, such "objectification" of a woman clearly represents the polar opposite of feminism. Yet Blixen's fascination with the Somali women, expressed in her letters between 1928 and 1930, becomes admiration for their dignity vis-à-vis modern women of her own class and culture: "Of course I can see that there is something quite poetic in the Muhammadan view of woman and her position in life as its crown and greatest treasure for man; . . . and they are not subjected to many of the nightmares that oppress European women."[34]

Feminism colors a great deal of Blixen's writing, although it is often hidden in her art of narration. In addition to her talent for metaphor, erasure, and time navigation, she deploys the techniques of nonlinear storytelling, nested tales, and masks to conceal her deeper layers of thought. Yet another feature that marks *Out of Africa* as a feminist text involves the ways in which the narrator's best intentions are often undermined, disrupted, or drastically rerouted by events beyond her control. As Susan Hardy Aiken explains, this essentially self-reflective device mirrors the disjointed rhythm of Blixen's life experience during her African years. It is no accident that this rhythm is repeated throughout the memoir, as Aiken analyzes with rigorous eloquence, whether Blixen is writing in first person, as she does in "A Shooting Accident on the Farm," or writing a parable such as "The Roads of Life."[35] There is, most certainly, tension in the air as the fragility of the narrator's world accumulates on the page with changing relationships, unexpected weather conditions, and dashed hopes as elements of her lived experience. The impact of these events is orchestrated by the narrator of *Out of Africa,* who finds herself destabilized as she is constantly forced to relocate her inner self on the ever-shifting stage of the story. Insofar as the narrator of *Out of Africa* is a "character" in a story, this is a character who can never be "fixed" in one place or state of mind for long, a reality that contrasts with the stability of the hierarchical, titled male roles in British colonial society, or in Danish society for that matter, as Uncle Aage demonstrates. Perhaps this explains why "Baroness" was a title Blixen kept long after her African years as a one-word marker of place and purpose that required no further explanation or justification. Ultimately, however, her keen awareness of instability, caused by powerlessness and conveyed with words, "translates" in Aiken's lexicon as a self-portrait of feminist consciousness.

Blixen's memoir felt startling in its originality when it appeared in 1937, yet it joined centuries of women's fragmented writing and anticipated the late twentieth-century emphasis of "*her*story" as a hidden world within the "*his*tory" of civilization. By 1975, Jane Austen's tightly constructed "marriage plots" and the repressed passions of the Brontë sisters were reappearing in bookstores along with the confessional poetry of Anne Sexton and Erica Jong's best-selling novel *Fear of Flying* (1973). In the same era, Virginia Woolf's *A Room of One's Own* acquired feminist reverence as a "classic" and became a useful argument for individual space as foundational to a woman's creativity. In the midst of this sea change, Susan Gubar's 1981 article on Blixen's tale "The Blank Page," from *Last Tales* (1957), explores feminine creativity as it observes an important source of hidden and/or untold stories in the detritus of women's lives: "The attraction of women writers to personal forms of expression like letters, autobiographies, confessional poetry, diaries, and journals points out the effect of a life experienced as an art or an art experienced as a kind of life, as does women's traditional interest in cosmetics, fashion, and interior decorating."[36] By contrast, Blixen's "The Blank Page" honors blood-stained bridal sheets as records of women's lives and recognizes an unstained sheet as an untold story, a life without a mark.

Somewhere between the vanished archives of daily life and women's stories suddenly valued in the late twentieth century, we arrive at Blixen's intention to validate her experience in *Out of Africa*. This is what Susan Hardy Aiken interprets as "engendered" narration that strives to make sense out of the scattered days of a woman's life. "Like the shimmering, mirage-laden landscapes of Africa, in whose mutabilities and 'irregularity' Dinesen implicitly figures both the 'self' and the text that represents them, *Out of Africa* constitutes the ever-belated testimony that what it describes cannot be fixed. . . . Like the dreams and echoes with which it compares itself, the narrative is ultimately both product and producer of radical displacement," Aiken writes.[37] This, in essence, describes Blixen's dilemma and her solution in the world she ages into where voices try to define her by continually asking: *Was she a feminist?* Clearly, this is a very different question than *What kind of feminist was she?*, with its whiff of accusation. Or *What did she do to advance the feminist cause in the twentieth century?*, which demands sociopolitical engagement in a community of women. Yet as Stecher-Hansen suggests, Blixen was too individualistic to identify herself with organizations or slogans, even if she made efforts to express her solidarity in public appearances at the Danish Women's Citizens Society, or by delivering her lecture at Nathalie Zahle's Teachers College, or with her frail presence at Radcliffe College in Cambridge, Massachusetts, during her only visit to the United States in 1959.[38]

And so we arrive at a "reading" of Blixen in the mid-1920s as a woman conscious of a "women's movement" that might involve her somehow and might even improve her life, despite the "upheavals it has caused." We also arrive at a reading of *Out of Africa* as a feminist work of art because not only does it model feminized power, it actively *extends* feminized power by producing a book that tells a woman's story of her own, unique experience in her own, unique voice. Just as Blixen's existence far from home allowed her to explore herself, it also enabled her to confront confusion, contradiction, and change as a matter of personal and moral responsibility. If we dare to ask *What does a feminist life represent in the world?*, the answer inevitably involves a willingness to shape a life beyond prescriptive roles of "womanliness," such as the Dinesen sisters were offered as young girls growing up at Rungstedlund. By contrast, feminism is an active state that resists and rejects a great deal, yet accepts contradiction, negotiation, and a long view of history with its vision of women as agents of change—internally and externally. One of Blixen's paradoxes is that she never quite sees herself as an agent of change in *Out of Africa,* even as she writes her changing self into and out of her Africa. Yet even as a passing shadow on a train or a woman waving from a ship, she becomes what Susan Hardy Aiken describes as "only one among many moving figures, gliding in and out of 'history,' in and out of a 'dream,' sometimes receding . . . sometimes addressing us with astonishing immediacy"?[39] In any of these visions Karen Blixen holds her place as a modern woman on the move.

CHAPTER TEN

I Had a Farm in Hollywood

Looking back on a sojourn in the African highlands, you are struck by your feeling of having lived for a time up in the air.

—Karen Blixen, *Out of Africa*

Karen Blixen's *Out of Africa* lives up to Sven Birkerts's assertion that memoir is a genre in which "every remembered moment, every characterization of a person, every suggestion of causality—*everything* is staged."[1] Readers of memoir accept its arts of illusion as long as the story offers a personal connection between reader and writer. The "seventh art" of film invents a different kind of illusion as it relocates the reader as a spectator attuned to visual and auditory aspects of performance. Time constraints on the big screen demand compression in ways that words on the page do not, which invites a blurring of historical facts. If memoir is a reinvention, a film based on memoir is a reinvention of a reinvention made possible by a small army of talented artists, technicians, investors, and the most courageous creature of all, the script writer whose words exist at the mercy of those paid to pronounce them with convincing emotion. When the subject of a film is a slice-of-life, such as Blixen's years in Africa (1914–31), the film becomes part of that life's legacy, bibliography, and iconography.

Karen Blixen created her own script with her memoir *Out of Africa*, but a film based on a book inevitably lacks that mysterious reader-author connection. It also lacks the pleasure of fine writing, which a film script must dismantle into fragments in order to produce dialogue. This translation from one genre to another raises important questions for writers and readers, beginning with the essential question of *Whose story is it to tell?* This quickly expands to a longer list of questions including, *What if the film director's reinventions of a story misread the author's intentions? What happens when a life and legacy are manipulated as a cultural artifact without the author's permission? And how and why does market value shift over time?* All of these questions emerge as we turn to the film titled *Out of Africa,* which quickly recouped a $31 million budget when it grossed $227,000,000 in its first six months in movie theaters.[2] It takes very little imagination to realize that the profits exceeded anything Karen Blixen earned from the entirety of her work in her lifetime.

It was, nevertheless, a brilliant decision to entrust the filming of *Out of Africa* to Sydney Pollack (1934–2008), whose prior successes included *The Way We Were* (1973), *Absence of Malice* (1981), and *Tootsie* (1982), among others. As Pollack pulled the pieces of *Out of Africa* together on both sides of the camera, his instincts included a healthy respect for the challenge of adapting a slice-of-life story for Hollywood, which explains why he turned to Blixen's award-winning biographer Judith Thurman, listed in the film credits as "associate producer." He also had the good sense to hire screenwriter Kurt Luedtke (1939–2000), who brought prior experience with Pollack and Robert Redford to the task, to say nothing of his Academy Award nomination for *Absence of Malice.* No one was surprised when Luedtke's screenplay for *Out of Africa* earned him an Academy Award and a BAFTA for Best Adapted Screenplay of 1985. As Pollack acknowledged in his introduction to the shooting script, "It was Kurt's perceptions and grasp of the material and Judith's insights that enabled us to make the film of Karen Blixen's years in Africa."[3]

In one of the first reviews written within days of the premiere, film historian and critic Richard Schickel, writing for *Time Magazine,* focused on its emotional power. He begins with his expectation that Blixen's book would be untranslatable to the big screen because it was "so dependent for its haunting power on the tonalities of her prose, at once specific and mysteriously reticent." Yet he applauds the solution found by Pollack—perhaps with the advice of Thurman and/or Luedtke—to "make bold with the material by taking care only to retain its important truth, which is an emotional one." In the end, Schickel sees *Out of Africa* on the big screen as "the free-spirited, fullhearted gesture that everyone has been waiting for the movies to make all decade long. It reclaims the emotional territory that is rightfully theirs."[4] For him, and millions of others, the feeling of the film was like discovering a new friend or regaining an old one—or maybe even like falling in love.

Many other critics were less enthusiastic and, like the influential television team of Siskel and Ebert, were split on *Out of Africa* at the time. Roger Ebert was enthralled with the "great epic romance . . . breathtakingly filmed on location" while Gene Siskel, unlike millions of American women, felt distracted by the idea of Robert Redford as a love object.[5] Quite apart from Siskel's quip that Redford "looks and acts as if he just walked out of the safari fitting room at Abercrombie & Fitch," he laments that "it's a shame to have to knock the otherwise beautiful and haunting picture, but when you're watching a love story and you can't stand the character who is being loved, that makes for a very frustrating movie-going experience."[6] Some years later, Jane Kramer wrote an extensive cover feature headlined as "The Isak Dinesen Fantasy" for the July 17, 1986, issue of *New York Review of Books* in which she described the film as "a lovely and inane Lotusland product." Kramer deconstructs her sharp opinion with a turn toward the contradiction at the center of *Out of Africa*—as memoir and/or film—that remains problematic in the twenty-first century: "It enjoys (and so do we) its plantations and white lawn dresses and gentle servants—and never considers the possibility that anything that looks as good as its fantasy of British rule might be troubling (or even false)."[7]

Paradoxically, it was the film's visual appeal that propelled a late-century wave of nostalgia for the casual elegance of colonial manners so successfully captured by Ralph Lauren's first "safari chic" ad campaign of 1982. Yet by the mid-1980s, the "lost paradise" effect was crashing into a wave of postcolonial analysis eager to interpret Karen Blixen's book and moral character as representative of the shameful history of colonialism. In 1990, Blixen scholar Susan Hardy Aiken wryly noted that as a book *Out of Africa* is as much an illusion as the recent motion picture for which it served as pretext—a film released under the apt rubric 'a Mirage Production.'"[8] In any case, it seemed clear to those with insight that the Best Picture of 1985 lost sight of the memoir's underlying existential struggle for meaning and replaced it with an "epic romance" brought to life by cinematographer David Watkin and a film-editing team, all of whom won Academy Awards for their talents.[9] In this performance, Blixen's displacements, emotions, and encounters with Black Africans became a moving testimony to a lost Garden of Eden for some and a prime example of the arrogance of privilege for others.

The question I would put to Sydney Pollack, if I could, would be: *Why did you make it so beautiful?* In retrospect, his golden vistas, birds in flight, cheerful children, and inviting veranda perched on the edge of Paradise distract the viewer from Blixen's nonconforming individuality, since so little context for nonconformity is provided. While the film offers condensed flashes of illness that were, in fact, debilitating for Blixen from the age of thirty, Pollack colludes with her to omit painful disputes with Uncle Aage, days of despair expressed in her letters, and her sinking physical and mental state that reached its nadir just as Thomas Dinesen met her ship in Marseille: "It was as if I were looking at a stranger, the shadow of woman I had once known," he wrote.[10] A visualization of her inner drama reflected in her indifference to external life would have been just the sort of thing a film could do better than a memoir. Instead, Pollack's shimmering light, gentle pacing, and emphasis on romance—all played against the Academy Award-winning musical score by John Barry—create a buffer against the discomfort of revealing that Karen Blixen was physically ill and suicidally depressed when she left Ngong in 1931. She, naturally, had nothing to do with Pollack's Hollywood portrayal of herself, or her friends, or of the men she loved a half-century later. She did, however, have an inkling that a movie might happen one day once the idea was floated in the mid-1950s with Greta Garbo imagined in the leading role, a thought that must have made her smile.[11] That movie, like many others might have happened, but never did.

In 1960, a young, rich, talented, and charismatic American visited Karen Blixen at Rungstedlund. Peter Beard was an artistic wildlife photographer who, by the time of Blixen's death in September 1962, held the film rights to *Out of Africa*—or so he thought. As his biographer put it, "Blixen saw Beard as a soulmate and fully trusted his judgement," a sentiment that apparently extended to the implicit trust of the Rungstedlund Foundation created in 1958 to manage Blixen's property—real and intellectual—as well as her legacy in perpetuity.[12] This connection explains why the Danish Ministry of Culture financed an exploratory trip to Kenya in 1963 with Rungstedlund support for Danish filmmaker Johan Jacobsen, screenwriter Anneliese Hovmand, and Blixen's brother Thomas Dinesen, who had become a friend of Peter Beard. The first challenge, however, was the widespread "antipathy" the three encountered a few short years after the bloody Mau-Mau (Gikuyu) Rebellion (1952–58) that paved the way to Kenyan independence. Ultimately, the timing was terrible for white people in Kenya discussing a film set in the colonial era and the Danish group went home with nothing more than a draft of a script and the intriguing idea of Vanessa Redgrave in the leading role.[13]

In 1967, Peter Beard's own idea for a film faltered when it became clear that the verbal "permission" expressed by the Rungstedlund Foundation in a cordial letter was not legally binding. In fact, the film rights were owned by Random House as part of the publishing contract signed years earlier by Blixen herself. Peter Beard charged ahead anyway in talks with British director Nicolas Roeg, whose imagined film would feature Julie Christie of *Dr. Zhivago* fame as Karen Blixen with music composed by Mick Jagger, then twenty-four years old. This idea, like others, ran out of steam by the time Universal Pictures entered the discussion, negotiated rights with the Rungstedlund Foundation, and signed a contract with Sydney Pollack, whose "big pictures" mentioned above had led to a genuine friendship with Robert Redford.[14] Meryl Streep was another likely choice after winning Academy Awards for *Kramer vs. Kramer* (1980) and *Sophie's Choice* (1983). By 1980, a dream team with a big budget was finally in place.

The project was, nevertheless, a difficult one, as Pollack expected. "As in every case in which film is based on literary material, selection is a major problem. What stays? What goes?" At least the script had a place to start since he had "inherited" two drafts from the well-known Hollywood screenwriter Judith Rascoe before hiring Kurt Luedtke. "We incorporated some of her material into this final version," he writes, although very few of Blixen's words were actually used.[15] Instead, Pollack and Luedtke came up with the effective device of "voice-over" monologues read by Streep in an accent presumed by millions to be Danish beginning with the first line of the memoir: "I had a farm in Africa at the foot of the Ngong Hills." This line serves as a gentle "opening" to the past in the first minutes of the film after a glance at what we are meant to see as the aging storyteller tossing in a restless sleep filled with dreams of life in Ngong, then sitting at her writing desk in her bedroom beneath the rafters on a snowy day. The fact that she actually wrote most of the book in a small hotel room in the remote village of Skagen, Denmark, in the fall and winter of 1936–37 is never mentioned or shown. Yet Pollack's "tricks" of compression place us "in the story" quickly enough before the film begins to unfold in a recreated city of colonial Nairobi with its hot, dusty streets and cacophony of sounds.

"Trying to make a film out of something that has become a classic piece of literature is worrisome," Pollack writes. "Making films in general is worrisome, but this one was more so."[16] Long before the filming began, Pollack worked with Luedtke to establish essential ideas that could be visualized onscreen. "We spent two years trying to find the 'spine' or 'armature' of this piece, trying to distill the idea down to one or two clear sentences." In Pollack's words, this spine came down to "Possession. Freedom vs. Obligation. If I say I love you, what price am I expected to pay? To what extent am I obligated?"[17] Even as a filmmaker's "shorthand," this breakdown confirms Pollack's conscious intention to find a plot large enough to frame the unresolved needs, feelings, and contradictions embedded in Karen Blixen's love for Denys Finch Hatton. That love was real, though never expressed as well as Blixen described it in her letter to Thomas Dinesen in 1924: "I believe that for all time and eternity I am bound to

Denys, to love the ground he walks on, to be happy beyond words when he is here, and to suffer worse than death many times when he leaves."[18] Yet it is curious that her relationship with Denys receives little exploration in the memoir itself until she recounts his death and funeral in "The Grave in the Hills."[19] More often than not, this legendary aristocrat is simply "there"—or not there—as part of her ever-changing world after their meeting at a dinner party in 1918. Clearly, the film, like the memoir, was never intended to dig too deep into her personal relationships or into Blixen's financial predicament, much less become sociopolitical exposé or an argument for the evolution of her feminism—although each of these themes gets a nudge here and there in the film. Ultimately, the overarching themes of the movie are the simplest and most universal: The passing of time and the fragility of love.

Pollack does, nevertheless, rely on the "spine" he and Luedtke articulated through the invention of six scenes within carefully plotted boundaries, each of which constitutes an "act" in theatrical terms. This structure allows the voice of the memoir and the characters within it to move in and out of the narrator's layered stories within the larger, ever-expanding story of impending loss. Seven monologues inspired by Blixen's memoir in spirit, tone, and syntax serve to introduce, connect, or end the scenes with words that sound very much like her own, although only the final monologue is a precise quote from the memoir:

> If I know a song of Africa,—I thought,—of the Giraffe, and the African moon lying on her back, of the ploughs in the fields, and the sweaty faces of the coffee pickers, does Africa know a song of me? Would the air over the plain quiver with a color that I had had on, or the children invent a game in which my name was, or the full moon throw a shadow over the gravel of the drive that was like me, or would the eagles of Ngong look out for me?[20]

In the memoir, these lines come early, in "Part I: Kamante and Lulu" as the narrator laments the absence of the small bushbuck gazelle, a species of antelope, that lived in and around the house for a time then suddenly kept away and remained in the forest. The story of Lulu "fits" well in the beginning because as it represents the idea of rejection and learning how to recognize the dangers of *possession,* as do the parable of the iguana and snippets of Blixen's dialogue with Denys Finch Hatton designed to represent human respect for Nature. Meanwhile, Lulu's absence is more than a charming example of Blixen's human-animal connection. Rather, it serves to foreshadow unexpected loss.

Another device deployed by Pollack is the injection of a metaphorical scene that "speaks 1,000 words" when Karen Blixen strides into the Muthaiga Men's Club in Nairobi to ask for help in locating Bror. Time stops, eyes roll, and newspapers drop into well-fed laps before a turbaned bartender of Indian origin escorts her out as he repeats a stern "*Memsaabs* (Women) must not be here. *Memsaabs* must *not* be here." This says a great deal about the patriarchal society Blixen has entered, which comes full circle when she exits that world through the same bar in the final ten minutes of the film. It was a clever idea to echo the earlier scene in reverse by having her *invited* into the strictly male preserve of the Muthaiga Club at the end of her "story" for a stiff drink and a toast for which a roomful of well-heeled gentlemen kindly stand to raise a glass. The toast is understood as a measure of how far she had come in their esteem, despite the farm's failure, as she mumbles a few words of poetry before downing her whiskey and leaving the room: "Rose-lipt maidens, light foot lads," she says, quoting a stanza from A. E. Housman's 1896 classic, "A Shropshire Lad," a poem that every man in that room, at that time, could have recited by heart:

With rue my heart is laden
For golden friends I had,
For many a rose-lipt maiden
And many a lightfoot lad.

By brooks too broad for leaping
The lightfoot boys are laid;
The rose-lipt girls are sleeping
In fields where roses fade.

Clearly, this time-conscious moment invented by Sydney Pollack captures the contrast of Blixen's coming and going with radically different identities.

Pollack's revisions are more problematic when stories written in the memoir are merged or relocated. One example is the scene in which Kamante enters Karen Blixen's room late at night and urges her to get out of bed and look out of the window. "I think that you had better get up. I think that God is coming," he says with great solemnity. She gets up to try and see what he sees when he directs her attention to a strange grass fire on a distant hill. I read this mysterious moment between Blixen and Kamante as a spiritual moment that illustrates her growing comprehension of people who simply see the world and everything in it differently than she does, and vice versa. In the movie, the same scene is played halfway when Kamante comes to Blixen in the middle of the night with the same announcement of "God is coming." Yet this time the fire is not in the distance but on the farm itself where it destroys the barn, seedlings, wooden table for sorting coffee beans, and turns equipment to ash. In the midst of irrevocable loss, the fire becomes the last straw and a symbol of inevitable loss before Blixen decides to sell out and leave Africa for good. Pollack and Luedtke's version moves the plot forward in a dramatic way, yet something is sacrificed here that relates to the important theme of Blixen's encounter with otherness. Pollack has changed the context and with that change, the meaningful juxtaposition of Karen and Kamante's worldviews is lost.

Memoir and film based on memoir are decidedly different art forms, yet both approach biographical material as malleable, unlike traditional biography with its tedious adherence to chronology and documentation. Karen Blixen's *Out of Africa* endorses the malleability of memory through her use of metaphor, erasure, and—in fact—utter silence, when it suits her to avoid the memory of consequential events that include family visits throughout the 1920s. In "Farah and I Sell Out," she carefully choreographs entrances and exits including those of Bror, Denys, and her Swedish friend Ingrid Lindstrom, the only other Scandinavian woman she knew who also managed a farm in the region.[21] In Lindstrom's place, Pollack invents a woman friend for Blixen in the form of the fictional Felicity—a cute, sexualized rival for the attentions of Denys Finch Hatton and a dim reflection of the indomitable Beryl Markham. Most of what Blixen says about friends in Ngong Africa is condensed into anecdotes gathered under "Visits of Friends" in Part III: Visitors to the Farm. Her portraits of Berkeley Cole, "The Noble Pioneer," followed by "Wings," an ode to Denys Finch Hatton, are rightfully set apart as something we might think of as "characters" in a novel whose life journeys happen to intersect with hers.

Blixen loved the journey metaphor and often used it in her tales. In a sense, *Out of Africa* is a "real life" journey tale imbued with a storyteller's imagination. *Out of Africa* onscreen is another kind of journey that owes its existence to the talents of hundreds of well-paid professionals who worked very hard to shape the story in Sydney Pollack's image and make it believable enough for a moviegoing audience to sit still for over two and a half hours. Shooting on location in the Highlands southwest of Nairobi in the suburban area now called "Karen Lang'ata" expressed Pollack's desire for authenticity, as did the rebuilding of colonial Nairobi as a movie set with human-drawn rickshaws and horse-drawn carriages. He even found a block of administrative buildings at the Nairobi School that worked well for scenes calling for a glimpse of Governor's House with its green lawn.[22] The vistas, sunsets, skies, and wildlife that earned David Watkin his Academy Award for Cinematography were real, of course, as were the more scenic Chyulu Hills substituted for the Ngong Hills. Pollack even managed to shoot some scenes near Mbagathi House, the original house that Karen and Bror inhabited from 1914 to 1917.[23]

Despite these impressive efforts, however, Pollack's translation tends to approach Karen Blixen as a "made for Hollywood" muse. Not only is she manipulated for maximum effect as a tragic heroine, her tragedy is staged as a romantic triangle rather than as the larger problem of becoming a modern woman in the shifting sands of the early twentieth century. Some of Pollack's decisions can be rationalized by the necessity of compression in a film under contract to run a maximum length of two hours and fifteen minutes. "To violate this (which I did) would theoretically mean I would lose control of the picture—or, more precisely, lose the much-protected final cut."[24] This explains why early scenes feel rushed and jumbled, as when Farah meets Karen's train in Nairobi then dashes her off to the Muthaiga Club, where she is thrown out of the bar before she finds Bror in the lobby, just in time to change into her wedding suit in his room and marry him an hour later. From her *Letters from Africa,* we know that Karen encountered Farah at the Port of Aden and was subsequently met by Bror in Mombasa. They married the next day, not on her day of arrival, and enjoyed a wedding lunch on the train ride to Nairobi.[25] Pollack's urge to get past the "Bror Years" as quickly as possible also establishes Karen's first meeting with Denys Finch Hatton in the opening scene dating to 1914, not at a dinner party four years later in 1918.[26] Such "fast-forwarding" obviously foregrounds the love story with Finch Hatton, although her lifelong friendship with the reportedly charming and recklessly adventurous personality of Bror von Blixen would make a very interesting movie in itself.

In a similar romanticized "tweak," the dramatic ordeal of reaching Bror on the Tanganyika border with a caravan of supplies patronizes her feat as the remarkable accomplishment of a "little woman." In truth, the experience was far more empowering than sexy for Karen Blixen, as she explains in her memoir.[27] Pollack also applies his own mid-twentieth-century male filter to a misreading of the moment when she meets the new governor of colonial Kenya, Sir Joseph Byrne. In the movie, Meryl Street falls to her knees at his feet to plead her case for the relocation of two thousand squatters, as if she were a girl pleading with Daddy to let her stay up late. Blixen did, indeed, plead with the authorities to keep those people together and was much relieved when they were relocated to the Dagoretti Forest Reserve. Yet she did so patiently and diplomatically in the offices of the British Colonial Administration, not on her knees at a public event after which she was gallantly escorted out by Denys Finch Hatton. She states this clearly toward the end of her memoir: "In the end, just as I was beginning to feel that I must drive into Nairobi and back, and talk on in Government Offices all my life, I was suddenly informed that my application had been granted."[28] Once again, the film gratuitously emphasizes Karen Blixen's lack of emotional control and the presumption of "feminine weakness."

Denys Finch Hatton's death, which is conflated with his funeral and her departure, also places Blixen on the receiving end of male approval. He died in a fiery airplane accident on May 14, 1931, a date that precedes Blixen's departure by three months. Contrary to Pollack's decision to inject a final moment with Bror by having him come to tell her of her lover's death, it was Lady McMillan, wife of Sir William Northrup McMillan, who gently informed Karen Blixen of the accident in her private sitting room.[29] This occurred after she noticed Blixen's confusion as people were avoiding her in the street in Nairobi. Lady McMillan rightfully deduced that she had not yet heard the tragic news and invited her to come home with her. Staging a scene with the perfect-pitch performance of Klaus Maria Brandauer in an empty house naturally highlights a love-triangle sadly resolved by death.[30] Yet, a dramatic woman-to-woman scene with Lady McMillan—perhaps played by Judi Dench or Maggie Smith?—might also have been packed with emotion of a different kind.

Pollack's focus on romance also deploys Finch Hatton's death as the true "end of the story" when he injects classic English poetry into the closing scenes. In addition to A. E. Housman's "My Heart with Rue Is Laden," which enters into the final toast at the Muthaiga Club, Housman's poem of untimely death titled "To an Athlete Dying Young" is read in the film by Blixen at the gravesite. In fact, she did not read that or any other poem aloud on that day. Rather, a priest read Psalm 121:1: "I will lift up mine eyes unto the hills, from whence cometh my help. My help cometh from the LORD, which made heaven and earth. He will not suffer." Furthermore, if there is a poem associated with Denys Finch Hatton's gravesite, it would be "The Rime of the Ancient Mariner" by Samuel Taylor Coleridge. From this poem Finch Hatton's brother had the closing line inscribed on a stone obelisk sent to Kenya to be placed at his brother's grave some months after Karen Blixen's departure: "He prayeth well who loveth well, both man and bird and beast." These words are, in fact, Pollack's most appropriate use of poetry and a fitting line to place in the mouth of Robert Redford in the midst of the memorably sensuous, *plein air* shampoo he gives to Meryl Streep.

Memoir, as we have seen, represents a peculiarly personal space balanced between truth and fiction that allows readers to hear—and feel—the inner voice of another individual. As a cross-genre translation of *Out of Africa* onscreen, the larger-than-life story elicits a different response as we shift from the private experience of reading a book in relative solitude to a work of art made for mass consumption and aimed at box-office success or, here in the twenty-first century, at streaming subscriptions. Even if the movie has inspired new generations to read Karen Blixen's story, each generation of readers brings its own interpretation to a book that can be read and critiqued from various angles of vision. Yet the "truth" of the story will always come close to the complex journey that Judith Lee described as "the story of a woman who must come to terms with the fact that she can fulfill her nature only through acting out an imagined identity."[31]

Sydney Pollack's masterpiece leads with beautiful scenery in which he places Karen Blixen between two men, rather than between different visions of individual identity that may or may not have included marriage, or a life in Denmark, or a life in Kenya, or a career as a writer. In this way, Pollack's telling of her story shifts her boundaries to such an extent that he tells a different story than her memoir intends to tell. Boundaries beyond geographical exist in *Out of Africa* as they do in any *authorized* telling of a slice-of-life. In fact, it is part of the "job" of writing memoir to impose a frame in which many things are included or excluded as the author establishes a place to meet, a line of communication, and a view of the past through a subjective reorganization of memory. In this sense, memoir is a historical genre because it reflects on the past in the present as a means of understanding human experience and the power of experience to alter one's sense of self.

In the flow of narration, it is good if the reader feels that the author has engaged in a process of discovery, since we are, as readers of memoir, always hoping to discover a hidden truth of human experience. It is, in other words, entirely possible that the book we know as *Out of Africa*—with its multiple genres, rich layers of meaning, and moments of self-revelation—may not have been the book Blixen set out to write when she summarized the book she planned to write, in a letter to her Random House editor, in 1934 as "a few short, quite truthful accounts of my life on the African farm, particularly about my relations with the Natives."[32] It is even possible that she never quite understood the meaning of the book she was writing until she discovered herself in the process of writing it. By almost any measure, the film titled *Out of Africa* was arguably less complex as a project than the memoir because it began with a clear foundation, including a beginning and an end, even if the themes allowed for artistic manipulation.

Ultimately, Karen Blixen's most famous work of literature poses critical questions to readers and writers of memoir: What does memoir owe to its readers? How much erasure is acceptable before a memoir becomes a novel? Where is the boundary between fidelity to inner life and the facts of each writer's historic moment, which—intentionally or not—dares to represent the collective experience of others who happened to share that moment, perhaps from a different vantage point? Was Karen Blixen's writing an attempt to reinvent herself or to reinvent the world? And with a question like that, we are obligated to ask "Whose world?"

At the risk of oversimplification, I have considered such questions across these chapters and reflected on them through a critical filter that could be formulated as a three-pronged "guide" to reading memoir:

- Consider and contextualize how and when and why the memoir was written.
- Consider and contextualize who wrote it and how s/he became that person.

- Consider and contextualize the world of the memoir and how the world has changed.

I believe that Karen Blixen's reinventions were consciously done with a sense of artistic purpose. I also believe that she was a contradictory figure whose embodiments included negative aspects of a colonial era and a colonized mind as well as a desire to know and love the unknown. I believe that she was aware of her contradictions, just as she was aware of her fragility and her oddity—her otherness—from an early age. I also believe she was a "feminist," regardless of how anyone wishes to define that term, because the only meaningful definition of that word is a claim to a woman's non-negotiable freedom to describe herself and her relationship with the world.

For all of these reasons, Karen Blixen owns the story she told in *Out of Africa* in ways that include how it should be told. She owns the story because it remains her vision of her personal struggle to find a sense of belonging in a world irrevocably altered by her father's suicide in 1895, as much as by war or technological innovation. And she owns it because she traveled through seasons and landscapes and time zones and years in order to both author and authorize a work of literature. Some of the most reflective pages of *Out of Africa* occur as she studies the night sky just before everything is shattered by a "shot in the dark." In those moments before the tragedy of the shooting accident, her mind runs free on a moonlit night and she is reminded that "people who dream when they sleep at night know of a special kind of happiness which the world of the day holds not, a placid ecstasy, and ease of heart, that are like honey on the tongue."[33] This may be a common experience to writers of lyrical memoir, who, as Sven Birkerts points out, "are all, in their fashion, ecstatic dreamers."[34] In the dreamscape of *Out of Africa* Karen Blixen achieved what drives so many memoirists to go back and bring forward a different kind of truth through the mask and magic of words.

APPENDIX

A Brief Chronology of *Out of Africa*

January 1914	Karen Christentze Dinesen arrives in Africa, from Italy, after three weeks at sea, and marries her cousin Bror von Blixen-Finecke in Mombasa on January 14, 1914.
1915	She writes a poem titled "Ex Africa" from a hospital bed during four months of hospitalization at the National Hospital in Copenhagen during her first trip back to Denmark. She shows the poem to her brother Thomas when he visits her. The title becomes her first choice for the memoir she eventually writes in 1935–37.
1926	As a distraction from the farm, Blixen turns to writing at night. In a letter to Thomas, she mentions that her "little African travel accounts, which Flesborg Newspaper are now benevolently awaiting, are like parroting the Angel's Songs of Praise, and I can't do that any more; they become *mbuni* (coffee berries) before they get onto my pen."
August 19, 1931	Karen arrives in Marseille on the SS *Mantola* in a weakened state of physical and emotional health. Thomas meets her and accompanies her back to Denmark after a few days of consultation at the Clinique de Valmont in

the Swiss village of Glion overlooking Montreux, Switzerland, and Lake Leman.

1932 As she recovers from the trauma of failure in Ngong, she turns to writing intricate tales set in the nineteenth century. Sometime in 1932, she invents her pseudonym "Isak Dinesen," which combines the Hebrew name meaning "one who laughs" and her paternal family name.

1934 A well-known Danish photographer, Reimert Kehlet, creates a mysterious full-length portrait of the new author for her American readers in a flowing, white evening dress. This will be the first image of Isak Dinesen to appear in the United States.

January 1934 After a long recovery and gradual return to writing, *Seven Gothic Tales* is published by Random House with her pseudonym "Isak Dinesen" on the cover. It becomes a Book-of-the-Month Club selection with a print run of 50,000. By comparison, the tepid response in Denmark leaves her depressed, especially after Danish translation rights are sold to Reitzel, her brother-in-law Knud Dahl's firm. He is in no hurry to publish the book and grows weary of Karen's heavy hand in the translation. Blixen will do her own translations from English to Danish from then on.

March 1934 Blixen authorizes her Random House editor Robert Haas to divulge her true identity to her American readers. She also writes that "I have got a few short, quite truthful accounts of my life on the African farm, particularly about my relations with the Natives. I have to have these published under my real name, as they deal with real facts and people. I should like to get them out in a *good* magazine, if possible, and I suppose that this cannot interfere with our contract, since the stories can not in any way be classed as a book. Will you give me your kind assistance to find such a magazine, if you think it could be found?"

Fall 1934 — She is in an emotional crisis—fatigue, lack of direction, sense of failure, loss of confidence. Her December departure for London cheers her up as she is welcomed there as a literary star among illustrious people. Among other things, she discusses her idea of creating a hospital for Masai children in Kenya with Albert Schweitzer, founder of a well-known hospital in French Equatorial Africa, who is in London to perform a concert. She accepts his advice not to pursue the project she refers to as her "bridge to the Masai Reserve."

1935 — Karen Blixen celebrates her fiftieth birthday in Denmark on April 17. After this, she is in London through November, except for September in Geneva, where she attends a League of Nations session with her aristocratic friend Moura Budberg to protest Mussolini's threat to Ethiopia. (He invades the country in October 1935.) She does little or no writing in 1935, but is thinking seriously about how to approach "a book about Africa."

January 29, 1935 — Karen Blixen tells an interviewer for *Møns Folkeblad* (Danish daily newspaper) that she is planning to write a book "in which all things are true, where everything that is told truly happened. It shall be the truth about Blacks."

May 1935 — Thomas urges her, in a letter, to get out of her rut by either devoting herself to religion or hiring a secretary so that

	she could "put everything else aside" and get to work on the book she has had in mind "on the Masai."
1935–36	She is working on *Out of Africa* in earnest and feels generally confident that Robert Haas at Random House will be happy to publish it. Meanwhile, the Danish firm Reitzel purchases rights to Bror Blixen's book *Nyama* (The African Hunter), which causes stress and leads to more acrimony with Knud Dahl and his wife, Karen's sister Elle.
September 1936	Having finally reached a point where she needs solitude and uninterrupted time to complete her book, Karen Blixen drives across Zealand Province on September 21, 1936, ferries across the Kattagat Strait to Jutland, and continues on to the village of Skagen at the northern tip of Jutland Province. There, she settles into Brøndums Hotel, where she stays for nearly six months. Thomas Dinesen visits her at Christmastime 1936, despite family obligations, when she reads to him from pages rapidly becoming *Out of Africa*.
1937–38	*Out of Africa* by Isak Dinesen is published in English in the U.K. and in Danish as *Den afrikanske farm* late in the fall of 1937. To Blixen's consternation, the American edition was slightly delayed until January 1938, when it became a bestselling Random House Book-of-the-Month Club selection.

Sources for the appendix include Karen Blixen's *Letters from Africa* and *Letters from Denmark;* Thomas Dinesen's *My Sister, Isak Dinesen;* Robert Langbaum's *Isak Dinesen's Art: The Gayety of Vision;* and Judith Thurman's *Isak Dinesen: The Life of a Storyteller.*

NOTES

PROLOGUE

1. Karen Blixen's actual time in Kenya between 1914 and 1931 works out to about fourteen years, if travel to Europe for medical treatment and family visits are taken into account.

2. Susan C. Brantly, "Karen Blixen's Challenges," 40.

3. References throughout are keyed to the 1992 Modern Library Edition of *Out of Africa,* originally published under Blixen's pseudonym of "Isak Dinesen."

4. Sven Birkerts, *Nabokov's Speak, Memory,* 77.

5. Maureen Murdock, *Unreliable Truth,* 13.

6. Susan Tiberghien, *One Year to a Writing Life,* Kindle, loc 1616–18.

7. Judith Lee, "The Mask of Form," 280.

8. Isak Dinesen, *Letters from Africa, 1914–1931,* is the source for Karen Blixen's letters quoted throughout this book, unless otherwise noted.

9. S. Birkerts, *Nabokov's Speak, Memory,* 78.

10. David Ward, "Karen Blixen," in *Chronicles of Darkness,* 51.

11. Isak Dinesen, Part V: Farewell to the Farm, *Out of Africa,* 389.

12. Susan C. Brantly, *Understanding Isak Dinesen,* 77.

13. Simon Lewis, "Culture, Cultivation, and Colonialism in *Out of Africa* and Beyond," in *White Women Writers and Their African Invention,* 119.

14. Ibid., 112.

15. Karen Blixen to Thomas Dinesen, April 1–3, 1926.

16. The essay is first referenced in K. Blixen to T. Dinesen, April 27, 1924.

17. Judith Thurman, *Isak Dinesen: The Life of a Storyteller* identifies the two stories as "The Dreamers" and "The Old Chevalier," 255n.

18. American sales figures for *Out of Africa* as of April 1938 were estimated at 7,000 copies sold in book shops vs. 92,000 sold through the Book-of-the-Month Club system by Olga Anastasia Pelensky, in *Isak Dinesen: The Life and Imagination of a Seducer,* 142.

19. Isak Dinesen, *Shadows on the Grass,* 114.

20. J. Thurman, *Isak Dinesen,* 443n17.

21. Qtd. in Ebbe Mørk, *Karen Blixen at Home,* 176.

22. Jane Kramer, "The Eighth Gothic Tale," *New York Review of Books* (July 17, 1986).

23. Thomas Knipp, "Kenya's Literary Ladies," 3.

24. K. Blixen to T. Dinesen, April 1–3, 1926, *LFA*. Also qtd. in T. Dinesen, *My Sister, Isak Dinesen,* 99.

25. Frans Lasson, "Introduction to the Letters of Isak Dinesen," *LFA,* xxv.

1. THINKING BACKWARDS, MOVING FORWARD

1. K. Blixen to Gustav Mohr, Rungstedlund, September 20, 1936. *Lettres du Danemark* (Selected), in *Karen Blixen: Afrique.*

2. T. Dinesen to K. Blixen, May 16, 1935, as qtd. in J. Thurman, *Isak Dinesen,* 276.

3. F. Lasson and Clara Svendsen, eds., *Life and Destiny,* 147.

4. J. Thurman, *Isak Dinesen,* 279–80.

5. Isak Dinesen, "Daguerreotypes," in *Daguerreotypes and Other Essays,* 22.

6. Isak Dinesen, *SGT,* 79.

7. Olive Schreiner, *The Story of an African Farm: A Novel,* is compared with Isak Dinesen's *OA* in Simon Lewis's *White Women Writers and Their African Invention* (2003). Blixen wrote an introduction to a special edition of the nineteenth-century classic, which was published in the U.K. in 1961.

8. J. Thurman, *Isak Dinesen,* 127.

9. Isak Dinesen, *SG,* 4.

10. Parmenia Migel, *Titania,* 108–10.

11. Ibid., 109.

12. Note that a revised version of "Ex Africa" appeared in the Danish daily *Berlingske Tidende* on December 6, 1942, and also in a holiday edition from Gyldendal Publishers titled *Osceola* in 1962. As the poem is not available in English, my translations here are based on the French translation by Alain Gnaedig in *Karen Blixen: Afrique* (Gallimard, 2006), 327–28.

13. Note that *Out of Africa* was titled *Den Afrikanske gård* in Danish and *La ferme africaine* in French, both translatable in English as "The African Farm." In German, the emphasis falls on unknowable distance with *Jenseits in Afrika* (literally: "Beyond in Africa" and equally correct as "Somewhere in Africa").

14. Marcel Proust, *In the Shadow of Young Girls in Flower,* Vol. 2 of the multivolume novel *In Search of Lost Time,* won the Prix Goncourt in 1919. Blixen's 1925 French edition remains in her library in Rungstedlund, which was catalogued at the time of her death in 1962.

15. S. Brantly, Understanding Isak Dinesen, 72.

16. *Politken,* May 1, 1934. Qtd. in J. Thurman, *Isak Dinesen,* 264.

17. *Politken,* 10 September 1934. Qtd. in J. Thurman, *Isak Dinesen,* 281.

18. *Møns Folkeblad,* January 29, 1935. Qtd. in J. Thurman, *Isak Dinesen,* 281.

19. J. Thurman, *Isak Dinesen,* 274.

20. Thorkild Bjørnvig, *The Pact: My Friendship with Isak Dinesen,* 47.

21. K. Blixen to T. Dinesen. Ngong. April 1, 1926. See also T. Dinesen, *My Sister,* 98.

22. See Isak Dinesen, *LFA,* for a photo of Thomas Dinesen on Mt. Kenya in 1923 taken by Gustav Mohr.

23. Robert Langbaum quotes Blixen's letter to Robert Haas of Random House in *Isak Dinesen's Art: The Gayety of Vision,* 120 [emphasis mine]. Langbaum's source for the letter is "Random House Files, New York," which are now located at the Columbia University Library Archives.

24. Karen Blixen left for London shortly after her fiftieth birthday in April 1935 and stayed with her friend Moura Budberg. See J. Thurman, *Isak Dinesen,* 272–77.

25. Albert and Helene Schweitzer established a hospital in Lambarene, French Equatorial Africa (Republic of Gabon), in 1913. Note that Blixen met Schweitzer twice in her life: once in London, where he often came to raise funds by performing organ concerts, and a second time in 1954 in the airport in Copenhagen, where he stopped en route to his Nobel Peace Prize ceremony in Oslo, Norway.

26. R. Langbaum, *Isak Dinesen's Art,* 97.

27. T. Bjørnvig, *The Pact: My Friendship with Isak Dinesen,* 46.

28. Skagen, in the 1880s, was a well-known European art colony, and Brøndum's Hotel was owned by the family of Anna and Michael Ancher, both painters. Anna was born in the hotel when Hans Christian Andersen was staying there. This cultural nexus surely inspired Karen Blixen's imagination, as Hans Christian Andersen had not only been the author of the beloved fairy tales of her childhood, but a friend of her paternal grandfather, Adolph Wilhelm Dinesen (1808–1876). The two men traveled together in Italy between Milan and Rome in 1833. See F. Lasson and C. Svendsen, eds., *Life and Destiny,* 18.

29. Susan Brantly references a Danish source, Marianne Juhl, for the length of time spent in Skagen as "almost six months." S. Brantly, *Understanding Isak Dinesen,* 72n2.

30. Ibid., 73n5.

31. Ibid., 74n9.

32. Ibid., 74.

33. https://www.randomhousebooks.com/imprint/modern-library/.

2. ORIGINS OF IMAGINATION

1. Isak Dinesen, "Radio Address—Rungstedlund," in *Daguerreotypes,* 195–218.

2. Donald Hannah, *"Isak Dinesen" and Karen Blixen: The Mask and the Reality,* 14. Brandes was a Danish literary icon, biographer of Søren Kierkegaard, and family friend admired by Karen Blixen in her youth.

3. Over 20,000 Parisians died in the Paris Commune, many executed by the French Army, during the Bloody Week of May 21–28, 1871. Note that Babette Hersant, heroine of Blixen's "Babette's Feast," was a *pétroleuse* (a female arsonist) and survivor of the conflict in which working-class women played an active role.

4. Richard B. Vowles, "Boganis, Father of Osceola; or Wilhelm Dinesen in America 1872–1874," 369–83.

5. Anders Westenholz, *The Power of Aries*, 54.

6. K. Blixen to Thomas Dinesen, Ngong, April 10, 1931.

7. Folehave Farm was part of the Rungstedlund estate. Ingeborg's mother ("Mama") and sister Mary Bess Westenholz lived at Folehave.

8. P. Migel, *Titania*, 14.

9. F. Lasson and C. Svendsen, *Life and Destiny*, 43.

10. Thomas Dinesen, *My Sister, Isak Dinesen* 11–15.

11. Ingeborg Dinesen (Private) to T. Dinesen, Rungstedlund, May 9, 1931. Note that nearly a century after this letter was written, Karen Blixen's grand-nephew Morten Keller asserted that Wilhelm's "dishonorable" death by hanging was a decision made after having fathered a child outside of his marriage to Ingeborg. (See Graham Boynton, *Wild: The Life of Peter Beard—Photographer, Adventurer, Lover*, 54n4.)

12. Ibid.

13. T. Dinesen, *My Sister, Isak Dinesen* 31–33.

14. J. Thurman, *Isak Dinesen*, 42.

15. T. Dinesen, *My Sister, Isak Dinesen* 34–35. The "heroic poem" was written to mark five centuries since three Scandinavian countries—Denmark, Norway, Sweden—had come together under one monarch as the Kalmar Union (1397–1523).

16. J. Thurman, *Isak Dinesen*, 42–43.

17. Ibid., 40.

18. Note that Blixen's early drawings, notebooks, and letters are housed in the Karen Blixen Archives. The Royal Danish Library, Copenhagen.

19. Anne Barton, *The Shakespearean Forest*, 2017, loc 336.

20. P. Migel, *Titania*, 20–31.

21. Isak Dinesen, *Carnival: Entertainments and Posthumous Tales*, 1.

22. Isak Dinesen, "The Art of Fiction No. 14," Interview by Eugene Walter.

23. Isak Dinesen, "Roads to Life," in Part IV: From an Immigrant's Notebook, *OA*, 259–61.

24. J. Thurman, *Isak Dinesen*, 40.

3. TRUTH AND REVENGE

1. J. Thurman, *Isak Dinesen*, 275. Note that Blixen writes on the role of witches in her essay "Daguerreotypes" in *Daguerreotypes and Other Essays*, 33.

2. D. Hannah, *The Mask and the Reality,* 151.

3. Anders Westenholz, *The Power of Aries,* 36.

4. Karen Blixen, "The Revenge of Truth," Appendix in D. Hannah, *The Mask and the Reality,* 182.

5. Aage Henriksen, *The Work and the Life,* 19.

6. Ibid., "Afterword," 193.

7. A. Henriksen, "Karen Blixen and Marionettes," in *The Work and the Life,* 20.

8. K. Blixen, "The Revenge of Truth," Appendix in D. Hannah, *The Mask and the Reality,* 181.

9. T. Dinesen, *My Sister, Isak Dinesen,* 36.

10. J. Thurman, *Isak Dinesen,* 205.

11. Anders Westenholz, *The Power of Aries,* 44.

12. K. Blixen to Mary Bess Westenholz, Mbagathi Estate, April 1, 1914.

4. METAPHORS OF TRUTH

1. J. Thurman, *Isak Dinesen,* 161.

2. Isak Dinesen, "The Ngong Farm," Part I: Kamante and Lulu, *OA*, 8.

3. Susan Hardy Aiken, "Transporting Topologies: *Out of Africa* and the Poetics of Nostalgia," in *Engendering of Narrative,* 229.

4. O. Pelensky, *The Life and Imagination of a Seducer,* 141–42.

5. Isak Dinesen, "Farewell," Part V: Farewell to the Farm, *OA*, 391.

6. Margaret Atwood, "Margaret Atwood on the Show-Stopping Isak Dinesen," *Guardian Online.*

7. Isak Dinesen, "Deluge at Norderney," *SGT,* 79.

8. Elisabeth Bronfen, *Over Her Dead Body,* xii.

9. Note that a 1986 article published by Elisabeth Bronfen in her native German places Miss Malin's quote at the end of "Deluge at Norderney" in the title: "'Scheherazade sah den Morgen dämmern und schwieg diskret': Zu der Beziehung zwischen Erzählen und Tod in den Geschichten von Isak Dinesen (Karen Blixen)." [Scheherazade saw the dawn and remained discreetly silent: On the relationship between storytelling and death in the stories of (Karen Blixen) Isak Dinesen].

10. S. Brantly, *Understanding Isak Dinesen,* 18.

11. Isak Dinesen, "Somali Women," Part IV: From an Immigrant's Notebook, *OA,* 188.

12. Isak Dinesen, "Wings," Part III: Visitors to the Farm, *OA,* 234.

13. Ngũgĩ wa Thiong'o, "Detained: A Writer's Prison Diary," 1.

14. Judith Lee, "The Mask of Form," 270–71.

15. Mads Bunch, *Isak Dinesen Reading Søren Kierkegaard,* xii.

16. S. H. Aiken, "Introduction," in *Engendering of Narrative,* xx.

17. Isak Dinesen, “Farewell,” Part V: Farewell to the Farm, *OA,* 397.

18. Isak Dinesen, “A Native Child,” Part I: Kamante and Lulu, *OA,* 39.

19. Ibid., 42.

20. S. H. Aiken, *Engendering of Narrative,* 64.

21. Ngũgĩ wa Thiong'o, *Decolonising the Mind: The Politics of Language in African Literature,* 3.

22. Ibid., 13.

23. Isak Dinesen, “The Iguana,” Part IV: From an Immigrant's Notebook, *OA,* 265–69.

24. Ibid., 265.

25. Ibid.

5. A TRACE OF ERASURE

1. S. Lewis, “Culture, Cultivation, and Colonialism,” 126–27.

2. R Langbaum, *Isak Dinesen's Art,* 119.

3. T. Knipp, “Kenya's Literary Ladies,” 3.

4. S. Brantly, *Understanding Isak Dinesen,* 82.

5. Isak Dinesen, “Farah and I Sell Out,” Part V: Farewell to the Farm, *OA,* 385.

6. Isak Dinesen, “A Native Child,” Part I: Kamante and Lulu, *OA,* 25–26.

7. S. Brantly, *Understanding Isak Dinesen,* 79.

8. R. Langbaum, *Isak Dinesen's Art,* 121.

9. Jean Stafford, “Lioness—*Titania: The Biography of Isak Dinesen,*” NYRB Archives Online, January 18, 1968.

10. Karen Blixen's eventual diagnosis of “tertiary syphilis” attacked her digestive system and led to chronic pain, repeated hospitalizations, disfigured facial features, and astonishing frailty in her final decade, even after penicillin became available in the 1940s.

11. Hannah Arendt, “Isak Dinesen: 1885–1961,” 100.

12. R. Langbaum, *Isak Dinesen's Art,* 121.

13. K. Blixen to Ingeborg Dinesen, Ngong, Oct. 30, 1921.

14. K. Blixen to Ingeborg Dinesen, Ngong, Nov. 24, 1921.

15. K. Blixen to Ingeborg Dinesen, Ngong, Jan. 13, 1922.

16. K. Blixen to Ingeborg Dinesen, Ngong, Jan. 23, 1922.

17. Ibid.

18. Quoted in Anders Westenholz, *The Power of Aries,* 22–24. Note that Anders Westenholz (1936–2010) was a grandson of Aage Westenholz.

19. Ibid., 24–25.

20. Ibid., 26. Aage Westenholz to T. Dinesen, Sept. 1, 1922.

21. T. Knipp, “Kenya's Literary Ladies,” 6.

22. S. Lewis, “Culture, Cultivation, and Colonialism,” 127.

23. Janet McIntosh, *Unsettled: Denial and Belonging,* Kindle, loc 2961–2967.

24. Elspeth Huxley, *White Man's Country,* Vol. 2, 207.

25. Ibid., 200.

26. Aage Westenholz to K. Blixen, Mar. 8, 1923. Quoted in Anders Westenholz, *The Power of Aries,* 26–27.

27. K. Blixen to T. Dinesen, April 1923. Ibid., 28.

28. Isak Dinesen, "Farewell to the Farm," Part V: Farewell to the Farm, *OA,* 329.

29. E. Huxley, *White Man's Country,* 207.

30. Bror Blixen was killed in an auto accident in Sweden in 1946.

31. Isak Dinesen, "Farewell to the Farm," Part V: Farewell to the Farm, *OA,* 331.

32. Ibid., 334.

33. R. Langbaum, *Isak Dinesen's Art,* 121–22.

34. T. Knipp, "Kenya's Literary Ladies," 7.

35. Ngũgĩ wa Thiong'o, "Her Cook, Her Dog: Karen Blixen's Africa," 158–59

36. Ngũgĩ, "*Decolonising the Mind,*" 3.

37. Ngũgĩ, "Detained," 613.

38. J. Lee, "The Mask of Form," 271.

6. IN SEARCH OF VANISHED TIME

1. Philippe Lançon, *Le Lambeau* (Gallimard, 2018). Note that "Disturbance" is a debatable English translation from the French by Steve Rendall. A literal English translation of the title would be "The Shred" or "The Flap of Skin" and could be understood to refer to the author himself.

2. Isak Dinesen, "The Ngong Farm," Part I: Kamante and Lulu, *OA,* 3.

3. Isak Dinesen, "Farewell," Part V: Farewell to the Farm, *OA,* 399.

4. M. Proust. *In Search of Lost Time, Vol. 5: The Prisoner,* 119, and Vol. 7: *Finding Time Again,* 387. Note that *Arabian Nights* and *1001 Nights* are interchangeable titles.

5. I am grateful to Likke Littrup at the Karen Blixen Museum (Rungstedlund) for confirming this.

6. M. Proust, *In Search of Lost Time,* Vol. 7: *Finding Time Again,* 388.

7. Isak Dinesen, "A Gazelle," Part I: Kamante and Lulu, *OA,* 77.

8. M. Proust, *In Search of Lost Time,* Vol. 5: *The Prisoner,* 244.

9. S. Lewis, "Culture, Cultivation, and Colonialism," 114.

10. T. Knipp, "Kenya's Literary Ladies," 7.

11. Isak Dinesen, "The Shooting Accident," Part II: A Shooting Accident on the Farm, *OA,* 89–162. The five chapters are "The Shooting Accident," "Riding in the Reserve," "Wamai," "Wanyangerri," and "The Gikuyu Chief."

12. Ibid., 92.

13. Ibid., 93–94.

14. K. Blixen to Ingeborg Dinesen, Ngong. December 23, 1923.

15. Judith Lee, "Mask of Form," 272.

16. S. H. Aiken, "Transporting Topologies: *Out of Africa* and the Poetics of Nostalgia," in *Engendering of Narrative*, 217.

17. Susan Horton, *Difficult Women, Artful Lives*, 244.

18. S. Lewis. "Culture, Cultivation, and Colonialism," 114.

7. OTHERNESS AS REVELATION

1. Janet McIntosh, *Unsettled: Denial and Belonging*, 2.

2. For population data for colonial Kenya and factors that influenced it over time, see "White People in Kenya," https://en.wikipedia.org/wiki/White_people_in_Kenya.

3. Abdullahi Ahmed Weid (Judge). Qtd. in S. Brantly, *Understanding Isak Dinesen*, 81, within her discussion of Tove Hussein's *Africa's Song of Karen Blixen* (1998).

4. Errol Trezbinski, *Silence Will Speak*, 66.

5. Isak Dinesen, "The Noble Pioneer," Part III: Visitors to the Farm, *OA*, 223–24.

6. Ngũgĩ, "Karen Blixen's Africa," 158–59.

7. Peggy McIntosh, "Unpacking the Invisible Knapsack," 10.

8. See Robin DiAngelo, *White Fragility: Why It's So Hard for White People to Talk about Racism* (2018).

9. Ibram X. Kendi, *How to be an Anti-Racist*, 13.

10. Rob Nixon, "Out of Africa," 219.

11. S. Brantly, *Understanding Isak Dinesen*, 81n30.

12. J. Thurman, *Isak Dinesen*,128.

13. Isak Dinesen, "Farah and I Sell Out," Part V: Farewell to the Farm, *OA*, 388.

14. Isak Dinesen, "A Gazelle," Part I: Kamante and Lulu, *OA*, 67.

15. S. Lewis, "Culture, Cultivation, and Colonialism," 117. Note that Blixen was not the only person to fix on Kamante Gatura as a symbolic figure. Photographer Peter Beard gave him a home on his Hog Ranch near the farm, as well as a chance to exhibit his drawings and contribute to *Longing for Darkness: Kamante's Tales from Out of Africa* (1975/1990).

16. Peter Mortensen, "'Both Men and Beasts,'" 508.

17. S. Brantly, *Understanding Isak Dinesen*, 84.

18. Isak Dinesen. "Mottoes of My Life," 8.

19. Isak Dinesen, "Pania," Part IV: From an Immigrant's Notebook, *OA*, 296–97.

20. Ngũgĩ, "Detained," 617.

21. P. Mortensen, "'Both Men and Beasts,'" qtd. on p. 508.

22. Ibid.

23. hooks, "Eating the Other," loc 506.

24. Ibid., loc 556–561 (emphasis mine).

25. K. Blixen to Ingeborg Dinesen, May 28, 1914. The India rupee used at the time was worth approximately $45 each in today's value. When the East Africa Protectorate became a British Colony in 1920, the currency used was called the African rupee.

26. K. Blixen to Mary Bess Westenholz, Mbagathi House, April 1, 1914.

27. K. Blixen to T. Dinesen, February 24, 1926.

28. S. Brantly, "Karen Blixen's Challenges," 30.

29. Ibid., 40.

30. S. Horton, *Difficult Women, Artful Lives,* 218.

31. Isak Dinesen, "A War-Time Safari," Part IV: From an Immigrant's Notebook, *OA,* 274–81.

32. Ibid., 276.

33. K. Blixen to Ingeborg Dinesen, September 23, 1914.

34. Isak Dinesen, "Somali Women," Part IV: From an Immigrant's Notebook, *OA,* 185.

35. Ibid., 186.

36. J. Lee, "Mask of Form," 274–75.

37. hooks, "Eating the Other," loc 478–855.

38. K. Blixen to T. Dinesen, February 24, 1926. Also qtd. in T. Dinesen, *My Sister, Isak Dinsen,* 94–95.

39. Ibid. Note that "posho" is a porridge made of corn meal.

40. K. Blixen to T. Dinesen, April 5, 1926. Also qtd. in T. Dinesen, *My Sister, Isak Dinsen* 103.

41. Karen Blixen, "Noirs et Blancs en Afrique" [Blacks and Whites in Africa] was first published posthumously in the Danish journal *Blixeniana* in 1977 and eventually incorporated into a Danish volume of essays, which is not available in English. All quotes are my translations from the French source, "Noirs et Blancs en Afrique," in *Essais* (Paris: des femmes, 1987).

42. Ngũgĩ, "Detained," 617.

43. Isak Dinesen, "Kitosch's Story," Part IV: From an Immigrant's Notebook, *OA,* 287.

44. Ibid., 291.

45. K. Blixen to Gustav Mohr, Rungstedlund, Rungsted Kyst, July 3, 1936, in Karen Blixen, *Afrique: Lettres de Danemark* (1932–58), 769. (My translation from the French.)

46. Ngũgĩ, "Detained," 617.

47. Isak Dinesen, "Kitosch's Story," Part IV: From an Immigrant's Notebook, *OA,* 288–90.

48. Ibid., 291–92.

49. David Anderson, "Punishment, Race and 'The Raw Native,'" 1.

50. K. Blixen, "Noirs et Blancs en Afrique," 98.

51. K. Blixen uses of the politically charged "native" in English editions of *Out of Africa.* However, her Danish *infødt* and the French *indigène,* which appears in the French translation of the Danish essay, both translate as "indigenous," which currently enjoys a positive connotation.

52. K. Blixen, "Noirs et Blancs en Afrique," 85.

53. Ibid., 86. Both "Blacks" and "Whites" are capitalized in the French edition of the essay that I have consulted and translated in my references. I therefore retain the capitalization here.

54. Ibid., 91.

55. Ibid., 99.

56. Ibid., 96.

57. Ibid., 97.

58. Ibid., 108.

59. Ibid., 112 [emphasis mine].

60. Ibid., 102.

8. KAREN BLIXEN'S CLOSET

1. F. Lasson and C. Svendsen, *Life and Destiny,* 65.

2. The "helmet" mentioned should be understood as a soft, close-fitting hat inspired by medieval sources. For numerous possibilities, see the Danish website https://postej-stew.dk/2016/11/female-headgear-and-hairstyles-in-the-middle-ages/.

3. K. Blixen to Mary Bess Westenholz and Ingeborg Dinesen, Mbagathi Estate, April 1, 1914.

4. Isak Dinesen, "The Ngong Farm," Part I: Kamante and Lulu, *OA,* 14.

5. Karen Blixen describes the momentous dinner party in a letter to her sister. See Karen Blixen to Ellen Dahl, Bogani House, April 6, 1918.

6. Isak Dinesen, "Wings," Part III: Visitors to the Farm, *OA,* 235.

7. Melissa Sones, "Designing for 'Out of Africa'; NEWLN: 'Out of Africa' a challenge for costume designer." UPI, Inc. January 28, 1986. https://www.upi.com/Archives/1986/01/28/Designing-for-Out-of-AfricaNEWLNOut-of-Africa-a-challenge-for-costume-designer/2828507272400/.

8. T. Knipp, "Kenya's Literary Ladies," 5.

9. K. Blixen to Ingeborg Dinesen, Mbagathi Estate, June 6, 1914.

10. K. Blixen to Ingeborg Dinesen, Mountain Health Resort, "Kijabe Hill," British East Africa. July 14, 1914.

11. See https://www.gettyimages.com/photos/roosevelt-safari.

12. See G. Boynton, *The Life of Peter Beard,* 51–63.

13. K. Blixen to Thomas Dinesen, Mbagathi Estate, Undated but noted by T.D. as "(Received) 17 Oct. 1914?"

14. K. Blixen to Ingeborg Dinesen. Ngong. Sunday, November 24, 1923.

15. Elliot Ross, "When Melania went to Africa wearing a pith helmet." October 7, 2018.

16. See Ulinka Rublack Interview: "A Feather in Your Cap: Inside the Symbolic Universe of Renaissance Europe," Cambridge Research Note Online; and Dean Sanchez: "The

Meaning of White, Black, and Gray Feathers: A Message from the Divine," www.finefeatherheads.com.

17. K. Blixen to Ingeborg Dinesen, January 3, 1923 (emphasis in original).

18. K. Blixen to Ellen Dinesen. Mbagathi Estate, May 13, 1914.

19. S. Lewis, "Culture, Cultivation, and Colonialism," 122–23.

20. Anders Westenholz, *The Power of Aries,* 9.

21. S. Brantly, *Understanding Isak Dinesen,* 9–10.

22. Isak Dinesen, *SG,* 44–45.

23. See Susan Hardy Aiken, "Consuming Isak Dinesen," 1994.

24. Ralph Lauren, *Ralph Lauren,* 213.

25. Ibid., 132.

26. See Caroline Elkins, *Imperial Reckoning;* Elspeth Huxley, *White Man's Country;* and Janet McIntosh, *Unsettled: Denial and Belonging among White Kenyans,* among many other books on this vast topic.

27. Isak Dinesen, "Visits of Friends," Part III: Visitors to the Farm, *OA,* 214.

28. R. Langbaum, *Isak Dinesen's Art,* 119.

29. Peter Mortensen, "Greening Karen Blixen," 226.

30. Ibid., 225.

31. Ibid., 227–28.

32. Ibid., 231.

33. Ibid.

34. Ibid., 238.

35. Meera Selva, "Woman who swapped London fashion scene for a Kenyan warrior," *Sunday Independent,* October 23, 2005. Independent.co.uk.

36. See Anna Trezbinski Online Shop at www.annatrezbinski.com

37. J. McIntosh, *Unsettled: Denial and Belonging,* 8–9.

38. J. Thurman, *Isak Dinesen,* 274.

39. S. Horton, *Difficult Lives,* 53.

40. Isak Dinesen, "The Art of Fiction, No. 14," Interview by Eugene Walter.

41. Jean Stafford, "Lioness—*Titania: The Biography of Isak Dinesen,*" NYRB Archives Online, January 18, 1968.

42. Isak Dinesen, "Daguerreotypes," 33.

43. See the Schlesinger Library Photo Archives, Radcliffe Institute.

44. Isak Dinesen, "Oration at a Bonfire, Fourteen Years Late," 76.

9. ON THE QUESTION OF FEMINISM

1. The most accessible version of "Oration at a Bonfire, Fourteen Years Late" appears in *Isak Dinesen: Daguerreotypes and Other Essays,* 1979. For this reason, "Isak Dinesen" is

noted in citations, although Karen Blixen originally delivered the lecture in person under her own name.

2. Isak Dinesen, "Oration," 77.

3. J. Thurman, *Isak Dinesen,* 348.

4. K. Blixen to Mary Bess Westenholz, Ngong, May 23, 1926.

5. Isak Dinesen, "Oration," 77 (emphasis in original).

6. Marianne Stecher-Hansen, "Karen Blixen on Feminism and Womanliness," 202.

7. Universal suffrage in Denmark (1915) was followed by Germany (1918), the United States (1920), Sweden (1921), the United Kingdom (1928), and France (1944).

8. S. Brantly, "Karen Blixen's Challenges," 29–30.

9. Ibid.

10. Susan Hardy Aiken, "The Uses of Duplicity," 400–411.

11. Isak Dinesen, "Oration," in *Daguerreotypes,* 83.

12. S. H. Aiken, *Engendering of Narrative,* 35–36.

13. Ibid., 213.

14. Ibid., 215.

15. Ibid., 211–12.

16. J. Thurman, *Isak Dinesen,* 192.

17. K. Blixen to Thomas Dinesen, Ngong, April 27, 1924.

18. K. Blixen to Thomas Dinesen, Ngong, August 3, 1924.

19. M. Stecher-Hansen, "Karen Blixen on Feminism and Womanliness," 197n3.

20. Isak Dinesen, "On Modern Marriage," 42.

21. Ibid., 43.

22. Ibid., 54.

23. Isak Dinesen, "The Young Man with the Carnation," *WT,* 16–17.

24. Ibid., 22.

25. Isak Dinesen, "On Modern Marriage," 91.

26. Else Cederborg, "Introduction," in *On Modern Marriage,* 31.

27. Isak Dinesen, "Mottoes of My Life," in *Daguerreotypes,* 8.

28. K. Blixen to T. Dinesen, April 3, 1926.

29. K. Blixen to Mary Bess Westenholz, Ngong, May 23, 1926.

30. M. Stecher-Hansen, "Karen Blixen on Feminism and Womanliness," 193.

31. K. Blixen to Ellen Dahl, January 13, 1928.

32. S. Brantly, *Understanding Isak Dinesen,* 9–10.

33. Isak Dinesen, "Somali Women," Part IV: From an Immigrant's Notebook, *OA,* 188–89.

34. K. Blixen to Ingeborg Dinesen, Ngong, Sunday, March 17, 1929.

35. Isak Dinesen, "The Shooting Accident," Part II: A Shooting Accident on the Farm, *OA,* 89–102; and "The Roads to Life," Part V: From an Immigrant's Notebook, 259–61.

36. Susan Gubar, "'The Blank Page' and Female Creativity," 257.

37. S. H. Aiken, *Engendering of Narrative,* 223.

38. See J. Thurman, *Isak Dinesen,* 275n4, and Schlesinger Library Photo Archives, Radcliffe Institute.

39. S. H. Aiken, "Consuming Isak Dinesen," 15.

10. I HAD A FARM IN HOLLYWOOD

1. S. Birkerts, *Nabokov's Speak, Memory,* 77.

2. See BoxOfficeMojo.com.

3. Sydney Pollack, "Introduction," in Kurt Luedtke, *The Shooting Script,*" vii.

4. Richard Schickel, "Where the Wild Things Were Out of Africa," *Time Magazine,* December 16, 1985.

5. Roger Ebert, Review of *Out of Africa,* https://www.rogerebert.com/reviews/out-of-africa-1985.

6. Gene Siskel, "Redford Mars the Beauty of 'Out of Africa,'" *Chicago Tribune,* December 20, 1985.

7. J. Kramer, "The Eighth Gothic Tale," *New York Review of Books* (July 17, 1986).

8. S. H. Aiken, *Engendering of Narrative,* 212.

9. David Watkin won the Academy Award for cinematography while the Best Film Editing award went to Frederic and William Steinkamp, Pembroke J. Herring, and Sheldon Kahn.

10. T. Dinesen, *My Sister, Isak Dinesen,* 125.

11. Isak Dinesen, "The Art of Fiction No. 14," Interview by Eugene Walter.

12. G. Boynton, *The Life of Peter Beard,* 136. Note that Blixen contributed her posthumous royalties from her work to the foundation, which continues to support her house museum with its library, bookshop, café, garden, and bird sanctuary in Rungsted Kyst, Denmark.

13. Ibid., 136–38.

14. Note that Sydney Pollack directed Robert Redford in *Jeremiah Johnson* (1972), *The Way We Were* (1973), *Three Days of the Condor* (1975), and *The Electric Horsemen* (1979).

15. S. Pollack, "Introduction," in Kurt Luedtke, *The Shooting Script,* x.

16. Ibid., xiii.

17. Ibid., xix.

18. K. Blixen to Thomas Dinesen, August 3,1924.

19. Isak Dinesen, "The Grave in the Hills," Part V: Farewell to the Farm, *OA,* 353–71.

20. Isak Dinesen, "A Gazelle," Part I: Kamante and Lulu, *OA,* 83.

21. Isak Dinesen, "Farah and I Sell Out," Part V: Farewell to the Farm, *OA,* 380–83.

22. Sources for these details are included in the article found online at en.wikipedia.org/wiki/Out_of_Africa_(film).

23. The larger house, Mbogani House, was not available in the early 1980s and had not yet become the Karen Blixen Museum.

24. S. Pollack, "Introduction" in *The Shooting Script,* xii (emphasis in original).

25. See J. Thurman, *Isak Dinesen,* 114–17.

26. See Karen Blixen to Ellen Dahl, Bogani House, April 6, 1918.

27. Isak Dinesen, "A War-Time Safari," Part IV: From an Immigrant's Notebook, *OA,* 274–81.

28. Isak Dinesen, "Farah and I Sell Out," Part V: Farewell to the Farm, *OA,* 388.

29. William Northrup McMillan was a gregarious, wealthy American who settled in colonial Kenya and contributed to its development. The McMillan Library in Nairobi was founded by the McMillans.

30. Isak Dinesen, "The Grave in the Hills," Part V: Farewell to the Farm, *OA,* 330–71.

31. J. Lee, *Mask of Form,* 279.

32. K. Blixen to Robert Haas, March 24, 1934. Qtd. in R. Langbaum, *Isak Dinesen's Art,* 120.

33. Isak Dinesen, "The Shooting Accident," Part II: A Shooting Accident on the Farm, *OA,* 91.

34. *The Art of Time in Memoir,* 49.

BIBLIOGRAPHY

Author names "Blixen" and "Dinesen" are listed as they appear on the edition noted.

PRIMARY SOURCES

Archives

Karen Blixen Museum, Rungstedlund, Denmark.

Messums London Museum. Collection of fifteen photographs taken in Africa by Thomas Dinesen. https://messumslondon.com/tales-of-africa-photography-and-fiction/.

Royal Danish Library Digital Photo Archives. Karen Blixen and Rungstedlund Collections. www.kb.dk.

Schlesinger Library, Radcliffe Institute, Harvard University. Mary Ingraham Bunting Records of the President of Radcliffe College, 1960–72; Radcliffe College Photo Archive.

Books

Blixen, Karen. *Afrique.* A Gallimard Quarto Edition of Blixen's collected works related to Africa: *La Ferme Africaine,* "Ex Africa," *Lettres d'Afrique* (1914–1931), *Lettres de Danemark* (1932–1958), *Ombres sur la Prairie, Essais, Sept Lettres des "Natives."* Gallimard, 2006.

Dinesen, Isak. *Seven Gothic Tales.* Random House Vintage International Edition, 1934, 1991.

———. *Out of Africa.* 1937. Random House Modern Library Edition, 1992.

———. *Winter's Tales.* Random House and Editions for the Armed Services, Inc., 1942.

———. *Winter's Tales.* Knopf Doubleday, 1942, 1993.

———. *Last Tales.* Random House Vintage Reprint Edition, 1957, 1991.

———. *Anecdotes of Destiny and Ehrengaard, including Babette's Feast.* Random House, 1958, Vintage International Edition Reissue, 2011.

———. *Shadows on the Grass.* Random House, 1961.

———. "Introduction" to *The Story of an African Farm* by Olive Schreiner. Westerham Limited Editions Club of Kent, 1961.

———. *Carnival: Entertainments and Posthumous Tales.* Trans. P. M. Mitchell and W. D. Paden. University of Chicago Press, 1977.

———. *Letters from Africa, 1914–1931.* Edited by Frans Lasson. Translated by Anne Born. University of Chicago Press, 1981.

———. *Daguerreotypes and Other Essays.* Trans. P. M. Mitchell and W. D. Paden. Rungstedlund Foundation, 1979, and University of Chicago Press, 1984.

Dinesen, Thomas, V. C. *My Sister, Isak Dinesen.* Translated by Joan Tate. Michael Joseph, 1975.

Lasson, Frans, and Clara Svendsen, eds. *The Life and Destiny of Isak Dinesen.* University of Chicago Press, 1970.

Essays, Interviews, Speeches, Theater

Blixen, Karen. "The Revenge of Truth: A Marionette Comedy." Translated by Donald Hannah. Appendix to *"Isak Dinesen" and Karen Blixen: The Mask and the Reality,* by Donald Hannah. Random House, 1971.

———. *Essais.* Translated by Régis Boyer. des femmes, 1987.

———. "Noirs et Blancs en Afrique," Speech delivered in Stockholm and Lund, Sweden, 1938. In *Essais,* 1987.

Dinesen, Isak. "The Art of Fiction No. 14." Interview by Eugene Walter. *Paris Review,* no. 14 (Autumn 1956). https://www.theparisreview.org/interviews/4911/the-art-of-fiction-no-14-isak-dinesen.

———. "The Wine of the Tetrarch." In *Atlantic Monthly,* December 1959. Note: Story read aloud in NYC to celebrate her induction as Foreign Member of the American Academy of Arts and Letters.

———. "On Mottoes of My Life." Acceptance speech as a Foreign Honorary Member of the American Academy of Arts and Letters, 1959. In *Daguerreotypes and Other Essays.* Foreword by Hannah Arendt. Translated by P. M. Mitchell and W. D. Paden. University of Chicago Press, 1984.

———. "Oration at a Bonfire Fourteen Years Late." In *Daguerreotypes and Other Essays.* Rungstedlund Foundation 1979 and University of Chicago Press, 1984.

———. "Rungstedlund." Radio Address from 1958. In *Daguerreotypes and Other Essays.* Rungstedlund Foundation 1979 and University of Chicago Press, 1984.

———. *On Modern Marriage and Other Observations.* Translated by Anne Born. St. Martin's Press/Rungstedlund Foundation, 1986.

SECONDARY SOURCES

Aiken, Susan Hardy. "The Uses of Duplicity: Isak Dinesen (1885–1962) and Questions of Feminist Criticism." *Scandinavian Studies,* vol. 57, no. 4 (Autumn 1985): 400–411.

———. *Isak Dinesen and the Engendering of Narrative.* University of Chicago Press, 1990.

———. "Consuming Isak Dinesen." In *Isak Dinesen and Narrativity: Reassessments for the 1990s,* Edited by Gurli A. Woods. Carleton University Press for The Center for Textual Analysis, Discourse, and Culture, 1994. https://doi.org/10.1515/978 0773573949-003.

Anderson, David M. "Punishment, Race and 'The Raw Native': Settler Society and Kenya's Flogging Scandals, 1895–1930." *Journal of Southern African Studies,* vol. 37, 2011: 479–97. https://doi.org/10.1080/03057070.2011.602887.

Arendt, Hannah. "Isak Dinesen: 1885–1961." In *Men in Dark Times.* Harcourt, Brace, Jovanovich, 1968. Subsequently published as the Forward to *Daguerreotypes and Other Essays* by Isak Dinesen. University of Chicago Press, 1984.

Atwood, Margaret. "On the Show-Stopping Isak Dinesen," *Guardian Online* (November 29, 2013). https://www.theguardian.com/books/2013/nov/29/margaret-atwood-isak-dinesen.

Axel, Gabriel. *Babette's Feast.* The Criterion Collection, 1987. DVD, 1h 43min.

Barton, Anne. *The Shakespearean Forest.* Cambridge University Press, 2017.

Beard, Peter, and Isak Dinesen (Karen Blixen). *Longing for Darkness: Kamante's Tales from Out of Africa.* Photographs by Peter Beard with photographs and captions by Isak Dinesen. Chronicle Books, 1990.

Birkerts, Sven. *The Art of Time in Memoir: Then, Again.* Graywolf Press, 2008.

———. *Vladimir Nabokov's Speak Memory.* Ig Publishing, 2020.

Bjørnvig, Thorkild. *The Pact: My Friendship with Isak Dinesen.* Introduction and translation by William Jay Smith and Ingvar Schousboe. Louisiana State University Press, 1983.

Blixen, Bror. *The African Hunter.* Translated by F. H. Lyon. St. Martin's Press, 1986.

Boynton, Graham. *Wild: The Life of Peter Beard—Photographer, Adventurer, Lover.* St. Martin's Press, 2022.

Brantly, Susan C. *Understanding Isak Dinesen.* University of South Carolina Press, 2002.

———. "Karen Blixen's Challenges to Postcolonial Criticism." *KULT 11: Made in Denmark,* 29–44. Roskilde University Press, 2013.

Bronfen, Elisabeth. "'Scheherazade sah den Morgen dämmern und schwieg diskret': Zu der Beziehung zwischen Erzählen und Tod in den Geschichten von Isak Dinesen (Karen Blixen)," *Skandinavistik* 16, no. 1 (1986): 48–62.

———. *Over Her Dead Body: Death, Femininity, and the Aesthetic.* Routledge, 1992.

Bunch, Mads. *Isak Dinesen Reading Søren Kierkegaard: On Christianity, Gender, and Repetition.* Modern Humanities Research Association, 2017.

DiAngelo, Robin. *White Fragility: Why It's So Hard for White People to Talk about Racism.* Beacon Press, 2018.

Ebert, Roger. Review of *Out of Africa,* 1985. https://www.rogerebert.com/reviews/.

Elkins, Caroline. *Imperial Reckoning: The Untold Story of Britain's Gulag in Kenya.* Henry Holt, 2005.

Gubar, Susan. "'The Blank Page' and the Issues of Female Creativity." *Critical Inquiry* 8, no. 2 (Winter 1981): 243–63. https://doi.org/10.1086/448153.

Hannah, Donald. *"Isak Dinesen" and Karen Blixen: The Mask and the Reality.* Random House, 1971.

Henriksen, Aage. *Isak Dinesen/Karen Blixen: The Work and the Life.* Translated by William Mishler. St. Martin's Press, 1988.

hooks, bell. "Eating the Other: Desire and Resistance." In *Black Looks: Race and Representation.* Routledge, 2015. https://doi.org/10.1007/978-981-97-0285-5_3.

Horton, Susan R. *Difficult Women, Artful Lives: Olive Schreiner and Isak Dinesen, in and out of Africa.* Johns Hopkins University Press, 1995.

Huxley, Elspeth. *White Man's Country: Lord Delamere and the Making of Kenya.* Vol. 2: *1914–1931.* Chatto and Windus, 1935, 1980.

Kendi, Ibram X. *How to Be an Anti-Racist.* One World, 2019.

Kiselyak, Charles. *Song of Africa.* Producer, director, writer. Documentary extra to *Out of Africa* DVD. Universal Studios, 1999. 50 mins.

Knipp, Thomas R. "Kenya's Literary Ladies and the Mythologizing of the White Highlands." *South Atlantic Review* 55, no. 1 (1990): 1–16. https://doi.org/10.2307/3199869.

Kramer, Jane. Cover feature: "The Isak Dinesen Fantasy." Article titled "The Eighth Gothic Tale" includes reviews of *Out of Africa* (film) directed by Sydney Pollack, *Out of Africa* and *Shadows on the Grass* by Isak Dinesen, plus sixteen additional titles. *New York Review of Books,* July 17, 1986. NYRB Online Archives.

Langbaum, Robert Woodrow. *Isak Dinesen's Art: The Gayety of Vision.* Random House, 1965; University of Chicago Press, 1975.

Lasson, Frans. "The Rain at Ngong: An Introduction to the Letters of Isak Dinesen." In *Isak Dinesen: Letters from Africa, 1914–1931.* Edited by Frans Lasson. Translated by Anne Born. University of Chicago Press, 1981.

Lauren, Ralph. *Ralph Lauren.* Rizzoli, 2007.

Lee, Judith. "The Mask of Form in *Out of Africa.*" *Prose Studies* 8, no. 2 (1985). Republished in *Isak Dinesen: Critical Views.* Edited by Olga Anastasia Pelensky. Ohio University Press, 1993, 266–82. https://doi.org/10.1080/01440358508586242.

Lewis, Simon. "Culture, Cultivation, and Colonialism in *Out of Africa* and Beyond." In *White Women Writers and Their African Invention.* University Press of Florida, 2003.

Luedtke, Kurt. *Out of Africa: The Shooting Script.* Introduction and annotation by Sydney Pollack. Newmarket Press, 1987.

McIntosh, Janet. *Unsettled: Denial and Belonging Among White Kenyans.* University of California Press, 2016.

McIntosh, Peggy. "White Privilege: Unpacking the Invisible Knapsack." In *On Privilege, Fraudulence, and Teaching as Learning.* Routledge, 2019. https://doi.org/10.4324/9781351133791-4.

Migel, Parmenia. *Titania: The Biography of Isak Dinesen.* Random House, 1967.

Mørk, Ebbe. *Karen Blixen at Home: Scenes from Rungstedlund.* Photographs by Jens Lindhe. Translated by John Kendall. Politiken, 2011.

Mortensen, Peter. "'The Grass Was Me . . . the Distant Invisible Mountains Were Me, the Tired Oxen Were Me': Greening Karen Blixen." *Scandinavian Studies* 88, no. 3 (2016): 225–45. doi:10.5406/scanstud.88.3.0225.

———. "'Both Men and Beasts': Rereading Karen Blixen's Anthropomorphisms." *Orbis Litterarum* 73 (2018): 506–19.

Murdock, Maureen. *Unreliable Truth: On Memoir and Memory.* Seal Press, 2003.

National Museum of Denmark. "Always in Style: Dresses from 1775 to 1969." Highlights from the Collection of the National Museum of Denmark. Photographs by Roberto Fortuna and Peter Danstrøm.

Ngũgĩ wa Thiong'o. *Decolonising the Mind: The Politics of Language in African Literature.* James Currey and Heineman, 1986.

———. "Her Cook, Her Dog: Karen Blixen's Africa." Lecture in Copenhagen 1980. Reprinted in *Moving the Center: The Struggle for Cultural Freedoms.* James Currey and Heineman, 1993.

———. "Detained: A Writer's Prison Diary." In *Perspectives on Africa: A Reader in Culture, History, and Representation.* Edited by Roy Richard Grinker and Christopher B. Steiner. Blackwell, 1997.

Nixon, Rob. "Out of Africa." *Grand Street* 5, no. 4 (1986): 216–27. https://doi.org/10.2307/25006911.

Oe, Kenzaburo. "Speaking on Japanese Culture before a Scandinavian Audience—Lecture Series 1992." Translated by Kunioki Yanagishita. In *Japan, the Ambiguous, and Myself.* Kodansha America Inc., 1995.

Pelensky, Olga Anastasia. *Isak Dinesen: The Life and Imagination of a Seducer.* Ohio University Press, 1991.

———, ed. *Isak Dinesen: Critical Views.* Ohio University Press, 1993.

Pollack, Sydney. "Out of Africa." Film based on *Out of Africa* by Isak Dinesen. Screenplay by Kurt Luedtke. Universal Pictures Home Entertainment, DVD, 1985. 160 min.

———. "Introduction and Notes." In *Out of Africa: The Shooting Script* by Kurt Luedtke. Newmarket Press, 1987.

Proust, Marcel. *In Search of Lost Time.* Vol. 5: *The Prisoner,* translated by Carol Clark. Random House/Penguin: 2002.

———. *In Search of Lost Time.* Vol. 7: *Finding Time Again,* translated by Ian Patterson. Random House/Penguin: 2023.

Ross, Elliot. "When Melania Went to Africa Wearing a Pith Helmet." October 7, 2018. https://www.aljazeera.com/opinions/2018/10/7/when-melania-went-to-africa-wearing-a-pith-helmet.

Rublack, Ulinka. "A Feather in Your Cap: Inside the Symbolic Universe of Renaissance Europe." Cambridge Research Notes Online, 2017.

Sanchez, Dean. "The Meaning of White, Black, and Gray Feathers: A Message from the Divine." Feathermyhead.com, 2023.

Schickel, Richard. Review of film *Out of Africa* titled "Where the Wild Things Were Out of Africa." *Time Magazine,* December 16, 1985.

Schreiner, Olive. *The Story of an African Farm.* Chapman and Hall, 1883; Digireads.com, 2004.

Siskel, Gene. Review of film *Out of Africa:* "Redford Masks the Beauty of 'Out of Africa.'" *Chicago Tribune,* December 20, 1985.

Smith, William Jay. "Introduction" in *The Pact: My Friendship with Isak Dinesen* by Thorkild Bjornvig. Louisiana State University Press, 1983.

Sones, Melissa. "Designing for 'Out of Africa.'" UPI International, January 28, 1986.

Stafford, Jean. "Lioness." Review of *Titania: The Biography of Isak Dinesen* by Parmenia Migel. *New York Review of Books*, January 18, 1968.

Stecher, Marianne. "Karen Blixen on Feminism and Womanliness"—'En Baaltale med 14 Aars Fosinkelse.'" *Scandinavian Studies* 83 2 (2011): 191–232. https://doi.org/10.2307/23075457.

Thurman, Judith. *Isak Dinesen: The Life of a Storyteller.* St. Martin's Press, 1982.

Tiberghien, Susan. *One Year to a Writing Life: Twelve Lessons to Deepen Every Writer's Art and Craft.* Marlowe & Company, 2007.

Trezbinski, Anna. Online shop: annatrezbinski.com.

Trezbinski, Errol. *Silence Will Speak.* University of Chicago Press, 1977.

Ward, David D. "Karen Blixen ('Isak Dinesen'): *Out of Africa.*" In *Chronicles of Darkness.* Routledge, 1989. https://doi.org/10.4324/9781003477860-6.

Westenholz, Anders. *The Power of Aries: Myth and Reality in Karen Blixen's Life.* Translated by Lise Kure-Jensen. Louisiana State University Press, 1987.

Wivel, Ole. *Karen Blixen: Un Conflit personnel irrésolu.* Translated by Inès Jorgensen. Actes Sud, 2004.

INDEX

Note: Page numbers in italics indicate images in the text.

Aarhus, Denmark, 19

Absence of Malice (film), 154

Aiken, Susan Hardy, 51, 54–55, 57, 85–86, 103, 140–42, 150–52, 155–56

Amiane from *The Revenge of Truth* (Blixen), 38, 39–45, 129

Andersen, Hans Christian, 29, 38

Anderson, David M., 107–8

Anecdotes of Destiny (Dinesen), 7

animals in Blixen's life and work: "'Both Men and Beasts'" (Mortensen), 98; in fashion and style, 125–27; "The Iguana," 58–59, 91, 160; in memory of childhood, 18; metaphors of, in *Out of Africa,* 37, 93, 96–99

antiracism, 94–95, 108

Arabian Nights, 17–18, 38, 52–54, 73–74

Arendt, Hannah, 62, 138

aristocratic characters in "The DeCats Family," 36–37

aristocratic conventions and values, 92–93, 112–13, 119–20, 149

aristocratic origins of Scheherazade, 53

Atwood, Margaret, 52

Austen, Jane, 150

authenticity in fashion, 122–24

autobiography, 3–4

Babette's Feast (Dinesen), 37

Bardenfleth, Else, 33

Barry, John, 156

Barton, Anne, 36

Beard, Peter, 157

Becoming (Obama), 49

belonging, 55, 67, 77, 167

Birkerts, Sven, 3, 4, 50, 153, 167

Bjørnvig, Thorkild, 8, 24, 126

Black Africans, 70, 92–96, 100–101, 103–4, 108–11, 122, 146–47

"Blacks and Whites in Africa" speech (Blixen), 104, 108–11

"The Blank Page" in *Last Tales* (Dinesen), 151

Blixen, Bror (husband), 4, 6; disillusionment with, 20–21; divorce from, 143; erasures, 50, 62; farm in Ngong, 67, 69; feminized power acquired by marriage to, 119; in film version, 69, 160–64; and legal/financial matters, 65–66; in *Letters from Africa,* 63–66; pressure to divorce,

Blixen, Bror (*continued*)
63–64; rifle picture, 122–23; safari life and style, 115–17; separation from, 139; volunteered to join Lord Delamere, 102; wedding day, 113

Blixen, Karen (Isak Dinesen): in 1958, wearing a leopard stole from Africa, *136;* beginning to write for publication, 36–37; conversion experience, 99–100; divorce from Bror, 143; duplicity, in narrative voice, 103, 140–42; education, 35–36; emotional link to material, 21; exploitable image, 124; farm in Ngong, 68–70; fashion and style, 112–30; father's suicide, 8–9, 32–33, 63, 167; feminism, 137–52, 159; *fermière générale,* role as, 5, 64–65, 68; first safari, 1914, *133;* full-length portrait, 1922, 114–15, *132;* hunting, 49, 117–20; intention to validate her experience in *Out of Africa,* 151; and legal/financial matters, 62–66; "Lioness" nickname, 97–98; otherness, 91–96; personal and feminized power, 39–43, 45, 53, 118–22, 139, 152; personas, 17, 40, 45, 54, 95, 111, 112, 114–15, 117–20, 126–27, 128–30; photographic record of life in Africa, 121–24; photographs of, 131–36; race relations, 71, 99–102; reinventions, 8, 44, 86–88, 166–67; rifle picture, 122–23; safari life, 99, 114, 115–18, 121–24, 125–26, *133–34,* 149; safari style, 113–15, 116–21; self-mythology, 51, 93, 121–24; separation from Bror, 139; sociocultural position in Africa, 139; studio portrait by Reimert Kehlet, 128–29, *135;* suicidal depression, 30; syphilis, 30, 32, 62, 115, 129; as Tanne Dinesen, 6, 18, 29–32, 34–39, 41, 45, 66, 99, 112; and witches, 39–40, 129, 149; as a young woman, *131*

Blixen, Karen, works of: "Blacks and Whites in Africa" speech, 104, 108–11; "The DeCats Family" (writing as Osceola), 36–37; "Ex Africa," 20–21; "The Hermits" (writing as Osceola), 36; "The Plowman" (writing as Osceola), 36; "The Revenge of Truth," 38, 39–46, 129, 146. *See also* Dinesen, Isak, works of

"'Both Men and Beasts'" (Mortensen), 98

bourgeois life and marriage, 30, 32, 42, 45, 143–44

bourgeois values, 34, 149

Brandauer, Klaus Maria, 69, 164

Brandes, Georg, 29

Brantly, Susan, 21, 24–25, 53, 62, 95–96, 97, 101, 121, 139–40, 149

British Colonial Administration, 5, 60, 163–64

British colonialism/colonial society, 2, 4–5, 61–62, 96, 100–102, 110–11, 124, 125, 141–42, 150. *See also* postcolonial analysis and critiques

British women, fashion and style, 119

Brøndums Hotel, 15, 24

Bronfen, Elisabeth, 53

Brontë sisters, 150

Bunch, Mads, 54

Byrne, Sir Joseph, 163

Canonero, Milena, 114

"Cassandra's Journey" (Dinesen), 35, 41

Cederborg, Else, 146

Chanel, Coco, 129

characters, 34, 36, 39–42, 55–56, 70, 159

Chippewa, 29–30

Christie, Julie, 157

Chyulu Hills, 162

class distinctions in colonial Kenya, 76, 95–96, 101, 102–4, 112, 119–20, 125, 128, 149

Clinique de Valmont, 10
clothing. *See* fashion and style
Cole, Berkeley, 70, 93, 162
Coleridge, Samuel Taylor, 164–65
colonization, 5, 71, 77
commedia dell'arte, 34–35, 40–41
Conference of the International Women's Suffrage Alliance, 137
confessional poetry, 150–51
Conrad, Joseph, 77
consumption in the western world, 121, 127–28
contradiction(s), 54, 70, 87, 91, 105, 115, 141–42, 152, 155, 158, 167
Conversations of German Emigrants (Goethe), 53
Copenhagen, 1, 27, 28, 33–36, 40, 45, 63, 96, 112, 137, 138, 144
cosplay, 119
Council on Books in Wartime, 7
country life, 120
cultural appropriation, 59
cultural time, 76–77

Dagoretti Forest Reserve, 5, 61, 163
Daguerreotypes and Other Essays (Dinesen), 138
Dahl, Ellen (Elle) (sister), 14, 18, 35, 119, 148–49
Dahl, Knud (brother-in-law), 14
Danish Ministry of Culture, 157
Danish Women's Citizens Society, 151
Dano-Prussian War, 29
"The DeCats Family" (Blixen writing as Osceola), 36–37
deerhounds, 98, 120
"Deluge at Norderney" (Dinesen), 18, 52, 60
denial of oneself, 76–77
Denmark, 10, 14, 17, 19, 29–30, 37, 45, 64, 148; return to, in 1931, 71, 77–78, 87
Deraniyagala, Sonali, 49
desire(s), 56, 58, 98, 99
Destiny, 37, 41, 42, 43, 44, 87–88
"Detained" (Ngũgĩ wa Thiong'o), 53–54, 104–5
Diana (Goddess of the Hunt), 121, 149
DiAngelo, Robin, 94
Didion, Joan, 49
Difficult Women, Artful Lives (Horton), 87
Dinesen, Alvide (aunt), 27–28
Dinesen, Ingeborg (née Westenholz) (mother), 7, 13–14, 18, 27, 29–33, 35, 45, 62, 63–64, 100, 123, 143–44
Dinesen, Inger (Ea) de Neergaard (sister), 7, 31, 35, 143
Dinesen, Isak. *See* Blixen, Karen (Isak Dinesen)
Dinesen, Isak, works of: *Anecdotes of Destiny,* 7; *Babette's Feast,* 37; "The Blank Page," in *Last Tales,* 151; "Cassandra's Journey," 35, 41; *Daguerreotypes and Other Essays,* 138; "Deluge at Norderney," 18, 52, 60; "The Dreamers," in *Seven Gothic Tales,* 17, 129; *Last Tales,* 7, 151; *Letters from Africa,* 3, 8, 13, 18, 61–62, 63–66, 77, 116, 118, 163; "On Modern Marriage and Other Observations," 7, 142–46; "On Mottoes of My Life," 97–98; "Oration at a Bonfire, Fourteen Years Late," 137–39, 140–41, 146, 148–49; "Roads around Pisa," in *Seven Gothic Tales,* 45; *Seven Gothic Tales,* 1, 7, 10, 14, 17, 20, 21–23, 36, 45, 52, 67, 128; *Shadows on the Grass,* 7, 19, 123; *Winter's Tales,* 7, 145; "The Young Man with a Carnation," in *Winter's Tales,* 145. *See also* Blixen, Karen, works of

Dinesen, Tanne. *See* Blixen, Karen (Isak Dinesen)
Dinesen, Thomas (brother), 7–8; and Bror Blixen, 64; connections of, 14; early years of, 31–33; and epigraph to *Out of Africa*, 49; erasures, 50; and film's exploratory trip, 157; and legal/financial matters, 65–66; letters to, 9–10, 30, 31–32, 100, 104, 121, 143–44, 147, 158–59; love and marriage, 143–44; meeting ship in Marseille, 10, 156; *My Sister, Isak Dinesen*, 27, 35; safari life, 116; support of, 22–23
Dinesen, Wilhelm (father), 8–9, 15, 20, 27–28, 29–35, 37–38, 63, 167
Disturbance: Surviving Charlie Hebdo (Lançon), 72
double-consciousness, 59, 91, 101–2, 103
"The Dreamers," in *Seven Gothic Tales* (Dinesen), 17, 129
dress codes, 116, 120, 122
duplicity, in narrative voice, 103, 140–42

East Africa Federation, 67
East Africa Protectorate, 6, 64, 67, 99, 108–9, 147
Ebert, Roger, 155
ecocriticism, 98, 125–27
École Benet, 33
Educated (Westover), 49
Edward VIII (Prince), 123
emotions, in film version of *Out of Africa*, 153–54
English poetry, Pollack's use of, 164–65
erasures, 50, 60–71, 161
European culture, 40, 57, 76–78, 86, 112–15, 119–20
Ewald, Johannes, 28
Ewald's Hill, 28, 35
"Ex Africa" (Blixen), 20–21

Facing Mt. Kenya (Kenyatta), 25
Fall of Man theme, 34–35, 42
Farah, 18–19, 55–56, 69–70, 71, 102, 114, 163
"Farah and I Sell Out," in *Out of Africa* (Dinesen), 161–62
"Farewell to the Farm," section V in *Out of Africa* (Dinesen), 50, 68–70, 72–73
farm in Ngong. *See* Swedo Coffee Farm
fashion and style, 112–30; animals, 125–27; authenticity in, 122–24; and class, 112, 119–20, 125, 128; consumption in the western world, 121, 127–28; dress codes, 116, 120, 122; feminine ideal, 119; feminism, 118–19; feminized power, 118–22; hunting, 117–20; khaki, 113–15, 119–20, 125, 127; Nature, 120, 125–28; personas, 112, 117–20, 126–27, 128–30; "safari chic," 120–21, 124, 128, 155; safari style, 113–15, 116–21
Fear of Flying (Jong), 150
feminine death, in Bronfen, 53
feminism, 137–52, 159; fashion and style, 118–19; feminized power, 39–43, 45, 53, 118–22, 139, 152; modern womanhood, 5, 25, 49, 113, 118, 125, 143, 145–46, 149, 152, 162; "Oration at a Bonfire, Fourteen Years Late" (Dinesen), 137–39; postcolonial analysis and critiques, 101–2; womanliness, 148–49, 152; women's movement, 119, 137–40, 148, 152
film. See *Out of Africa* (film)
first-person voice, 60–61. *See also* narrative voice
Fisher, Dorothy Canfield, 14

Folehave Farm, 31, 33
Fontaine, Jean de la, 97
freedom, feminist sense of, 39, 139, 141, 167
freedom and death, 30
freedom and otherness, 102–3
freedom and technology, 127
free love, 142–46
Frijs, Agnes, 30
"From an Immigrant's Notebook," section IV in *Out of Africa* (Dinesen), 98, 102–4
From the Center (Lippard), 138

Gable, Clark, 118
Garbo, Greta, 156
gender, 39, 43, 101, 117–18, 120, 125–26
"Gibson Girl" drawings of Charles Gibson, 112
Gide, André, 77
Gilbert, Sandra M., 138
God's Will concept, 16, 34–35, 42, 44
Goethe, Johann Wolfgang von, 53
"The Grass Was Me . . ." (Mortensen), 126
"The Grave in the Hills," in *Out of Africa* (Dinesen), 159
Greene, Graham, 77
Greer, Germaine, 138
Gubar, Susan, 138, 151
"Gypsy-Moth" airplane, 127

Haas, Robert, 20, 24
Hannah, Donald, 40, 42
Hatton, Denys Finch, 6; and Blixen's approach to otherness, 93; and Blixen's sociocultural position in Africa, 139; death of, 9, 70; erasures, 62; feminized power over, 53; in film version, 158–65; "Gypsy-Moth" airplane, 127; in *Letters from Africa,* 114, 158–59; love and marriage, 143, 145; and Percival, 115–16; safari life, 114
Hein, Estrid, 137–38
Hemingway, Ernest, 116
Henriksen, Aage, 42–44
"Her Cook, Her Dog: Karen Blixen's Africa" (Ngũgĩ wa Thiong'o), 96
"The Hermits" (Blixen writing as Osceola), 36
High Court, 105–8
historical time, 77
hooks, bell, 99, 103
Hørsholm Cemetery, 31
Hørsholm Parish Council, 30
Horton, Susan, 87, 101, 129
Housman, A. E., 160, 164
Hovmand, Anneliese, 157
humanism, Mortensen's reflection on, 98, 126–27
hunting, 49, 117–20
Huxley, Aldous, 23
Huxley, Elspeth, 8, 66, 69, 123

idealized world, 9, 43, 51, 75, 99
identity/identities, 3, 17, 119–20, 126–27, 141, 161, 165
"The Iguana," in *Out of Africa* (Dinesen), 58–59, 91, 160
imagination, 3, 21, 27–38, 51
inner life, 4, 60–61, 86, 142, 166
In Search of Lost Time (Proust), 4, 21, 73–74, 86
Iron, Ralph. *See* Schreiner, Olive
Isak Dinesen and the Engendering of Narrative (Aiken), 140–41
"The Isak Dinesen Fantasy" (Kramer), 155
Isak Dinesen's Art (Langbaum), 8
Isak Dinesen: The Life of a Storyteller (Thurman), 8, 13, 138

Jacobsen, Johan, 157
Jagger, Mick, 157
Jong, Erica, 150
journey tales/journey metaphor, 52–54, 162. *See also* storytelling

Kamante, 18, 55–57, 59, 91, 93, 96, 159–61
"Kamante and Lulu," in *Out of Africa* (Dinesen), 159–60
Karen Blixen Archives, 144
Karen Blixen Museum and Bird Sanctuary, Rungstedlund, 10, 28
Karen Lang'ata, Nairobi, 162
Katholm Castle, Djursland peninsula, 15, 28, 34
Kattegat Strait, 19
Kehlet, Reimert, 128–29, *135*
Kelly, Grace, 118
Kendi, Ibram X., 94–95, 101
Kenya, 1–2, 4; Blixen as "notable figure" in, 66–67; and Blixen's manipulation of time, 86–87; Blixen's position in colonial Kenya, 101–2; closure of Blixen's life in, 70–71; colonization of, 71; and corporal punishment, 107–8; fashion and style, 127–28; film's exploratory trip, 157; and hunting, 115, 120; as a mythical space, 76; race relations, 91–94; safari life, 121; sunbeam period, 67. *See also* British colonialism/colonial society
Kenyatta, Jomo, 25
khaki, 113–15, 118, 119–20, 125, 127
Kierkegaard, Søren, 16
Kijabe, 102
"Kitosch's Story," in *Out of Africa* (Dinesen), 104–8
Klampenborg, Copenhagen, 34, 49, 112
Knipp, Thomas R., 9, 61, 66, 70, 76–77, 114
Kramer, Jane, 9, 155
Kramer vs. Kramer (film), 157

Ladies' Home Journal, 37
Lançon, Philippe, 72
Langbaum, Robert, 8, 61–62, 70–71, 125
language, politics of, 57
Lasson, Frans, 8
Last Tales (Dinesen), 7, 151
Lauren, Ralph, 124, 155
Lausanne, Switzerland, 33
Leakey, Louis, 67
leather boots, 117–18
Lee, Judith, 3, 54, 71, 85–86, 103, 165
Letters from Africa (Dinesen), 3, 8, 13, 18, 61–62, 63–66, 77, 116, 118, 163
Lewis, Simon, 4–6, 60, 66, 76, 77, 87, 96, 120
The Life and Destiny of Isak Dinesen (Svendsen), 8
Lindstrøm, Ingrid, 6, 162
Lippard, Lucy, 138
A Literature of Their Own (Showalter), 138
Lord Delamere, 67, 71, 102–4, 123
loss, 9, 17–18, 40, 50–52, 55, 70, 72–73, 78, 159, 160, 161
"lost place" of lived experience metaphor, 55
love and marriage, 142–46. *See also* free love
Luedtke, Kurt, 154, 158–59, 161

The Madwoman in the Attic (Gilbert and Gubar), 138
malaria, 115
marionettes. *See* puppet theater
Markham, Beryl, 9, 66, 162
Marseille, France, 10, 156
Masai Reserve, 115–16
mask(s), 3, 16, 17–18, 40, 42–43, 45, 54–55, 63, 70–71, 119–20, 122, 150
Mau-Mau (Gikuyu) Rebellion, 25, 157
Mbagathi House, 115, 122–23, 162
Mbogani House, 17
McIntosh, Janet, 67, 91, 128
McIntosh, Peggy, 94

McMillan, Sir William Northrup and Lady, 164
memoir, 2–4, 8, 49–52, 55, 60, 70, 72, 75–76, 79, 85–86, 153, 161, 165–67
mémoire involuntaire (involuntary memory), 4
memory, 3–4, 15–17, 21, 50–51, 54, 57, 73–75, 78–79, 87, 161–62. *See also* memoir
The Merchant of Venice (Shakespeare), 140
metaphors, 37, 52, 55–59, 93, 96–99, 107, 109, 110–11, 124, 160–62
A Midsummer Night's Dream (Shakespeare), 36, 40
Migel, Parmenia, 8, 19–20, 24
Milne, A. A., 97
Miss Sode's Drawing School, 33, 36
modern womanhood, 5, 25, 49, 113, 118, 125, 143, 145–46, 149, 152, 162
Mogambo (film), 118
Mohr, Gustav, 104–6
Mombasa, 18, 69, 71, 93, 113, 163
monologues in film of *Out of Africa*, 158, 159–60
Møns Folkeblad (People's Magazine), 22
Montreux, Switzerland, 10
Mortensen, Peter, 25, 97–99, 125–27
movement, 85–86
Murdock, Maureen, 3
Muthaiga Men's Club, Nairobi, 160–61, 163, 164
"My Heart with Rue Is Laden" (Housman), 164
My Sister, Isak Dinesen (Dinesen), 8, 27
myth, in description by Aiken, 51

Nabokov, Vladimir, 3
Nairobi, 4–6, 71, 93, 119, 125, 128, 158, 162–64
narrative voice, 21, 40, 45, 51, 52–55, 58, 60–61, 77, 78, 103, 140–42, 143, 159
Nathalie Zahle's Teachers College, 151
Nature, 4, 13, 58, 60–61, 68–69, 70, 74–75, 78, 84, 102, 120, 125–28, 160
New York Review of Books, 155
Ngong, 4, 16; Aage's visit to, 62; Blixen's sociocultural position in, 99–101, 120–21, 139; closure of Blixen's life in, 70–71; failure of the farm, 66, 68–70; in film version, 162; horses, 49; mask(s), 42–43; and otherness, 91–96; race relations, 93–95; safari life photograph, 122, *134;* and Somali women, 102–3; Thomas Dinesen's visit to, 116; and vanished time, 72–75
Ngũgĩ wa Thiong'o, 2, 53–54, 57, 59, 71, 93–94, 96, 98–99, 104–7
Nixon, Rob, 95
"The Noble Pioneer," in *Out of Africa* (Dinesen), 162
noblesse oblige, 61, 95–96
Nochlin, Linda, 138
nonlinear writing, 10, 85–86, 150
Norway, 139
nostalgia, 9, 50, 54, 61, 70–71, 74–75, 77, 87, 124, 128, 137, 155

Obama, Michelle, 49
The Obstacle Race (Greer), 138
1001 Nights. See *Arabian Nights*
One Year to a Writing Life (Tiberghien), 50–51
"On Modern Marriage and Other Observations" (Dinesen), 7, 142–46
"On Mottoes of My Life" (Dinesen), 97–98
"Oration at a Bonfire, Fourteen Years Late" (Dinesen), 137–39, 140–41, 146, 148–49
"Osceola" pseudonym, 20, 36–37
otherness, 55–57, 58–59, 91–96, 99, 101–2, 103, 108–9, 161, 167. *See also* "Kitosch's Story," in *Out of Africa* (Dinesen)
Other(s), 59, 99, 109

Out of Africa (Dinesen): anthropomorphism and zoomorphism in, 96–98; authority of Blixen to tell her own story, 121, 141–42, 165–67; as autobiography, 3–4; and belonging, 167; and boundaries, 165; characters, 55–56, 70, 159; and cultural time, 76–77; and discovery, 166; double-consciousness, 59, 91, 101–2, 103; ecocritical approach to in Mortensen, 97–99, 125–27; ending of, 70–71; epigraph, 49; erasures, 50, 60–71, 161; exile theme, 55–57; "Farah and I Sell Out," 161–62; "Farewell to the Farm," section V, 50, 68–70, 72–73; as feminist work, 141–42, 149–52; and film, 153–54; film rights to, 157; "From an Immigrant's Notebook," section IV, 98, 102–4; "The Grave in the Hills," 159; "The Iguana," 58–59, 91, 160; internal/external quest, 51–52; "Kamante and Lulu," 159–60; "Kitosch's Story," 104–8; Knipp's critique of, 66; and loss, 50–52, 55, 70, 72–73, 78, 159, 160, 161; mask(s), 42–43; and memory, 161–62; metaphors, 37, 55–59, 93, 96–99, 161–62; mythical tone and structure, 52–55; narrative voice, 45, 140–42, 159; Nature, 160; "The Noble Pioneer," 162; otherness theme, 91–96; pastoral, Langbaum's designation, 61, 125; possession theme, 55, 58–59; possessive pronouns, 96; postcolonial analysis and critiques of, 4–6, 25, 56, 139–42, 155–56; reception of, 7, 24–26; "The Roads to Life," 37, 150; and self-mythology, 93, 121–24; "A Shooting Accident on the Farm," 79–86, 92, 150; the shot in the dark, 84–85; time navigation, 84–88; travelogue pages, 50; and truth, 49–59; and vanished time, 72–75, 78–79; "Visits of Friends," 162; "Wings," 162

Out of Africa (film), 2, 25, 49, 55–56, 69, 102, 109, 114, 118–19, 120, 153–66

Over Her Dead Body (Bronfen), 53

The Pact (Bjørnvig), 8, 24

Paris Commune, 29–30

Paris Review, 129

Paris under the Commune and Boganis (Wilhelm Dinesen), 30

Pelensky, Olga, 51

Pellegrina Leoni from *The Dreamers*, 17, 19, 24, 129

Percival, Philip, 115–16

personas, 17, 40, 45, 54, 95, 111, 112, 114–15, 117–20, 126–27, 128–30

pith helmet, 117

pledge, 6, 43, 62–63, 64–65

"The Plowman" (Blixen writing as Osceola), 36

Politken, 21–22

Pollack, Sydney, 2, 8, 13, 25, 154–61, 162–65

Port of Aden, 18, 163

possession, 55, 58–59. *See also* "The Iguana," in *Out of Africa* (Dinesen)

possessive pronouns, 93, 96

postcolonial analysis and critiques, 4–6, 25, 56, 95–96, 101–2, 139–42, 155–56

Pride before Fall (Dinesen), 35

primitive time, 77

prolongation, 73, 86

prosthesis machines, 127

Proust, Marcel, 4, 21, 73–75, 76, 86

provocation, 103, 126, 141, 142

pseudonyms, 1, 14, 20, 36, 40, 54–55

puppet theater, 35–36, 40–42

race relations, 71, 92–96, 99–102, 104–5

racial codes, 120

Radcliffe College, Cambridge, MA, 151

Random House, 1, 7, 14, 20, 23, 157

Rascoe, Judith, 158
Redford, Robert, 154–55, 157, 165
Redgrave, Vanessa, 157
reinvention(s), 4, 8, 10, 44, 76, 86–88, 153–54, 166–67
Reitzel (Danish publishing house), 14
"The Revenge of Truth" (Blixen), 38, 39–46, 129, 146
"The Rime of the Ancient Mariner" (Coleridge), 164–65
"Roads around Pisa," in *Seven Gothic Tales* (Dinesen), 45
"The Roads to Life," in *Out of Africa* (Dinesen), 37, 150
Roeg, Nicolas, 157
A Room of One's Own (Woolf), 150–51
Roosevelt, Teddy, 115–16
Rose, Helen, 118
Roskilde, Denmark, 19
Ross, Elliot, 117
Royal Academy School, Copenhagen, 33, 36
Royal Library, Copenhagen, 144
Royal Theater, Copenhagen, 45
Rungsted Kyst, 28
Rungstedlund, 10, 14, 15–17, 19, 27–29, 33–34, 42, 45, 57, 74, 76, 99, 152
Rungstedlund Foundation, 157

"safari chic," 120–21, 124, 128, 155
safari life, 99, 114, 115–18, 121–24, 125–26, *133–34*, 149
safari style, 113–15, 116–21
Scheherazade, 17–18, 52–53, 73–74
Schickel, Richard, 154–55
Schreiner, Olive, 18, 87
Schweitzer, Albert, 23, 117
selective memory, 50, 87
self, search for, 16, 17–18, 58, 74, 86–88, 151, 165
Seven Gothic Tales (Dinesen), 1, 7, 10, 14, 17, 20, 21–23, 36, 45, 52, 67, 128
Sexton, Anne, 150
sexuality, 146, 149
Shadows on the Grass (Dinesen), 7, 19, 123
Shakespeare, William, 36, 40, 41, 140
Shaw, George Bernard, 23
"A Shooting Accident on the Farm," in *Out of Africa* (Dinesen), 79–86, 92, 150; passages from, with annotations, 80–83
Showalter. Elaine, 138
"A Shropshire Lad" (Housman), 160
Siskel, Gene, 155
Skagen, Denmark, 1, 10, 13, 15–16, 19–20, 21, 76, 158
Smithsonian Institute, 115
social norms, 39, 120, 142, 146
Somali women, 20, 53, 102–3, 149
Sophie's Choice (film), 157
Speak, Memory (Nabokov), 3
"squatters" (displaced people), 4–5, 25, 55, 61, 92, 95, 163
Squire, Sir John, 25
SS *Admiral,* 18
SS *Mantola,* 10
Stafford, Jean, 62, 129
Stecher-Hansen, Marianne, 139, 148, 151
The Story of an African Farm (Schreiner), 18
storytelling, 51, 52–55, 61–62, 73–74, 76. *See also* journey tales/journey metaphor
Streep, Meryl, 2, 114, 157–58, 163, 165
Sullivan, Heather, 127
Svendsen, Clara, 8, 31, 112
Swedo Coffee Farm, 6, 50, 60–63, 64–70, 72–73, 92, 113–14. *See also* "Farewell to the Farm," section V in *Out of Africa* (Dinesen)

Tanganyika, 102–3, 163
technology, human dependency on, 127

Thurman, Judith, 8, 13, 22, 34, 38, 39, 45, 96, 118–19, 128, 138–39, 140–41, 143, 154–55
Tiberghien, Susan, 3–4, 50–51
Tilskueren (The Spectator), 20, 36–37, 40, 42
Time Magazine, 154–55
time navigation, 72–88; Blixen's manipulation of time, 86–88; cultural time, 76–77; timelessness, 20–21, 51, 77, 87; time navigation analysis, 80–83; time regained, 74, 78, 87; vanished time, 78–79
Titania (Migel), 8, 19–20
Tivoli Gardens, Cophenhagen, 34–35, 40
"To an Athlete Dying Young" (Housman), 164
Tootsie (film), 154
Trader Horn (film), 118
travel literature, 76
"triple nostalgia," Knipp, 9, 61
Trump, Melania, 117
truth, 4, 13, 37, 39–46, 49–59, 74, 165–67
Trzebinski, Anna, 127–28

Uganda Railroad, 127
United Kingdom, 139
United States, 139
Universal Pictures, 157
Unreliable Truth (Murdock), 3
"The Uses of Duplicity" (Aiken), 140–42

vanished time, 72–75, 78–79
"Visits of Friends," in *Out of Africa* (Dinesen), 162

Ward, David, 4
Watkin, David, 156, 162
Wave (Deraniyagala), 49
The Way We Were (film), 154–55
Westenholz, Aage (uncle), 6, 43, 62–63, 64–68, 69, 123, 150, 156
Westenholz, Anders (brother), 15, 33
Westenholz, Anders (great-nephew), 30, 40–41, 45, 121
Westenholz, Mary Bess (aunt), 31, 33, 46, 100, 112–13, 138–39, 147–48
Westover, Tara, 49
White Fragility (DiAngelo), 94
whiteness, 101–2, 117
white privilege, 67, 94, 124
"White Privilege: Unpacking the Invisible Knapsack" (McIntosh), 94
Why Have There Been No Great Women Artists? (Nochlin), 138
"Wings," in *Out of Africa* (Dinesen), 162
Winter's Tales (Dinesen), 7, 145
witches, 38, 39–40, 129, 149
Wivel, Ole, 8
womanliness, 148–49, 152
women's memoirs, truth in, 49–50
women's movement, 119, 137–40, 148, 152
Woolf, Virginia, 50, 150–51
World War I, 102

The Year of Magical Thinking (Didion), 49
"The Young Man with a Carnation" (Dinesen), 145

Zealand ("Sea-land") Province, 19, 28
zoomorphism, 96–98
Zweig, Stephen, 23

ABOUT THE AUTHOR

Patti M. Marxsen is a biographer, translator, and independent scholar whose works have been published in the United States, Europe, and the Caribbean. She is the author of two essay collections—*Island Journeys: Exploring the Legacy of France* and *Rousseau's Refuge: Essays Out of Switzerland*—as well as two biographies: *Helene Schweitzer: A Life of Her Own* (Syracuse University Press, 2015) and *Jacques Roumain: A Life of Resistance* (Caribbean Studies Press, 2019). In addition to her work on Roumain, Marxsen has published numerous articles, translations, and reviews related to Haitian literature. Patti Marxsen lives in Midcoast Maine.